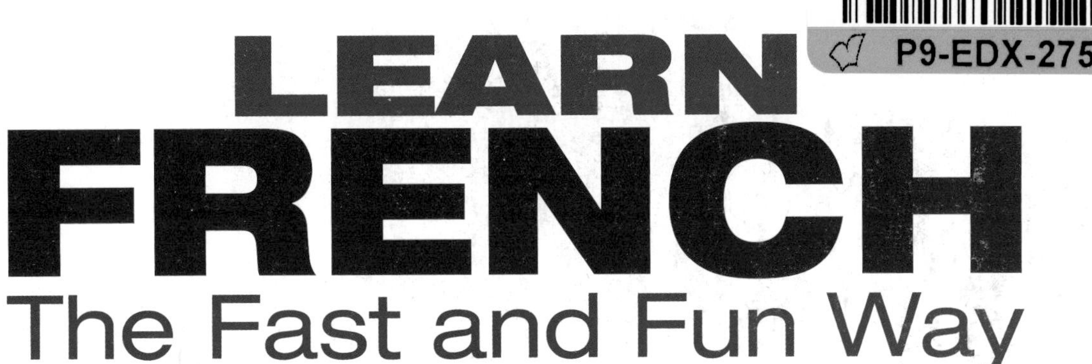

LEARN FRENCH
The Fast and Fun Way

FOURTH EDITION

Theodore Kendris, Ph.D.
Former Adjunct Instructor
Penn State University, Hazleton Campus

Elisabeth Bourquin Leete
Former Professor of French, International Language Institute
Northampton, Massachusetts

Heywood Wald, Coordinating Editor
Former Chairman, Department of Foreign Languages
Martin Van Buren High School, New York

A Word to the Reader

Because exchange rates of foreign currencies against the U.S. dollar vary from day to day, the actual cost of a hotel room, taxi ride, or a meal may be more or less than the amounts in the book. Please consult a newspaper, bank, or Internet web site for the most up-to-date exchange rate.

Photo Credit: Shutterstock.com

It was with great sadness that we learned of the passing of Mme Elisabeth Bourquin Leete. The goal of the current edition is to update the vocabulary and modernize the presentation while retaining the fun and humorous style of the author.

All inquiries should be addressed to:
Barron's Educational Series, Inc.
250 Wireless Boulevard
Hauppauge, NY 11788
www.barronseduc.com

ISBN: 978-1-4380-7494-8

Library of Congress Control Number: 2014931298

Printed in China

9 8 7 6 5 4 3 2 1

To help you pace your learning, we've included stopwatches like the one to the left throughout the book to mark each 15-minute interval. You can read one of these units each day or pace yourself according to your needs.

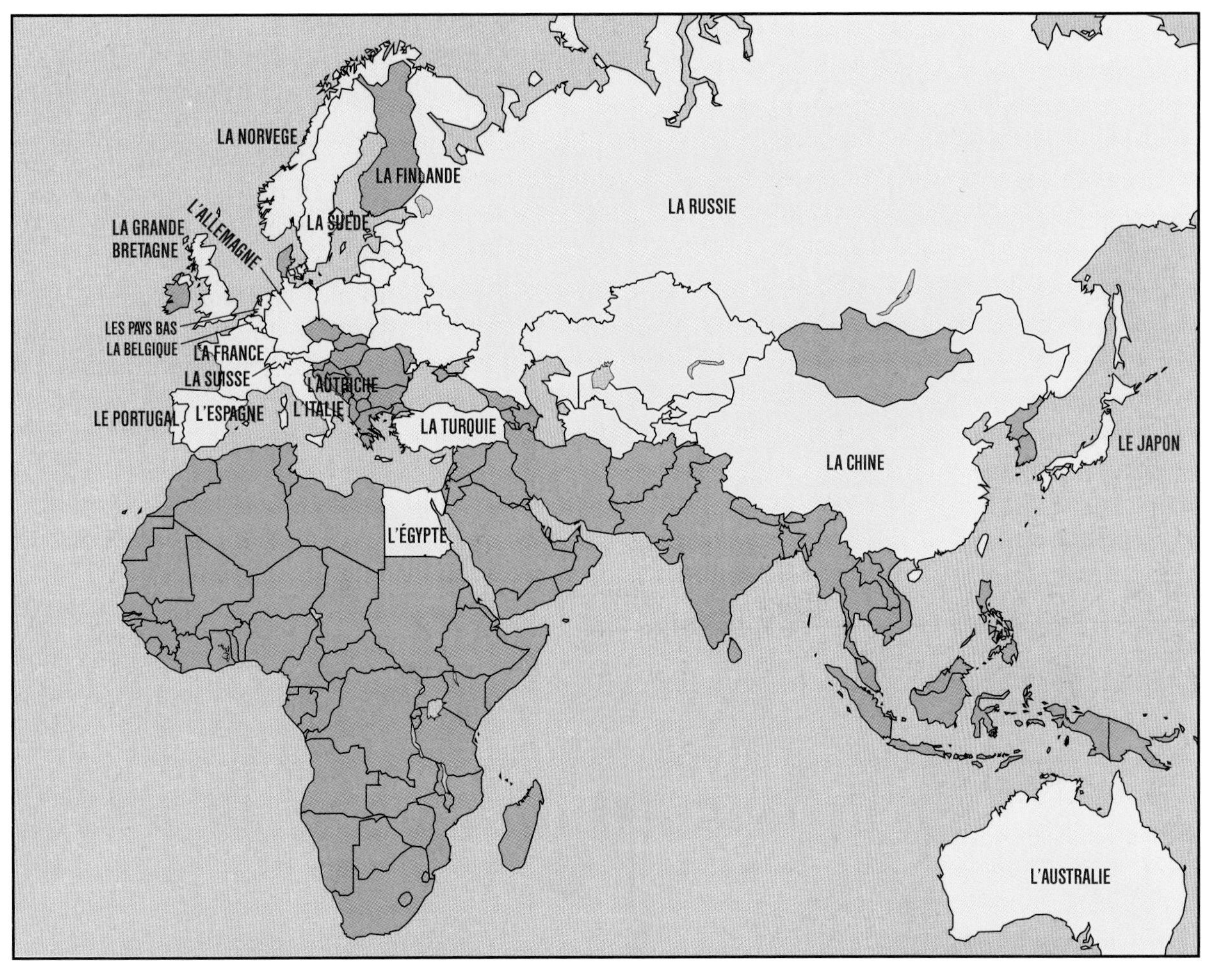

French is a language and culture shared not only by the 65 million people of European France but by many millions more in adjoining Belgium, Luxembourg and Switzerland and in the Canadian Province of Quebec, the Carribbean islands of Martinique, Guadeloupe and Haiti, French possessions in the Atlantic and Pacific, and former French colonies in South America, Asia and, especially, Africa. French is also employed extensively as an international language of diplomatic exchange.

Shaped somewhat like a hexagon, France comprises nearly 213,000 square miles. It is bounded by the English Channel in the north, the Atlantic Ocean in the west, the Pyrénées, Spain and the Mediterranean in the south, and in the east by Italy, Switzerland, the Rhine River, Germany, Luxembourg and Belgium. Its modern history dates to the Roman Conquest of Gaul in the first century B.C. Before that, France was inhabited by early modern humans, including those who created the famous cave paintings over 17,000 years ago in the Lascaux Cave (*la grotte de Lascaux*) in Dordogne, in southwest France.

From Paris, the nation's political and cultural capital, the visitor may strike out in any direction assured that the trip will be rewarding in every sense—historically, culturally, scenically, with the happy bonus of fine wines and cuisine distinctive to every region of France. Paris itself has a concentration of magnificent sightseeing and entertainment opportunities—art museums such as the

Louvre and the Musée d'Orsay, echoes of France's days of glory and the Napoleonic era at the Hôtel des Invalides, the Île de la Cité and Notre Dame Cathedral, lovely parks such as the Tuileries and Bois de Boulogne. And, of course, there is the Eiffel Tower.

Public transportation by rail, air and bus is excellent, and France is also blessed with a network of **autoroutes** (highways) together with well-mapped secondary roads, favored by many motorists wishing to gain a more intimate sense of French village and country life. Much of what the traveler may wish to see lies within a day's journey from Paris—Normandy and Brittany to the north and northwest; Marseilles, the Côte d'Azur, the Provence and the Mediterranean beaches to the south; Bordeaux, the Bay of Biscay and the Pyrénées to the southwest; to the southeast, the Alps and Mont Blanc, the Rhône Alps, and the Jura and Vosges mountains; and, to the east, the Rhine River, Champagne, Lorraine and Alsace.

Learning the language adds much interest, pleasure and satisfaction to a trip to France. Of equal importance to many is the access gained to some of the important bases of Western civilization. French philosophers, political theorists, statesmen, artists, writers and scientists have substantially influenced the cultural and political aspects of our world.

Last but not least, you will find in French-speaking countries—as you would in any other part of the world—that your efforts to communicate in the language are rewarded by kindness and offers of friendship.

FRENCH PRONUNCIATION—A FEW SIMPLE RULES

Is French difficult to pronounce? Not at all. French follows a few simple rules, and once you know these, you'll have no problem saying what you want and understanding those who speak to you. There are two basic principles of French pronunciation:

1. Not all letters are pronounced, as they most often are in English. Remember, however, that even in English, we have some silent letters—the *p* in *pneumonia*, for example.
2. The French like to link words. This is called *la liaison* (*lee-eh-zOH*). Sometimes a whole sentence may sound to you like one long word, especially in the beginning. For instance, you will find in the dialogue in the first unit, the sentence:

   J'habite aux États-Unis. I live in the United States.

   The sentence should sound like:

   zha-bee-toh-zay-ta-zew-nee

Linking is required in many situations, especially between words that logically belong together, but is optional in other situations. In a few cases, it may seem appropriate to link the words, but it is not permitted (for example, after the conjunction et, which means "and"). You'll learn the rules for linking up words as you work your way through this book.

The pronunciation tables that follow will help you get started on the road to France and its language. Practice pronouncing the words a few times while you also learn some basic vocabulary. You'll become familiar with how French speakers pronounce their vowels and consonants, so you'll know how to pronounce a new word when you see it on a road sign or included in an informational brochure. But, to make it all even easier, every time we introduce a new word in this book, we show you how to pronounce it.

TRACK 1

VOWELS

French Letters	Symbol	Pronunciation/Example
a, à	a	This is a short *A*, a bit like the vowel sound in *Tom*. Example: *ma* (ma) my.
a, â	ah	A long *AH*, as in *father*. Example: *pas* (pah) step.
é, final er, ez, et	ay	*A* as in *day*. Example *musée* (mew-zay) museum.
e + 2 consonants, e, ê, è	eh	This is a short *E*, as in *ever*. Example: *appelle* (a-pehl) call.
e, eu	uh	*E*, as in English word *the* or the first *a* in the word *again*. Example: *le* (luh) the.
eu	ūh	This sound does not exist in English. The sound is between *UH* and *EW*. It is similar to the *u* in *pudding*. Example: *peu* (pūh) little.
i, y	ee	The sound of *EE*, as in *meet*. Example: *valise* (va-leez) suitcase.
o	o	A short *O*, as in *done*. Example: *homme* (om) man.
o, ô	oh	A long *O*, as in *open*. Example: *tôt* (toh) soon.
oi, oî	wa	Pronounced *WA*, as in *watch*. Example: *toi* (twa) you (familiar).
ou	oo	Pronounced *OO*, as in *tooth*. Example: *ouvrir* (oo-vreer) to open.
u	ew	This sound does not exist in English. It's similar to the word *few*, but without the *y* sound before *ew* or the *w* after it. Example: *tu* (tew) you (familiar) .
u + vowel	wee	Pronounced *WEE*, as in *whee*. Example: *huit* (weet) eight.

TRACK 2

CONSONANTS

French Letter(s)	Symbol	Pronunciation/Example
b, d, f, k, l, m, n, p, s, t, v, z	—	The corresponding English sound for these French consonants is the same.
c (before e, i, y)	s	This consonant is pronounced *SS*. Example: *merci* (mehr-see) thank you.
ç (before a, o, u)	s	This consonant is pronounced *SS*. Example: *garçon* (gar-sOH) boy.
c (before a, o, u)	k	The *c* without the accent mark is a hard *K*, as in *kind*. Example: *comment* (ko-mAH) how .
g (before e, i, y)	zh	Pronounced like the soft *S* in *pleasure*. Example: *rouge* (roozh) red.
ge (before a, o, u)	zh	Pronounced like the soft *S* in *pleasure*.
g (before a, o, u)	g	Pronounced like the hard *G* in *go*. Example: *Chicago* (shee-kah-goh).
gn	ny	Like the sound *NI* in *onion*. Example: *oignon* (o-nyOH) onion.
h	—	The *h* is always silent. Example: *hôtel* (oh-tehl) hotel.
j	zh	Pronounced like the soft *S* in *pleasure*. Example: *je* (zhuh) I.
qu, final q	k	Pronounced like the hard *K* in *kind*. Example: *cinq* (sank) five.
r	r	This sound does not exist in English; roll the *R* at the top of back of mouth, as for gargling. Example: *rouge* (roozh) red.
ss	s	The double *s* sound is pronounced *SS*. Example: *poisson* (pwa-sOH) fish.
s (at the beginning of word)	s	Pronounced *SS*. Example: *son* (sOH) his (or hers).
s (next to consonant between vowels)	z	Pronounced *Z*. Example: *poison* (pwah-zOH) poison.
t (before i + vowel)	s	Pronounced *SS*. Example: *nation* (na-syOH) nation.
th	t	Pronounced like the short *T* in *top*. Example: *thé* (tay) tea.
x	ks	Pronounced *EKS*, as in *excellent*. Example: *excellent* (eck-se-lAH).
x	s	Pronounced *SS* in these words only: *dix* (dees) ten , *six* (sees) six.

NASAL SOUNDS		
These are very common in French and occur when a *single* N or M follows a vowel. The N and the M are not vocalized. The tip of the tongue does not touch the roof of the mouth.		
French Letters	Symbol	Pronunciation/Example
an, am, en, em	AH	This is not a sound we find in English. It is close to *throng*. Example: *France* (*frAHs*).
in, im, ain , aim, ien, ym	EH	This is not an English sound. It is close to *sang*. Example: *vin* (*vEH*) wine.
on, om	OH	This is not a sound we use in English. It is close to *song*. Example: *bon* (*bOH*) good.
un, um	UH	This is not an English sound. It is close to *sung*. Example: *un* (*UH*) one.

When words LE, LA ("the"), and some pronouns, adverbs and conjunctions that end with an E precede a word that begins with a vowel sound, the final vowel is dropped and replaced by an apostrophe.

EXAMPLE: la + auto = l'auto
le + homme = l'homme

When words merge like this, it is called **elision**.

French syllables all have the same length and approximately the same amount of stress. The last syllable of a word group is slightly emphasized, not by saying it louder, but by making it a little longer.

HOW ENGLISH AND FRENCH ARE SIMILAR

In many ways, French is very much like English. For example, simple French sentences generally follow the same arrangement as English ones:

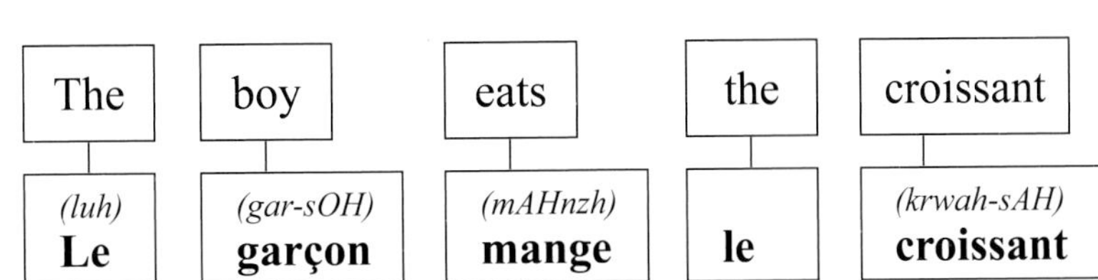
The
boy
eats
the
croissant
(luh)
Le
(gar-sOH)
garçon
(mAHnzh)
mange
le
(krwah-sAH)
croissant

We'll also show you some of the differences that exist between the two languages as you become more familiar with French. Let's look at one now.

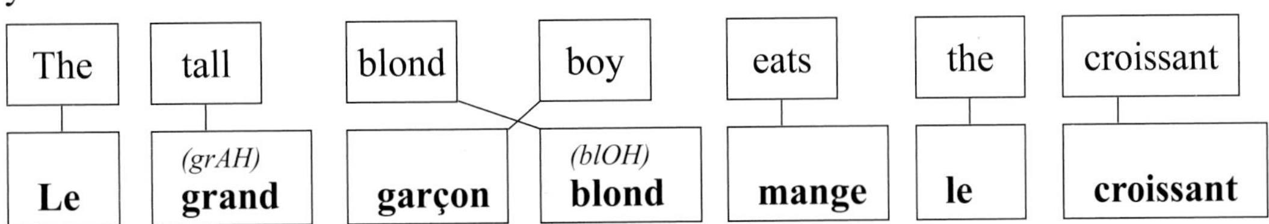
The
tall
blond
boy
eats
the
croissant
Le
(grAH)
grand
garçon
(blOH)
blond
mange
le
croissant

For now, think about the ways French and English words are alike. You can learn many French words simply by recognizing a few patterns in word endings.

ENGLISH WORDS ENDING IN	FRENCH WORDS ENDING IN
-ION	
correction	*(ko-rek-syOH)* **correction**
occasion	*(o-ka-zyOH)* **occasion**
nation	*(na-syOH)* **nation**
station	*(sta-syOH)* **station**
education	*(ay-dew-ka-syOH)* **éducation**
function	*(fohnk-syOH)* **fonction**

ENGLISH WORDS ENDING IN	FRENCH WORDS ENDING IN
-TY	-TÉ
city	*(see-tay)* **cité**
sincerity	*(sEH-say-ree-tay)* **sincérité**
unity	*(ew-nee-tay)* **unité**
possibility	*(po-see-bee-lee-tay)* **possibilité**

ENGLISH WORDS ENDING IN	FRENCH WORDS ENDING IN
-IST	-ISTE
dentist	*(dAH-teest)* **dentiste**
violinist	*(vyo-lo-neest)* **violoniste**
pianist	*(pya-neest)* **pianiste**

ENGLISH WORDS ENDING IN	FRENCH WORDS ENDING IN
-OR	-EUR
actor	*(ak-tūhr)* **acteur**
sculptor	*(skewl-tūhr)* **sculpteur**
vigor	*(vee-guhr)* **vigueur**
color	*(koo-lūhr)* **couleur**

Did you realize how much French you already know? In many cases, the only difference is the PRONUNCIATION. In fact, you may not have realized that you've been speaking French for years! Here are just a few expressions that are part of everyday American language.

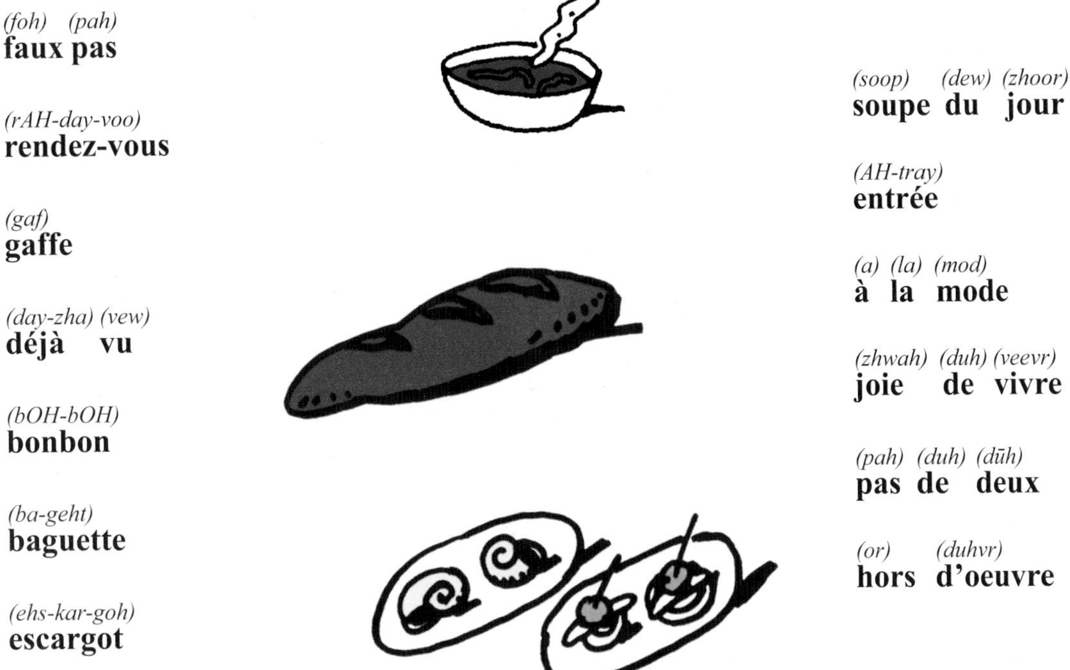

(foh) (pah)
faux pas

(rAH-day-voo)
rendez-vous

(gaf)
gaffe

(day-zha) (vew)
déjà vu

(bOH-bOH)
bonbon

(ba-geht)
baguette

(ehs-kar-goh)
escargot

(soop) (dew) (zhoor)
soupe du jour

(AH-tray)
entrée

(a) (la) (mod)
à la mode

(zhwah) (duh) (veevr)
joie de vivre

(pah) (duh) (dūh)
pas de deux

(or) (duhvr)
hors d'oeuvre

Now you can start building upon what you already know. We don't promise it will be a cinch, but we can guarantee it will be fun, especially when you begin trying to communicate with fluent French speakers. Just put in 15 minutes a day at a pace that is comfortable for you.

GETTING TO KNOW PEOPLE

(fuh-zOH) (ko-ne-sAHs)
Faisons Connaissance

1 Conversons

(kOH-vehr-sOH)
Let's Talk

Knowing how to greet people and how to start a conversation is important, and you should learn those skills first. Read the following dialogue several times, pronouncing each line carefully out loud. The dialogue contains some basic words and expressions that will be useful to you.

Mark Smith, his wife Mary, their daughter Anne, and their son Paul have just arrived at Charles de Gaulle Airport in Paris, and they can't find their luggage. Mark approaches an airline employee:

MARC	*(bOH-zhoor) (muh-syūh)* **Bonjour, Monsieur.**	Hello /Good day, Sir.
EMPLOYÉ	*(AH-plwa-yay) (voo) (day-zee-ray)* **Bonjour. Vous désirez** *(kehl-kuh) (shohz)* **quelque chose?**	Hello/Good day. May I help you? (*lit*. Do you want anything?)
MARC	*(wee) (zhuh) (shehrsh) (may)* **Oui. Je cherche mes** *(va-leez)* **valises.**	Yes. I am looking for my suitcases.
EMPLOYÉ	*(byEH) (ko-mAH) (voo)* **Bien. Comment vous** *(za-play) (voo)* **appelez-vous?**	Well/O.K. What is your name? (*lit*. How do you call yourself?)
MARC	*(zhuh) (ma-pehl))* **Je m'appelle Marc Smith.**	My name is Mark Smith.
EMPLOYÉ	*(luh) (new-may-roh) (duh) (votr) (vol)* **Le numéro de votre vol et** *(o-ree-zheen)* **l'origine?**	Your flight number and origin?
MARC	*(trwah) (sAH) (trAHt)* **Le vol Air France trois cent trente-** *(trwah) (duh)* **trois de New York.**	Air France flight 333 from New York.

EMPLOYÉ	*(UH) (mo-mAH) (seel) (voo) (pleh)* **Un moment, s'il vous plaît.**	One moment, please.

(zhahn)

As the clerk looks through some papers on his desk, Jean, a French business friend, sees Mark.

JEAN	*(sa-lew) (ko-mAH) (va-tew)* **Salut, Marc! Comment vas-tu?**	Hi, Mark. How are you?
MARC	*(zhuh) (vay) (byEH) (ay) (twa)* **Je vais bien, et toi?**	I am well. And you?
JEAN	*(treh) (tew) (eh) (ee-see) (ah)* **Très bien. Tu es ici en** *(va-kahns)* **vacances?**	Very well. Are you here on vacation?
MARC	*(zhuh) (tuh) (pray-zahnt) (ma) (fa-mee-y)* **Oui. Je te présente ma famille.** *(fam) (fee-y)* **Ma femme Marie, ma fille Anne, et** *(mohn) (fees)* **mon fils Paul.**	Yes. Let me introduce my family to you. My wife Mary, my daughter Anne, and my son Paul.
JEAN	*(AH-shAH-tay)* **Enchanté!**	Delighted!
EMPLOYÉ	*(ehks-kew-zay-mwa) (voh)* **Excusez-moi, Monsieur. Vos** *(a-reev) (a-vehk) (luh) (pro-shEH)* **valises arrivent avec le prochain** *(na-vyOH)* **avion.**	Excuse me, Sir. Your suitcases are arriving on the next plane.

MARC	*(zewt)* **Zut!**	Darn it!
JEAN	*(pa-syAHs)* *(neh)* *(pah)* *(AH)* **Patience Marc. Tu n'es pas en** *(na-may-reek)* **Amérique!**	Be patient, Mark. You are not in America!
MARC	(*à l'employé*) **Merci, Monsieur.** *(oh)* *(ruh-vwar)* **Au revoir!**	Thank you, Sir. Good-bye.
EMPLOYÉ	*(voo)* *(zAH)* *(pree)* **Je vous en prie.**	You are welcome.
JEAN	*(tool)* *(mOHd)* **Au revoir, tout le monde!**	Good-bye, everybody.
TOUT LE MONDE	*(a byEH-toh)* **À bientôt!**	See you soon!

Match the French expressions from the dialogue with their English equivalents:

1. Comment vous appelez-vous?
2. Je te présente ma famille.
3. Zut!
4. Vous désirez quelque chose?
5. Je vous en prie.
6. Je vais bien.
7. À bientôt.
8. Je m'appelle . . .
9. Enchanté!
10. Salut. Comment vas-tu?

a. May I help you?
b. My name is . . .
c. What's your name?
d. Hi, how are you?
e. I am well.
f. Let me introduce my family to you.
g. Delighted!
h. Darn it!
i. You are welcome.
j. See you soon.

ANSWERS

Matching **1.** c **2.** f **3.** h **4.** a **5.** i **6.** e **7.** j **8.** b **9.** g **10.** d

LES GENS ET LES CHOSES

(lay) (zhAH) (shohz)

People and Things

One of the first things you need to know is what to call certain things or people—words we call nouns. You will need to know what a French noun looks like and how to make it plural. Unlike English nouns, all French nouns have a gender (masculine or feminine); like English nouns, they can be either singular or plural. Look carefully at the following examples of nouns given in their singular and plural forms, and write them on the blank line in the space provided.

Masculine nouns singular and plural

(sEH-gew-lyay) SINGULIER	*(plew-ryel)* PLURIEL
(gar-sOH) **garçon** boy ________	*(gar-sOH)* **garçons** boys ________
(sha) **chat** cat ________	*(sha)* **chats** cats ________
(pyay) **pied** foot ________	*(pyay)* **pieds** feet ________
(arbr) **arbre** tree ________	*(arbr)* **arbres** trees ________
(pah) **pas** step ________	*(pah)* **pas** steps ________

(nuh-vūh)
neveu
nephew

(nuh-vuh)
neveux
nephews

(sha-poh)
chapeau
hat

(sha-poh)
chapeaux
hats

(zhoor-nal)
journal
newspaper

(zhoor-noh)
journaux
newspapers

These words you have just learned are masculine nouns. To form the plural, in most cases, you simply add S. If the singular noun ends with an S, don't change anything to form the plural. If it ends with EU or EAU, add X instead of S. If the noun ends in AL, the ending becomes AUX in the plural.

Feminine nouns singular and plural

Now look at the following feminine nouns:

SINGULIER

(meh-zOH)
maison
house, home

PLURIEL

(meh-zOH)
maisons
houses, homes

(oh-toh-mo-beel)
automobile
automobile

(oh-toh-mo-beel)
automobiles
automobiles

(mehr)
mère
mother

(mehr)
mères
mothers

Plural nouns formation

Simply add an S to form the plural of a noun. If the noun ends with an S or an X or a Z in the singular, don't change anything to form the plural. (The final S, X, or Z is not pronounced.)

Test your knowledge of singular and plural by making these nouns all plural:

(ka-yay)
cahier
workbook

1. cahiers
workbooks

(stee-loh)
stylo
pen

2. stylos
pens

(pehr)
père
father

3. des pères
fathers

(shuh-val)
cheval
horse

4. chevaux
horses

(fees)
fils
son

5. fils
sons

(mAH-toh)
manteau
coat

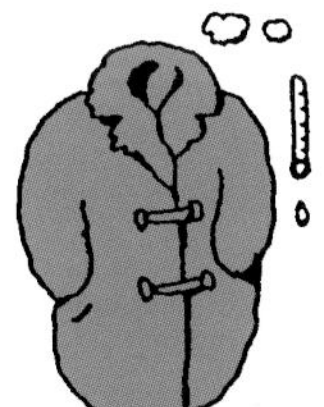

6. manteaux
coats

ANSWERS

Plural **1.** cahiers **2.** stylos **3.** pères **4.** chevaux **5.** fils **6.** manteaux

THREE EXCEPTIONS:

1. The following masculine nouns which end in EU take an S in the plural:
   (blūh) *(pnūh)*
   bleus (black and blue mark), **pneus** (tires).

2. The following masculine nouns which end in OU take an X in the plural:
   (bee-zhoo) *(ka-yoo)* *(shoo)* *(zhuh-noo)* *(ee -boo)*
   bijoux (jewels), **cailloux** (pebbles), **choux** (cabbages), **genoux** (knees), **hiboux** (owls),
   (zhoo-zhoo)
   joujoux (toys).

3. The following masculine nouns which end in AL take an S in the plural:
   (bal) *(kar-na-val)* *(fehs-tee-val)*
   bals (balls), **carnavals** (carnivals), **festivals** (festivals).

The indefinite articles

(UH) *(ewn)* *(day)*

un, une, des

A (An) , some

When we name something—use a noun—we often precede it in English with the words *a* or *some*. The same is true in French, and here is how to say these words, depending on whether the noun is masculine or feminine.

WITH FEMININE NOUNS

SINGULIER

(ewn) *(fee-y)*
une fille
a girl

(ew) *(na-mee)*
une amie
a female friend

PLURIEL

(day)
des filles
some girls, girls

(day) *(za-mee)*
des amies
some female friends

WITH MASCULINE NOUNS

(UH) *(nOHkl)*
un oncle
an uncle

(UH na-mee)
un ami
a male friend

(day zOHkl)
des oncles
some uncles

(day za-mee)
des amis
some friends

Note that in English, you often do not use some in the plural; you' ll say: "I have friends in Paris." In French, you **must** say "I have some friends in Paris": **J'ai des amis à Paris.** In other words, you need to use an article.

Now test yourself by putting the appropriate indefinite article in front of each noun.
Note: *m.* = masculine noun *f.* = feminine noun *pl.* = plural noun

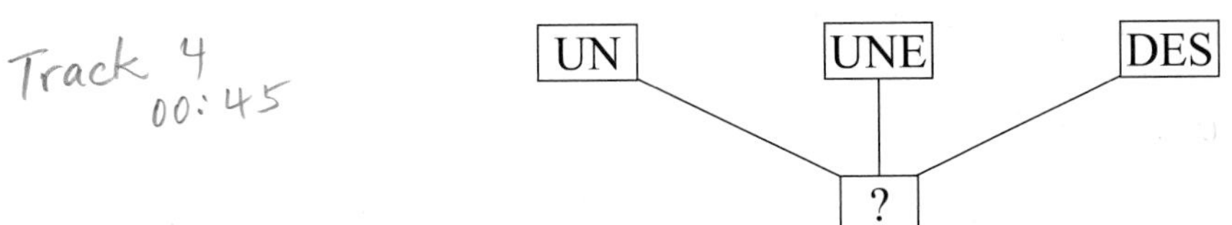

1. ___un___ chat (*m.*)
2. ___une___ fille (*f.*)
3. ___des___ oncles (*m. pl.*)
4. ___des___ journaux (*m. pl.*)
5. ___une___ amie (*f.*)
6. ___des___ maisons (*f. pl.*)
7. ___un___ manteau (*m.*)
8. ___un ami___ ami (*m.*)
9. ___un___ cheval (*m.*)
10. ___des___ automobiles (*f. pl.*)

Here's another chance to test yourself. Put the correct words on the lines below the pictures using the indefinite articles for "a" (an) and "some" and the French word for what is shown.

(kee) (ehs)
Qui est-ce?
Who is it?

(kehs) (kuh) (seh)
Qu'est-ce que c'est?
What is it?

(a) ___un garçon___

(b) ___un chat___

(c) ___un pied___

(d) ___des journaux___

(e) ___une mère___

(f) ___des pères___

ANSWERS

Conversation **1.** un chat **2.** une fille **3.** des oncles **4.** des journaux **5.** une amie **6.** des maisons **7.** un manteau **8.** un ami **9.** un cheval **10.** des automobiles

(a) un garçon **(b)** un chat **(c)** un pied **(d)** des journaux **(e)** une mère **(f)** des pères

Subject pronouns

(zhuh) (tew) (voo)

je, tu et vous

"I" and "you"

Track 4 00:50

It is also important to know how to say "I" and "you" in French. These words are called subject pronouns.

"I" is simply JE, (but J' before a vowel). Examples: *Je suis*. I am. / *J'ai*. I have.

"You" is given in three ways:

TU	— Familiar. When addressing one person: a friend, child, family member; also used for a pet.
VOUS	— Polite. When addressing anyone who is older or in a position of authority.
VOUS	— Plural form of both TU and VOUS

SUMMARY: "YOU"	
SINGULIER	**PLURIEL**
TU	VOUS
VOUS	VOUS

Which would you use—**tu** or **vous**—when speaking to the following? Write your answer in the space provided.

1. the doctor *Vous*
2. your brother *tu*
3. your sisters *tu*
4. your child *tu*
5. your teacher *Vous*
6. a police officer *Vous*
7. your dog *tu*
8. your roommate *tu*
9. your roommates *Vous*
10. the store clerk *Vous*

ANSWERS

Tu or vous **1.** vous **2.** tu **3.** vous **4.** tu **5.** vous **6.** vous **7.** tu **8.** tu **9.** vous **10.** vous

(par-lOH) *(mAH-bruh)* *(fa-mee-y)*

PARLONS DES MEMBRES DE LA FAMILLE

Let's Talk About the Members of the Family

Track 4 1:05

Here are the members of Paul's family.

(Note: The definite articles in French, which mean "the," are *le* (m.s.), *la* (f.s.), *les* (m./f. pl.). More details will follow on page 23.)

Henriette Dubois
(la) (grAH-mehr)
la grand-mère
grandmother

Pierre Dubois
(luh) (grAH-pehr)
le grand-père
grandfather

Jean-Pierre Dupont

le père
father

(ma-ree)
le mari
husband

Micheline Dupont
(née Dubois)
la mère
mother

(fam)
la femme
wife

Jean Dubois
(lOHkl)
l'oncle
uncle

Marie Dubois
(née Ogier)
(tAHt)
la tante
aunt

Michel Dupont
(frehr)
le frère
brother

le fils
son

Jeanine Dupont
(suhr)
la soeur
sister

la fille
daughter

Philippe Dubois
(koo-zEH)
le cousin
cousin (male)

Pierrette Dubois
(koo-zeen)
la cousine
cousin (female)

Identify the following members of the family:

1. **Henriette Dubois est la** grand-mère.
2. **Jean est l'** oncle.
3. **Pierrette est la** cousine.
4. **Jean-Pierre est le** père **et le** mari.
5. **Michel est le** frère **et le** fils.
6. **Jeanine Dupont est la** soeur **et la** fille.

Find the *plurals* of the following nouns hidden in the puzzle, write them down, and then circle them in the puzzle. We've done the first one for you, to show how easy it is.

1. **cousin** cousins
2. **cheval** chevaux
3. **fils** fils
4. **mère** mères
5. **chat** chats
6. **cousine** cousines
7. **genou** genoux
8. **fille** filles
9. **père** pères
10. **manteau** manteaux

C	O	U	S	I	N	S	J	E	S	U	F	I	L	L	E	S	X	A
H	U	L	A	L	G	M	A	N	T	E	A	U	X	S	O	U	P	U
E	E	N	M	M	E	O	E	C	H	A	T	S	I	E	O	T	O	P
V	A	U	C	E	D	R	U	N	A	M	D	E	S	N	T	A	I	E
A	L	A	I	R	R	A	C	O	U	S	I	N	E	S	P	O	U	R
U	N	M	O	T	M	E	A	C	H	A	N	G	P	L	U	M	E	E
X	J	A	I	T	U	A	S	I	L	A	N	O	F	I	L	S	O	S

ANSWERS

Family tree 1. grand-mère **2.** oncle **3.** cousine **4.** père . . . mari **5.** frère . . . fils **6.** soeur . . . fille
Word search 2. chevaux **3.** fils **4.** mères **5.** chats **6.** cousines **7.** genoux **8.** filles **9.** pères **10.** manteaux

Imagine you've begun your trip already. See how well you understand the following situation.

(sewr)
Monsieur Smith et la famille arrivent en France sur le vol 333 de New York. M. Smith
on

(dee)
dit "bonjour" à l'employé. M. Smith dit "merci" et l'employé dit "Je vous en prie."
says

(fee-nahl-mAH)
Finalement, M. Smith dit "Au revoir."
Finally

Are the following true or false?

1. **Monsieur Smith et la famille arrivent à New York.** T F
2. **Monsieur Smith dit "Je vous en prie" à l'employé.** T F
3. **Monsieur Smith et un ami arrivent en France.** T F
4. **Finalement, Monsieur Smith dit bonjour.** T F

ANSWERS

True or False 1. F 2. F 3. F 4. F

Have fun with the following crossword puzzle. The clues are English equivalents of French words.

ACROSS

3. I live
5. thank you
6. a, an (fem.)
7. I
9. sister

DOWN

1. grandmother
2. some
3. girls, daughter
8. horse

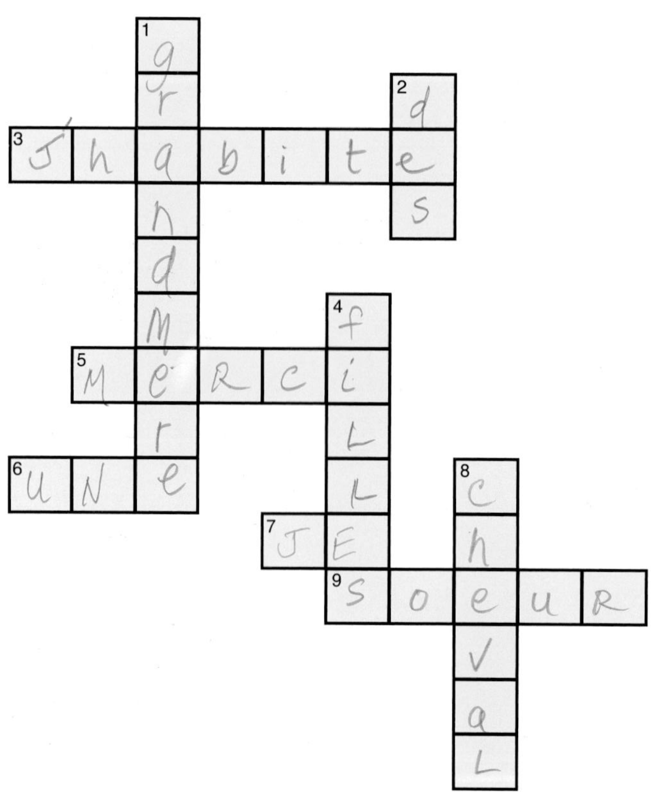

ANSWERS

Puzzle ACROSS **3.** j'habite **5.** merci **6.** une **7.** je **9.** soeur

DOWN **1.** grandmère **2.** des **4.** filles **8.** cheval

Now study and say aloud these parts of Paul's house.

UNE MAISON

A Home

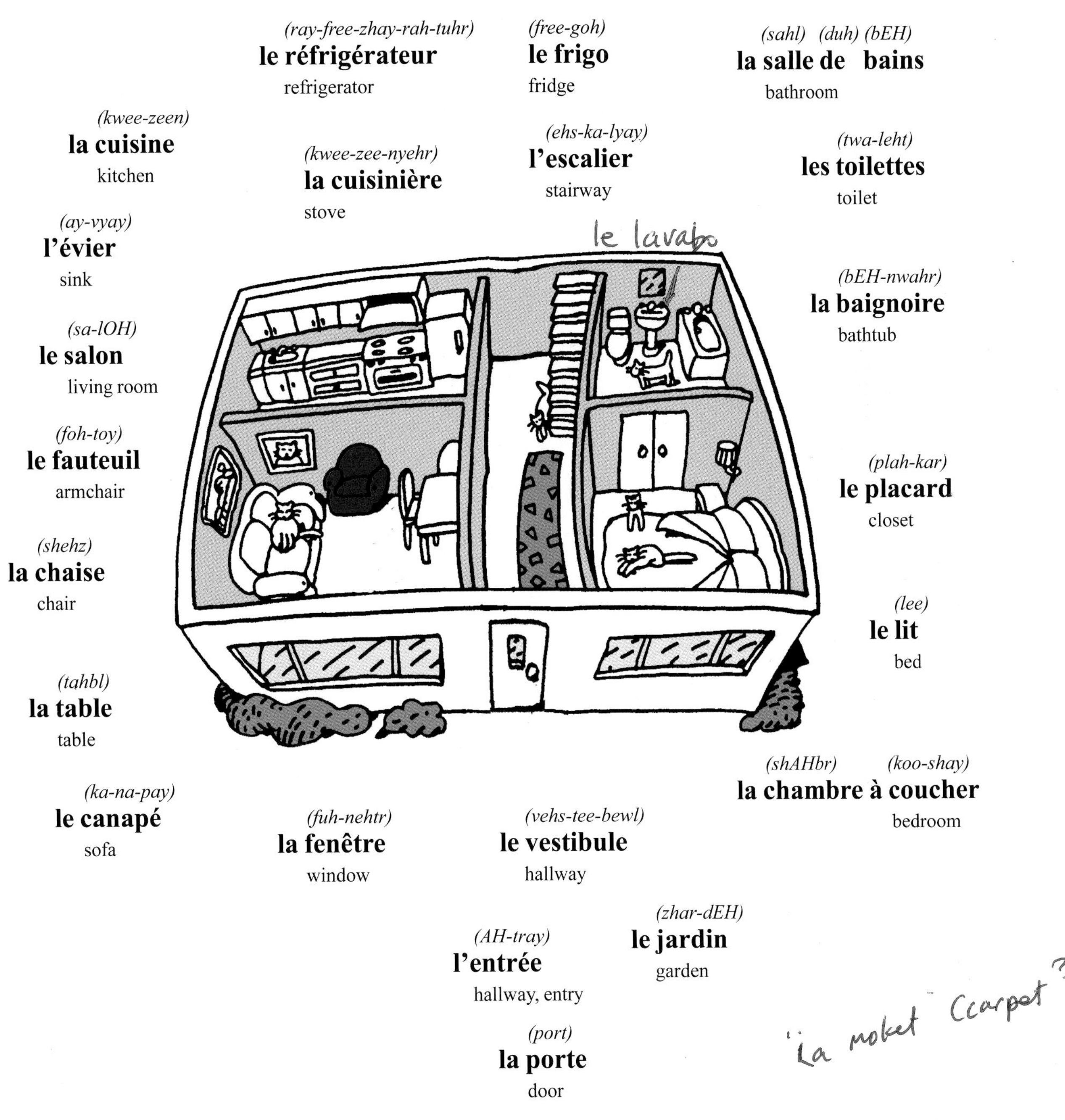

ARRIVAL

(la-ree-vay)
L'arrivee

2 — *(a)* *(la)* *(ruh-shehrsh)* *(dUH)* *(AH-drwah)* *(oo)* *(pa-say)* À la recherche d'un endroit où (where) passer *(la)* *(nwee)* la nuit

Finding a Place to Spend the Night

You'll probably book your hotel room from home—at least for your first night in France. But whether you have a reservation or not, you'll want to know some basic words that describe the services and facilities you expect to find at your hotel. Learn these words first, and notice how they are used in the dialogue you will read later.

(oh-tehl)
l'hôtel
Hotel

(shAHbr)
la chambre
Room

(pree)
le prix
Price

(sahl) (duh) (bEH)
la salle de bains
Bathroom

(ray-zehr-va -syOH)
la réservation
Reservation

(ray-zehr-vay)
réserver
To reserve

(pahs-por)
le passeport
Passport

(AH-plwa-yay)
l'employé/employée
Clerk (m.)/(f.)

(port)
la porte
Door

(fam) (duh) (shAHbr)
la femme de chambre
Maid

(fuh-nehtr)
la fenêtre
Window

Le, la, l', les

The many ways of saying "the" in French

Track 5 00:59

In English we use "the" to precede all nouns. In French, however, there are many ways of saying "the," depending on whether the noun is singular or plural, masculine or feminine.

WITH MASCULINE NOUNS	
SINGULIER	PLURIEL
Before a Consonant	
(luh) **Le père** father	**Les pères** fathers
Le garçon boy	**Les garçons** boys
Before a Vowel or silent *h*	
(lar-br) **L'arbre** tree	*(lay) (zarbr)* **Les arbres** trees
L'ami friend	*(lay) (zamee)* **Les amis** friends
(loh-tel) **L'hôtel** hotel	*(lay) (zoh-tel)* **Les hôtels** hotels

WITH FEMININE NOUNS	
SINGULIER	PLURIEL
Before a Consonant	
(la) **La maison** house	*(lay)* **Les maisons** houses
La fille girl	**Les filles** girls
La mère mother	**Les mères** mothers
Before a Vowel or silent *h*	
(luhr) **L'heure** hour	*(lay) (zhuhr)* **Les heures** hours
(la-mee) **L'amie** girlfriend	*(lay) (zamee)* **Les amies** girlfriends

Here's the same idea presented in a way that will make it easier for you to remember the forms of "the."

SUMMARY: "THE"			
WITH MASCULINE NOUNS		WITH FEMININE NOUNS	
Singulier	**Pluriel**	**Singulier**	**Pluriel**
Before a Consonant **LE**	**LES**	**Before a Consonant** **LA**	**LES**
Before a Vowel or silent *h* **L'**	**LES**	**Before a Vowel or silent *h*** **L'**	**LES**

Let's practice. Put the appropriate form of "the" before each noun listed below. We've done the first for you as an example.

ANSWERS

Definite article **1.** le prix **2.** la porte **3.** les chambres **4.** le passeport **5.** l'hôtel **6.** les fenêtres **7.** les réservations **8.** la salle de bains **9.** l'employé **10.** l'employée *(pro-nOH)* *(vehrb)*

Les pronoms et les verbes

Pronouns and verbs

Track 5 02:30

You've already learned how to say "I" and "You" in French. Now it's time to move on to the forms for "he," "she," "we," and "they." Here are your new words:

IL .... He (It)

ELLE .... She (It)

(OH)
ON .... One (people)

NOUS .... We

ILS .... They (masculine)

ELLES .... They (feminine)

Do you remember how to say "I"? And "You"

JE, **J'** I

TU .... You (familiar, singular)

VOUS .... You (polite, singular)

VOUS .... You (plural)

Use this table to help you remember the French pronoun:

SUMMARY: PRONOUNS			
SINGULAR		**PLURAL**	
je, j'	I	**nous**	we
tu	you (familiar)	**vous**	you (polite, singular)
		vous	you (plural)
il	he/it	**ils**	they (masculine)
elle	she/it	**elles**	they (feminine)
on	one (**On** is conjugated in the third person singular, like **il** and **elle**.)		

Now let's conjugate the verb **PARLER** *(par-lay)* (to speak). Conjugating the verb means changing the verb ending to agree with the subject. We do this automatically in English when we say "I speak" but "he speaks." Notice that the verb **PARLER** ends in **-ER**. **PARLER** is called the infinitive of the verb. The infinitive is the form of the verb corresponding to the English "to —" form. Many other verbs also end in **-ER**.: **CHANTER** (to sing), **ARRIVER** (to arrive). Watch how to conjugate them: drop the **-ER** and add the appropriate endings.

PARLER

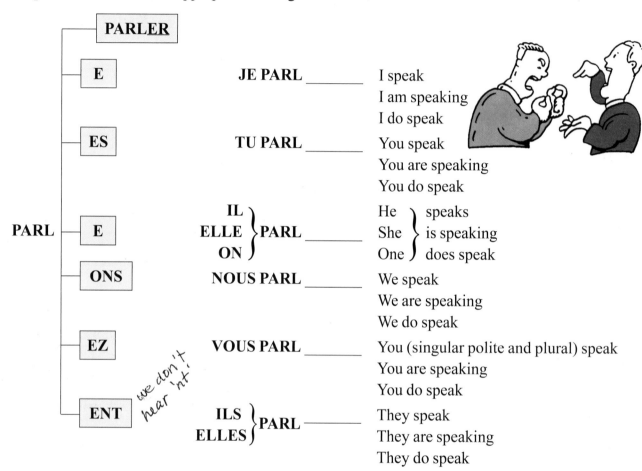

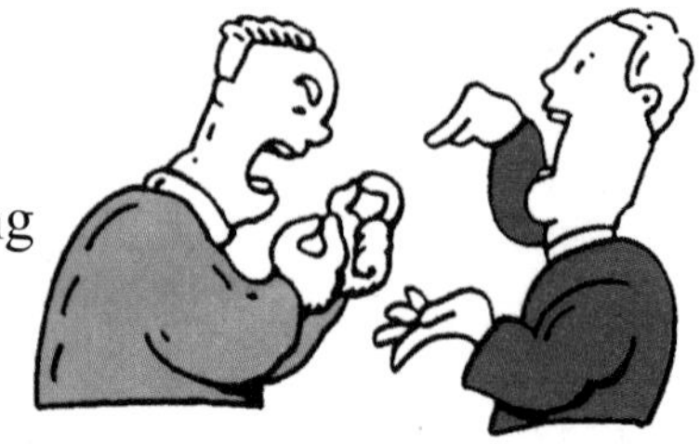

Stem	Ending		
PARL	**E**	**JE PARL** ______	I speak I am speaking I do speak
	ES	**TU PARL** ______	You speak You are speaking You do speak
	E	**IL / ELLE / ON PARL** ______	He / She / One speaks is speaking does speak
	ONS	**NOUS PARL** ______	We speak We are speaking We do speak
	EZ	**VOUS PARL** ______	You (singular polite and plural) speak You are speaking You do speak
	ENT	**ILS / ELLES PARL** ______	They speak They are speaking They do speak

NOTE: that the subject pronouns are always necessary, because after JE, TU, IL, ELLE, ON, ILS and ELLES, the verb sounds exactly the same:

je parle *(parl)*, tu parles *(parl)*, il/elle /on parle *(parl)*, ils /elles parlent *(parl)*:

je, il, elle, on	**parle**	**(parl)**
tu	**parles**	**(parl)**
ils, elles	**parlent**	**(parl)**

Notice that, exactly as in English, **IL**, **ELLE**, **ILS** and **ELLES** replace nouns:

Track 5 04:04

LE GARÇONS	PARLENT	FRANÇAIS.	ILS	PARLENT FRANÇAIS.
The boys	speak	French	They	speak French

DON'T FORGET THAT **JE** becomes **J'** before a vowel sound.

Now try to add the right endings to CHANTER and ARRIVER:

Je chant e	Nous chant ons	J'arriv e	Nous arriv ons
Tu chant es	Vous chant ez	Tu arriv es	Vous arriv ez
Il chant e	Ils chant ent	Il arriv e	Ils arriv ent
Elle chant e	Elles chant ent	Elle arriv e	Elles arriv ent
On chant e		On arriv e	

Bon! (Good) Now put the right endings on the verbs:

Le garçon parl e très bien.

Tu parl es et je chant e.

Les oncles arriv ent demain.

Nous chant ons et vous parl ez.

Marie chant e très bien.

Negatives

NOTE: To make any verb negative, put NE (N' before a vowel sound) before the verb and PAS after the verb:

AFFIRMATIVE		NEGATIVE	
JE PARLE	I speak	**JE NE PARLE PAS**	I don't speak

ANSWERS

Verb CHANTER

Je chante
Tu chantes
Il chante
Elle chante
On chante

Nous chantons
Vous chantez
Ils chantent
Elles chantent

Verb ARRIVER

J'arrive
Tu arrives
Il arrive
Elle arrive
On arrive

Nous arrivons
Vous arrivez
Ils arrivent
Elles arrivent

Verb PARLER, verb ARRIVER, verb CHANTER

Le garçon parle très bien.
Les oncles arrivent demain.
Marie chante très bien.
Tu parles et je chante.
Nous chantons et vous parlez.

(kee) (a-teel) (dAH) (zUH) (nOH)
Qu'y-a-t-il dans un nom?
What's in a name?

When you are settled in your room, get to know the names of the items there. You might need another towel, or find that your lamp doesn't work. Ask the hotel staff to help you, and explain what you need.

(ewn) (shAHbr) (doh-tehl)
UNE CHAMBRE D'HOTEL
A Hotel Room

1. I need a towel. Il me faut une serviette.
2. The lamp doesn't work. La lampe ne fonctionne pas.
3. Can you fix the toilet? Pouvez-vous reparer les toilettes?
4. Where is the shower? Où est la douche?
5. The bed is too small. Le lit est trop petit. peuti

ANSWERS

Hotel room **1.** une serviette **2.** la lampe **3.** les toilettes **4.** la douche **5.** le lit

Follow the adventures of the Smith family as they check into their hotel. Always read each line of dialogue out loud to practice your pronunciation.

MARC	**Excusez-moi, monsieur. J'ai réservé** *(ray-zehr-vay)* **deux chambres** *(shahnbr)* **pour ce soir.**	Excuse me, sir. I have a reservation for 2 rooms for tonight.
	Je m'appelle M. Smith.	My name is Smith.
EMPLOYÉ	**Bonjour. Oui, nous avons votre réservation** *(ray-zehr-va-syOH)* **pour deux chambres à deux lits** *(lee)* **avec salle** *(sahl)* **de** *(duh)* **bains** *(bEH)*. **Mais il y a un problème.**	Good afternoon. Yes, we have your reservation for 2 double rooms with bath. But there is a problem.
	What is it ~~tha~~ that there is?	
MARC	**Qu'est-ce qu'il y a?**	What's the matter?
EMPLOYÉ	**Dans une chambre, la douche** *(doosh)* **ne marche pas.**	The shower in one room is broken.
		Il n'importe pas.
MARC	**Ça** *(sa)* **ne** *(neh)* **fait** *(fay)* **rien** *(ryEH)*. **Les enfants peuvent se baigner** *(beh-nyay)* **chez nous.**	It doesn't matter. The children can use our bath.
EMPLOYÉ	**Bon. Mais il y a un autre problème. Dans l'autre chambre, on ne peut pas ouvrir** *(oo-vreer)* **la fenêtre** *(fuh-nehtr)*.	Good. But there is another problem. The window in the other room doesn't open.
MARC	**(à Marie) Qu'est-ce que tu en penses? Il n'y a pas de chambres dans ce quartier** *(kar-tyay)*. **Il y a une foule** *(fool)* **de touristes à Paris maintenant** *(mEH-tuh-nAH)*.	What do you think? There are no rooms in this neighborhood (area). Paris is full of tourists now.

MARIE	*(shoh)* **Il ne fait pas trop chaud. Prenons-** *(kahn) (mehm)* **les quand même.**	The weather isn't too hot. Let's take them anyway.
EMPLOYÉ	**Bon. Chaque chambre est à** *(swa-sAHt er-ro)* **60 euros par jour.**	Fine. Each room is 60 euros per day.
MARC	*(puh-tee) (day-zhūh-nay)* **Est-ce que le petit déjeuner est** *(kohn-pree)* **compris?**	Is breakfast included?

EMPLOYÉ	**Mais oui, monsieur.**	Oh yes, sir.
MARC	**Bon. Nous les prenons. Voici nos** *(pahs-por)* **passeports.**	Okay, we'll take them. Here are our passports.
EMPLOYÉ	*(vuh-yay) (rAH-pleer) (feesh)* **Veuillez remplir cette fiche.** *(klay)* **Voici votre clé. Les chambres sont** *(trwah-zee-ehm) (ay-tazh)* **au troisième étage.**	Please fill out this form. Here is your key. The rooms are on the third floor. (See page 56 for an explanation of how floors are numbered in French.)
MARC	*(a-sAH-suhr)* **Y a-t-il un ascenseur?**	Is there an elevator?
EMPLOYÉ	*(drwat)* **Oui, monsieur. À droite.**	Yes. To the right.
MARC	**Merci beaucoup, monsieur.**	Thank you very much, sir.
EMPLOYÉ	*(pree)* **Je vous en prie, monsieur.** *(a-mew-zay)* **Amusez-vous bien à Paris.**	You're welcome, sir. Have a good time in Paris.

Match these French expressions from the dialogue with their English equivalents:

1. J'ai réservé deux chambres pour ce soir.	a. It doesn't matter.
2. Il y a un problème.	b. What's the matter?
3. Qu'est-ce qu'il ya?	c. Have a good time in Paris.
4. N'importe.	d. Each room is 60 euros per day.
5. Chaque chambre est à 60 euros par jour.	e. There is a problem.
6. Est-ce que le petit déjeuner est compris?	f. Please fill out this form.
7. Veuillez remplir cette fiche.	g. I have a reservation for two rooms for tonight.
8. Amusez-vous bien à Paris.	h. Is breakfast included?

ANSWERS

Matching 1. g 2. e 3. b 4. a 5. d 6. h 7. f 8. c

(see) SI VOUS VOULEZ *(duh-mAH-day)* DEMANDER *(kehl-kuh)* QUELQUE *(shohz)* CHOSE

If You Want to Ask for Something

Track 6 02:32

You'll find yourself asking questions every day—of hotel clerks, tour guides, waitresses, and taxi drivers. To form a question from any statement, choose one of the three following methods:

TO FORM A QUESTION FROM ANY STATEMENT:

1. Just raise your voice in the normal way for questions:

   (gar-sOH) (mAHzh) (krwah-sAH)
   Le garçon mange le croissant.
   The boy eats the croissant.

   Le garçon mange le croissant?

2. Put the magical group of words **EST-CE QUE** *(es) (kuh)* (**QU'** before a vowel), which means literally "Is it that," at the beginning of a YES-NO question, or between the interrogative adverb and the rest of the question:

   Le garçon mange le croissant.

   (ehs-kuh)
   Est-ce que le garçon mange le croissant?
   Does the boy eat the croissant?

3. You can also invert the subject and the verb and put a hyphen between the two:

   (voo) (poo-vay)
   Vous pouvez.
   You can.

   (poo-vay) (voo)
   Pouvez-vous?
   Can you?

NOTICE: The previous inversion is rarely used after JE, which means "I." This is one of the times when **Est-ce que** comes in handy—and when the last letter of the verb and the first letter of the pronoun are vowels, you have to put -T- between them:

(eel)
Il mange.
he

(mAHzh) (teel)
Mange-t-il?

(el)
Elle mange.
she

(mAHzh) (tehl)
Mange-t-elle?

If the subject of the sentence is a noun or a name, the construction is as follows:

Le garçon mange le croissant.
Le garçon mange-t-il le croissant?

Marie mange le croissant.
Marie mange-t-elle le croissant?

BASIC QUESTION WORDS

(kuh)
QUE, QU' (+ vowel) __________ WHAT

(kee)
QUI __________ WHO

(oo)
OÙ __________ WHERE

(ko-mAH)
COMMENT __________ HOW

(poor-kwa)
POURQUOI __________ WHY

(kAH)
QUAND __________ WHEN

(kOH-byEH)
COMBIEN __________ HOW MUCH, HOW MANY

NOTICE: When COMBIEN is followed by a noun, the noun is preceded by DE *(duh)*, or D' (before a vowel):

Combien d'argent? *(dar-zhAH)* money	How much money?
Combien de garçons?	How many boys?
Combien de filles?	How many girls?

These words can be used to form a question by following one of the two following formulas:

1. Interrogative + **EST-CE QUE** (**EST-CE QU'**) + Subject + Verb

   Quand est-ce qu'ils arrivent? When do they arrive?
   Où est-ce qu'ils habitent? Where do they live?

   Note: **QUE** becomes **QU'** before **EST-CE QUE**

   Qu'est-ce qu'ils cherchent? What are they looking for?

2. Interrogative + verb (hyphen) subject (this is called *inversion*):

   Quand arrivent-ils? When do they arrive?
   Où habitent-ils? Where do they live?

Try it yourself. Match up each question in the left column with its answer in the right column.

1. **Qu'est-ce que Marie mange?**

   (parl) (tehl)
2. **Anne parle-t-elle français?**
   speak
3. **Quand arrivent-ils?**
4. **Où arrivent-ils?**

   (e-may)
5. **Est-ce que vous aimez les croissants?**
   like

A. **Oui, j'aime les croissants.**

B. **Marie mange le croissant.**

C. **Oui, elle parle français.**

(duh-mEH)
D. **Ils arrivent demain.**
tomorrow

(a) (la-ay-ro-por)
E. **Ils arrivent à l'aéroport.**
at the airport

The phrase "there is" is useful to know in French. And it is the same in the singular and in the plural:

Il y a une chambre = There is a room.

Il y a des chambres = There are some rooms.

You can use this phrase in another way to ask a question. To form a question, you can either use the inversion or **EST-CE QUE**:

Y a-t-il une chambre? = Is there a room?

Y a-t-il des chambres? = Are there any rooms?

Est-ce qu'il y a encore une chambre?
Is there still a room? (Is there a room left?)

Il n'y a pas de chambre = There is no room.

Il n'y a plus de chambres = There are no rooms left.

Note: *Un, une, des* = *de* in a negative sentence.

(eel-ya) **IL Y A**	*(eel) (nya) (pah)* **IL N'Y A PAS**	*(ya-teel) (ya-teel) (pah)* **Y A-T-IL ou N'Y A-T-IL PAS?**
There is There are	There is not (no) There are not	Is there or Isn't there? Are there? Aren't there?

ANSWERS

Questions/Answers 1. B 2. C 3. D 4. E 5. A

Slow down! If you are getting confused, just ease up on your pace and review what you've learned so far. **Vous comprenez?** (Do you understand?)

See how much French you already know by doing the following crossword puzzle. The puzzle contains verbs that you have already used: **parler** (to speak), **chanter** (to sing), **arriver** (to arrive), **habiter** (to live in a place).

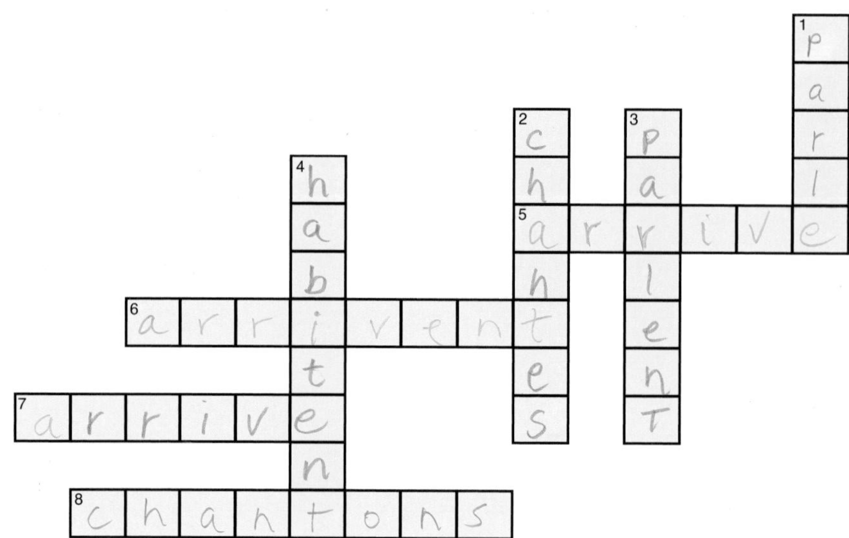

ACROSS

5. Elle (arrives)
6. Ils (arrive)
7. J' (live)
8. Nous (sing)

DOWN

1. On (speaks)
2. Tu (are singing)
3. Les garçons (speak)
4. Elles (live)

ANSWERS

Puzzle

ACROSS

5. arrive
6. arrivent
7. habite
8. chantons

DOWN

1. parle
2. chantes
3. parlent
4. habitent

Now test your comprehension of what you have learned in this unit about requesting a room at a hotel.

Fill in the blanks:

1. M. Smith a une réservation pour ___deux chambres___.
   two rooms
2. ___La douche___ ne marche pas.
   The shower
3. On ne peut pas ___ouvrir la fenêtre___.
   open the window
4. Le petit déjeuner ___est compris___.
   is included
5. Les chambres sont ___au troisième étage___.
   on the third floor

(See page 56 for tips on how floors are numbered in French.)

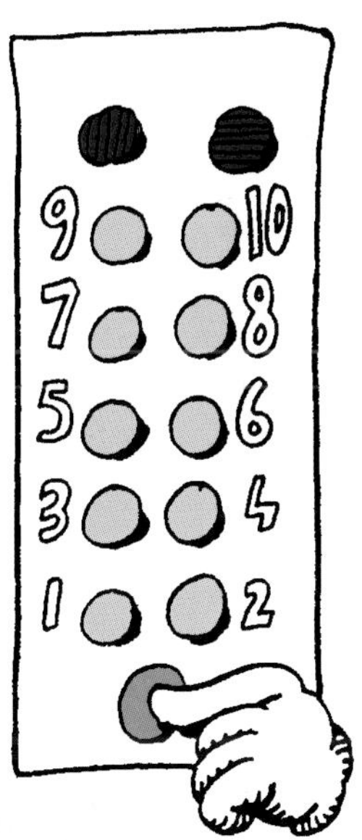

ANSWERS

Fill in blanks **1.** deux chambres **2.** La douche **3.** ouvrir la fenêtre **4.** est compris **5.** au troisième étage

SEEING THE SIGHTS

(vee-zee-tay) (veel)
Allons visiter la ville

(a-lOH-zee) (pyay)
3 Allons-y à pied

Let's Go on Foot

"How do I get to ... ?" "Where is the nearest subway?" "Is the museum straight ahead?" You'll be asking directions wherever you travel. Acquaint yourself with words and phrases that will make getting around easier. Don't forget to read each line aloud several times to practice your pronunciation. Act out each part to be certain you understand these new words.

(Paul and Anne Smith set out on their first day to visit a museum.)

ANNE	*(duh-mAH-dOH) (la-zhAH)* **Paul, demandons à l'agent de** *(pol-lees) (e) (mew-zay)* **police où est le musée.**	Paul, let's ask the policeman where the museum is.
PAUL	*(sewr) (ray-ew-seer)* **Je ne suis pas sûr de réussir . . .**	I am not sure of succeeding . . .
	Excusez-moi, Monsieur l'agent,	Excuse me, Sir,
	(deer) **pouvez-vous nous dire où est le musée?**	can you tell us where the museum is?

(sehr-ten-mAH) (kOH-tee-new-ay) (too)
AGENT **Certainement. Continuez tout**
(drwah) (zhews-ka) (rew) (mo-lyehr)
droit jusqu'à la rue Molière et
(toor-nay) (drwat)
tournez à droite. Continuez jusqu'à
(vol-tehr) (AH-sweet)
la rue Voltaire, ensuite tournez à
(gohsh) (ra-seen)
gauche et continuez sur la rue Racine
(zhews-koh) (fũh) (la) (a)
jusqu'aux feux. Le musée est là, à
(koh-tay) (lay-gleez)
côté de l'église.

Certainly. Continue straight ahead to Molière Street and turn right. Continue to Voltaire Street, then turn left and continue on Racine Street to the traffic lights. The museum is there, next to the church.

PAUL **Merci mille fois.**

Many thanks.

(ryEH)
AGENT **De rien.**

You are welcome. (*lit*. of nothing.)

After having followed the directions:

(suh) (nay) (pas) (luh) (mew-zay)
ANNE **Ce n'est pas le musée.**
(post)
C'est la poste.

This building is not the museum.
It's the post office.

(troh) (tar)
PAUL **Patience, Anne. Il est trop tard**
(poor)
pour visiter la ville.
(ruh-toor-nOH)
Retournons à l'hôtel.

Be patient, Anne. It's too late to go sightseeing in town.
Let's go back to the hotel.

Can you answer these true-false questions based on the dialogue? Write VRAI (true) next to each true statement. Correct any false statement.

le musée 1. Paul demande à l'agent où est *l'église*.
Vrai 2. L'agent dit de toumer *à droite*.
l'église 3. Le musée est à côté de *l'école*.
vrai 4. Ce n'est pas *le musée*.
la poste 5. C'est *l'aéroport*.

ANSWERS

True-false **1.** le musée **2.** VRAI **3.** l'église **4.** VRAI **5.** la poste

(oo) (a-lay) (voo)

OÙ ALLEZ-VOUS?

Where Are You Going?

You'll find yourself *going to* a museum, or being at a bakery or in a theater often if you go abroad, so knowing the following words will come in very handy.

(lom)
L'homme est à Paris.
in

(va)
L'homme va à New York.
goes to

L 'homme est ~~à + le~~ →
(oh)
AU cinéma.
at the

L'homme va ~~à + le~~ →
AU théâtre.
to the

Le garçon est à la
at the
boulangerie.
bakery

Le garçon va à la
to the
boulangerie.

Le garçon est à l'école.
at the

Le garçon va à l'école.
to the

Madame Dubois est
~~à + les~~ → AUX États-Unis.
in the

Madame Dubois va
~~à + les~~ → AUX États-Unis.
to the

(kel-kuh) (puh-tee) (moh) (kee) (see-nee-fee) (boh-koo)

Quelques petits mots qui signifient beaucoup

Some little words that mean a lot

The preposition **À** means "to" or "at" and is used before proper nouns:

Il parle à Jean.

The definite articles **LA** (used before feminine singular nouns beginning with a consonant) and **L'** (used before all singular nouns beginning with a vowel or silent *h*) can be placed after **À** to express "to the" or "at the":

Le garçon est À LA boulangerie. **Le garçon est À L' école.**

The definite articles **LE** (used before masculine singular nouns beginning with a consonant) and **LES** (used before all plural nouns) contract with **À** to form completely new words:

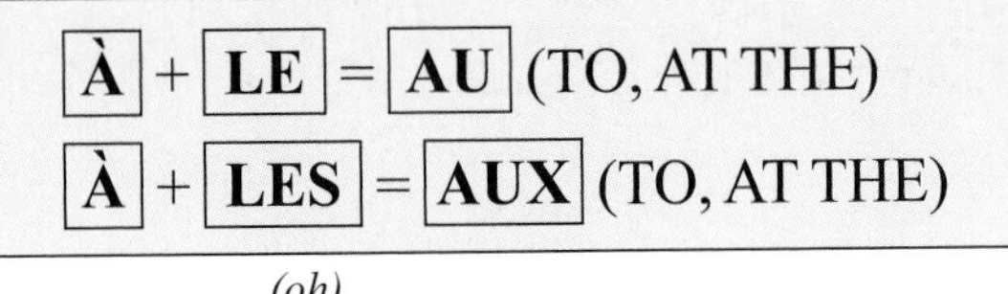

À + **LE** = **AU** (TO, AT THE)

À + **LES** = **AUX** (TO, AT THE)

(oh)

Il parle AU garçon.

(oh)

Il parle AUX garçons.

Try this exercise:

Jean va

1. ___au___ cinéma.
2. ___à l'___ école.
3. ___aux___ États-Unis.
4. ___à___ Paris.
5. ___à la___ boulangerie.

A similar change is made with **DE**, which means "from," "of," or "about":

Il parle DE Jean.

Il parle DE la boulangerie.

Il parle DE l'école.

DE + La = de la

But note:

DE + **LE** = **DU**

DE + **LES** = **DES**

Il parle du garçon.
Il parle des garçons.

ANSWERS

Prepositions **1.** au cinéma **2.** à l'école **3.** aux États-Unis **4.** à Paris **5.** à la boulangerie

Now do this exercise.

Jean parle 1. ________ école. 4. ________ New-York.

2. ________ théâtre. 5. ________ filles.

3. ________ boulangerie.

The other prepositions are easier. Some are followed by DE and the rule you just practiced applies.

(dAH)
Le garçon est dans la maison.
in house

(sewr)
Le chat est sur la chaise.
on

(shyEH) (soo)
Le chien est sous la table.
under

(soo-ree) (lwEH)
La souris est loin du chat.
mouse far from

(pwa-sOH)
La souris est près du poisson.
near fish

(gohsh)
Le réfrigérateur est à gauche de la table.
left

(drwat)
La table est à droite du réfrigérateur.
right

(koh-tay)
La chaise est à côté de la table.
next to

(duh-vAH)
Le dîner du chien est devant la chaise.
in front of

(deh-ryehr)
Le chien est derrière la chaise.
behind

Can you describe where everything and everybody is in this picture?

1. Le garçon est ________ la porte.
behind
2. M. Dubois est dans la ________.
kitchen
3. Le réfrigérateur est à côté de la ________.
stove

ANSWERS

Describe **1.** derrière **2.** cuisine **3.** cuisinière

About **1.** de l'école **2.** du théâtre **3.** de la boulangerie **4.** de New-York **5.** des filles

(AH-kor)

Encore des verbes

Verbs again

In the previous unit you learned how to conjugate verbs ending in -ER. These are known as verbs of the first conjugation. Now you will learn how to conjugate some common verbs of the second conjugation. These end in -IR. Drop **IR** and add the endings:

FINIR (TO FINISH)		**RÉUSSIR** (TO SUCCEED)	
je, **tu**	*(fee-nee)* **fin*is***	**je**, **tu**	*(ray-ew-see)* **réuss*is***
il, **elle**, **on**	*(fee-nee)* **fin*it***	**il**, **elle**, **on**	*(ray-ew-see)* **réuss*it***
nous	*(fee-nee-sOH)* **fin*issons***	**nous**	*(ray-ew-see-sOH)* **réuss*issons***
vous	*(fee-nee-say)* **fin*issez***	**vous**	*(ray-ew-see-say)* **réuss*issez***
ils, **elles**	*(fee-nees)* **fin*issent***	**ils**, **elles**	*(ray-ew-sees)* **réuss*issent***

Remember that to make verbs negative, you put NE (N') before the verb and PAS after.

Je ne finis pas. **Je ne réussis pas.**

Can you figure out each verb by unscrambling the letters? The only two verbs used are FINIR and RÉUSSIR.

a. Jean UÉRITSS Réussit à parler français.

b. Jean et Anne TNESSINIF finissent *(luhr)* leur sightseeing. (their)

c. Nous NFIISOSSN finissons le dîner.

d. IRZEEUSSSS réussissez-vous à parler français?

e. Je NIFIS finis ce *(tra-va-y)* travail.

f. Tu RIÉUSSS réussis.

g. On TFINI finit.

h. Vous EZNIFSSI finissez.

ANSWERS

Unscrambling IR verbs
a. Jean *réussit* à parler français.
b. Jean et Anne *finissent* leur sightseeing.
c. Nous *finissons* le dîner.
d. *Réussissez*-vous à parler français?
e. Je *finis* ce travail.
f. Tu *réussis*.
g. On *finit*.
h. Vous *finissez*.

(kel -kuh) (moh) (zew-teel)

Quelques mots utiles

Some useful words

(day-zee-nyay) (shohz) (AH)

Comment désigner les choses en français

How to point things out in French

Words like "this" and "that" are important to know, particularly when you go shopping, and want to buy that delicious-looking *éclair* at the *pâtisserie*. The French forms of these words vary, depending on whether the item is masculine or feminine, and whether you are pointing to one item or to many.

"THIS" OR "THAT" AND "THESE" OR "THOSE"	
WITH FEMININE NOUNS	
Singulier	**Pluriel**
(set) **cette fille**	*(say)* **ces filles**
cette amie	**ces amies**
(se tay-tew-dyAHt) **cette étudiante** this student—female	*(say zay-tew-dyAHt)* **ces étudiantes** these students
WITH MASCULINE NOUNS	
(suh) (bah-tee-mAH) **ce bâtiment** this building	*(bah-tee-mAH)* **ces bâtiments** these buildings
(se tay-tew-dyAH) **cet étudiant** this student—male	*(say zay-tew-dyAH)* **ces étudiants** these students

NOTE: CE becomes CET before masculine singular nouns that begin with a vowel.

(ee-see) *(la)*

ICI means "here" and LÀ means "there." So if you want to be more specific or to differentiate between this thing here and that thing over there, you simply add -CI or -LÀ to the noun.

"HERE" AND "THERE"

ICI	LÀ
cette fille-ci	**cette fille-là**
cette amie-ci	**cette amie-là**
ce garçon-ci	**ce garçon-là**
cet étudiant-ci	**cet étudiant-là**
ces filles-ci	**ces filles-là**
ces étudiants-ci	**ces étudiants-là**

Now, try the following: Put the appropriate form of "this" or "these" and "that" or "those" in each slot:

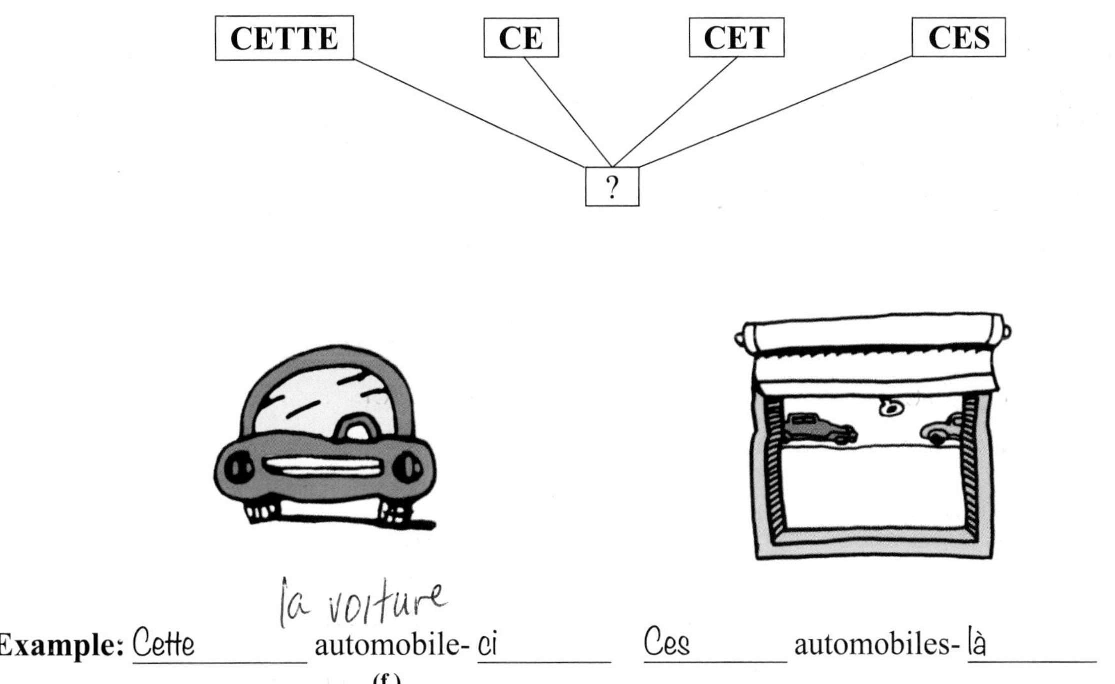

Example: Cette ________ automobile- ci ________ Ces ________ automobiles- là ________
(f.)

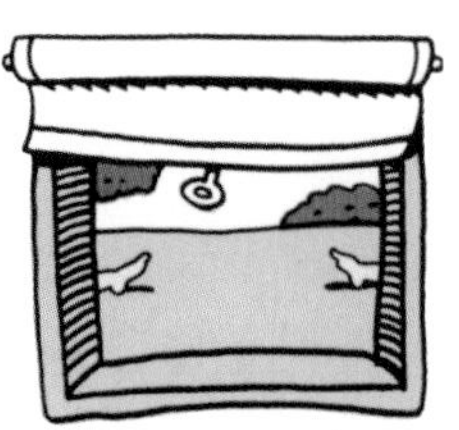

_____ chat- _____ (m.)

_____ chats- _____

_____ pied- _____ foot (m.)

_____ pieds- _____

_____ maison- _____ house (f.)

_____ maisons- _____

_____ étudiant- _____

_____ étudiants- _____

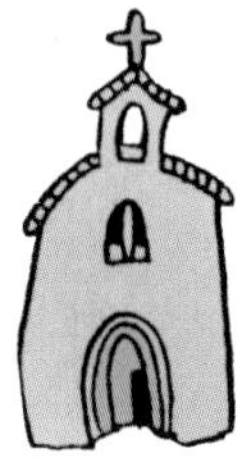

_____ église- _____ church (f.)

_____ églises- _____

(o-pay-rah)
_____ opéra- _____ opera (m.)

_____ opéras- _____

ANSWERS

Demonstrative adjectives

Ce chat-ci	Ces chats-là	Ce pied-ci	Ces pieds-là
Cette maison-ci	Ces maisons-là	Cet étudiant-ci	Ces étudiants-là
Cette église-ci	Ces églises-là	Cet opéra-ci	Ces opéras-là

Now have fun with the following crossword puzzle:

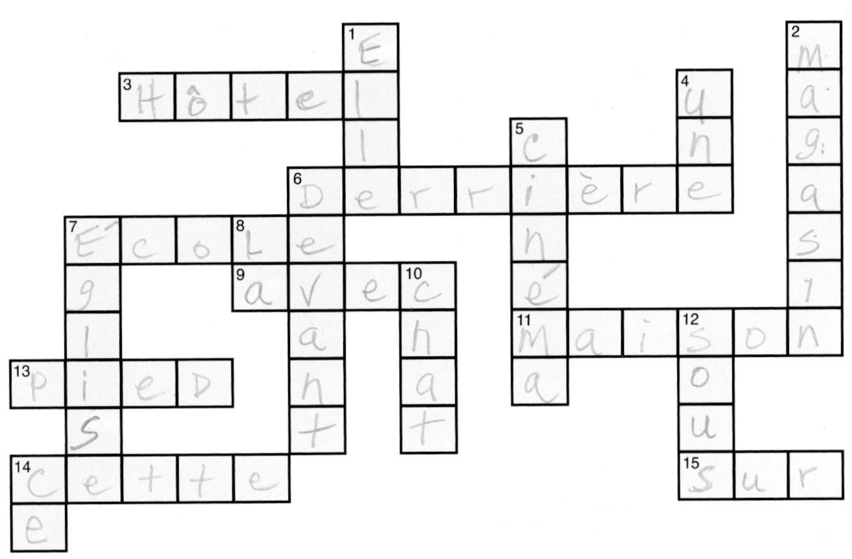

ACROSS

3. Hotel
6. Behind
7. School
9. With
11. House
13. Foot
14. This (f.)
15. On

DOWN

1. She
2. Store
4. One, a (f.)
5. Movies
6. In front
7. Church
8. The (f.)
10. Cat
12. Under
14. This (m.)

ANSWERS

Puzzle

ACROSS **3.** Hôtel **6.** Derrière **7.** École **9.** Avec **11.** Maison **13.** Pied **14.** Cette **15.** Sur

DOWN **1.** Elle **2.** Magasin **4.** Une **5.** Cinéma **6.** Devant **7.** Église **8.** La **10.** Chat **12.** Sous **14.** Ce

4 Le transport public

(tran-spor) *(pew-bleek)*

Le transport public

Public Transportation

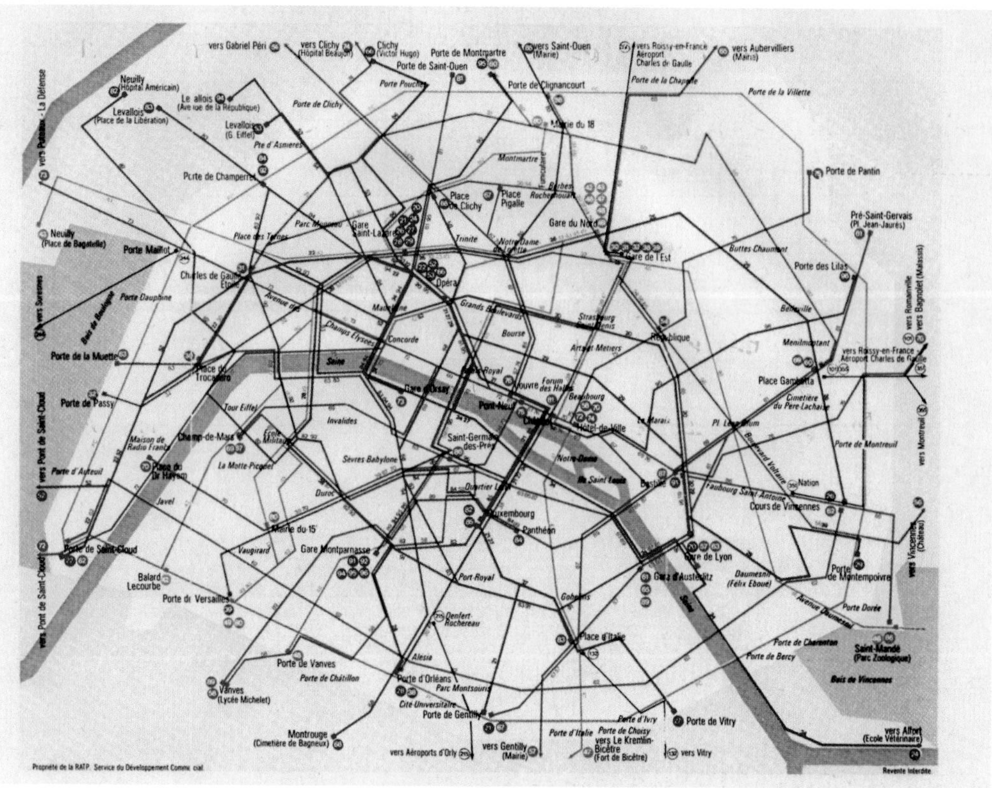

You will certainly want to take public transportation when you are in a foreign city. The following dialogue contains some words and expressions that you will find useful in order to get around easily using public transportation. Always read the dialogue carefully several times out loud to familiarize yourself with the meaning and pronunciation of the words.

(pruh-nOH) *(tak-see)* *(a-lay)*

MARIE **Prenons un taxi pour aller au cinéma.** — Let's take a taxi to go to the movies.

(troh)

MARC **Non. C'est trop cher.** — No. It's too expensive.

MARIE **Alors prenons le métro.** — **Then let's take the metro.**

(vwa) *(vew)*

MARC **Non. On ne voit pas la vue.** — No. One doesn't see the view.

	(keh) (lom) (ma-va) (ray) (dee-fee-seel)	
MARIE	**Quel homme avare et difficile!**	What a stingy and difficult man!
	(o-to-bews)	
	Alors prenons l'autobus.	Then, let's take the bus.
	(bee-yay)	
MARC	**D'accord. Notre billet est un passe**	Okay. Our unlimited ticket
	(ee-lee-mee-tay) (bohn)	
	illimité. Il est bon pour le métro et l'autobus.	is good for the metro and the bus.
	Dans l'autobus	On the Bus
	(de-sAH-dOH)	
MARC	**Pardon Madame, où descendons nous pour aller au cinéma Broadway?**	Excuse, me, Madam, where do we get off to go to the cinema "Broadway"?
	(a-reh) (a-preh) (kOH-kord)	
LA DAME	**À l'arrêt après la place de la Concorde.**	At the stop after the Concorde.
	(kom) (sOH) (teh-mahbl)	
MARC	**Comme les Français sont aimables!**	How kind the French are!

Circle the best answer to each question.

1. Marie désire prendre un taxi pour aller
   a. au musée (b.) au cinéma c. à l'hôtel d. à Paris

2. L'autobus
   a. ne va pas au cinéma b. est trop cher
   (c.) va directement au cinéma d. ne va pas à la place de la Concorde

3. Marie et Marc décident de prendre l'autobus et d'utiliser
   a. la carte de tourisme b. le billet de cinq euros
   c. le passeport (d.) le passe illimité

4. Le cinéma Broadway est
   a. tout droit b. à la rue Racine c. à côté du musée
   (d.) à l'arrêt apres la place de la Concorde

Qu'est-ce que c'est?

a. un taxi_______________ b. un autobus_______________

ANSWERS

Multiple choice 1. b 2. c 3. d 4. d

Qu'est-ce que c'est? **a.** un taxi **b.** un autobus

voitre la person

c. un Métro ______ d. une automobile ______

Encore des verbes

More Verbs

Now, you will learn how to conjugate third conjugation verbs like DESCENDRE *(de-sAHdr)* (to go down—to get off) and VENDRE *(vAHdr)* (to sell) and the irregular verbs ÊTRE *(ehtr)* (to be), AVOIR *(a-vwar)* (to have) and PRENDRE *(prAHdr)* (to take). Notice that third conjugation verbs end in -RE. Drop the -RE and add the following endings.

VENDRE (TO SELL)		DESCENDRE (TO GO DOWN, TO GET OFF)	
je, **tu**	*(vAH)* **vend*s***	**je**, **tu**	*(deh-sAH)* **descend*s***
il, **elle**, **on**	*(vAH)* **vend**	**il**, **elle**, **on**	*(deh-sAH)* **descend**
nous	*(vAH-dOH)* **vend*ons***	**nous**	*(deh-sAH-dOH)* **descend*ons***
vous	*(vAH-day)* **vend*ez***	**vous**	*(deh-sAH-day)* **descend*ez***
ils, **elles**	*(vAHd)* **vend*ent***	**ils**, **elles**	*(deh-sAHd)* **descend*ent***

Remember that you are saying "I sell," "I am selling" or "I do sell." In other words, one French structure can express three different ideas in English.

ANSWERS

Qu'est-ce que c'est? **c.** un métro **d.** une automobile

It's wise now to review the conjugations of the three groups of regular French verbs.

SUMMARY: ENDINGS FOR THREE TYPES OF REGULAR VERBS			
	PARL-*ER*	FIN-*IR*	VEND-*RE*
je	**-E**	**-IS**	**-S**
tu	**-ES**	**-IS**	**-S**
il, elle, on	**-E**	**-IT**	—
nous	**-ONS**	**-ISSONS**	**-ONS**
vous	**-EZ**	**-ISSEZ**	**-EZ**
ils, elles	**-ENT**	**-ISSENT**	**-ENT**

Do you begin to see a pattern? Now conjugate DESCENDRE:

1. Je descend s
2. Tu descend s
3. Il descend –
4. Nous descend ons
5. Vous descend ez
6. Ils descend ent
7. Le garçon descend –
8. Les hommes descend ent

COMMENT PARLER AU CONTRÔLEUR . . .

How to Speak to the Conductor . . .

As a tourist in a French-speaking city, you may want to speak with the **conducteur** (*kOH-dewk-tuhr*) or the **contrôleur** (*kOH-troh-luhr*) of the bus. A **contrôleur** is an agent who checks tickets and assures proper behavior on the train or bus. Don't smoke or put your feet up on the seat! Also, when you travel by bus or train, remember to keep your ticket until after the ride is over because you will have to use it for transfers and to leave the station at the end of your ride. You may also be asked by a **contrôleur** to show your ticket and you could pay a fine if you haven't validated it properly. Here are some questions that you may want to ask an agent.

(conducteur: driver)

ANSWERS

Descendre **1.** Je descends **2.** Tu descends **3.** Il descend **4.** Nous descendons **5.** Vous descendez **6.** Ils descendent **7.** Le garçon descend **8.** Les hommes descendent

Track 09 03:15

(puh) (ash-tay) **Est-ce que je peux acheter mon billet dans l'autobus?** (buy)	Can I buy my ticket on the bus?
(foh) (mOH-tay) **Est-ce qu'il faut monter devant ou derrière?** (get on)	Should one get on in the front or in the rear?
(koot) **Combien coûte le billet?**	How much does the ticket cost?
Pouvez-vous me dire quand il faut descendre?	Can you tell me when to get off?
(day-zo-lay) (mo-ne) **Je suis désolé, je n'ai pas de monnaie.**	I am very sorry, I don't have any change.

(lay) (vehrb) (kee) (nuh) (suh) (kOH-form) (pah) (zoh) (rehgl)

Les verbes qui ne se conforment pas aux règles

Verbs that don't follow the rules

You've learned how to use some common verbs that end in "er," "ir," and "re." Unfortunately, using verbs isn't that simple! *Naturellement*! There are exceptions to the rules, and we call them "irregular verbs." Here are two common irregular verbs. Notice how they take on different forms, depending upon the subject. It is hard work, but you just have to learn these well, because you will want to use them often.

PP été PP eu

(ehtr) **ÊTRE** (TO BE)		*(a-vwar)* **AVOIR** (TO HAVE)	
je	*(swee)* **suis**	**j'**	*(zhay)* **ai**
tu	*(eh)* **es**	**tu**	*(a)* **as**
il, elle, on	*(eh)* **est**	**il, elle, on**	*(a)* **a**
nous	*(som)* **sommes**	**nous**	*(a-vOH)* **avons**
vous	*(eht)* **êtes**	**vous**	*(a-vay)* **avez**
ils, elles	*(sOH)* **sont**	**ils, elles**	*(zOH)* **ont**

j'ai été I was j'ai eu I've had

You may have noticed these verbs in the previous chapters:

Je ne suis pas sûr de réussir. I am not sure of succeeding.
Demandons à l'agent où est le musée. Let's ask the policeman where the museum is.
Comme les Français sont aimables! How friendly the French are!

Now, write down the meaning of the next short sentences in English.

1. Nous sommes à Paris. We are in Paris.
2. Vous avez une réservation. You have a reservation.
3. L'hôtel est loin de la banque. The hotel is far from the bank.
4. Marc et Marie n'ont pas de réservation. Marc et Marie have no reservation.
5. Est-ce que vous avez de la monnaie? Do you have any change?

There are a few more irregular verbs that you'll need to know. Take a look at **prendre** *(prAHdr)* (to take), **apprendre** *(a-prAHdr)* (to learn), and **comprendre** *(kOH-prAHdr)* (to understand).

	PRENDRE (TO TAKE)	APPRENDRE (TO LEARN)	COMPRENDRE (TO UNDERSTAND)
je, j'	**prend*s***	**apprend*s***	**comprend*s***
tu	**prend*s***	**apprend*s***	**comprends**
il, elle, on	**prend**	**apprend**	**comprend**
nous	*(pruh-nOH)* **pren*ons***	*(a-pruh-nOH)* **appren*ons***	*(kOH-pruh-nOH)* **compren*ons***
vous	*(pruh-nay)* **pren*ez***	*(a-pruh-nay)* **appren*ez***	*(kOH-pruh-nay)* **compren*ez***
ils, elles	*(pren)* **pren*nent***	*(a-pren)* **appren*nent***	*(kOH-pren)* **compren*nent***

ANSWERS

English Translation **1.** We are in Paris. **2.** You have a reservation. **3.** The hotel is far from the bank. **4.** Mark and Mary have no reservation. **5.** Do you have any change?

This is how they would appear in context.

Prenons l'autobus! Let's take the bus! **J'apprends le français.** I am learning French.

(too) (ptee) (puh)

Je comprends le français un tout petit peu. I understand French a tiny little bit.

Write the meaning in English of the following sentences.

1. Marc et Marie comprennent le français. ____________________.
2. Est-ce que vous apprenez l'anglais? ____________________?
3. Jean ne comprend pas très bien le français. ____________________.
4. Prenons le métro! ____________________!
5. Prennent-ils un taxi? ____________________?

Now see if you can remember the regular and irregular verbs by writing in the appropriate forms on the blanks.

	ÊTRE	AVOIR	PRENDRE	DESCENDRE	FINIR
JE	______	______	______	______	______
TU	______	______	______	______	______
IL, ELLE, ON	______	______	______	______	______
NOUS	______	______	______	______	______
VOUS	______	______	______	______	______
ILS, ELLES	______	______	______	______	______

ANSWERS

English Translation **1.** Mark and Mary understand French. **2.** Are you learning English? **3.** John does not understand French very well. **4.** Let's take the metro. **5.** Are they taking a taxi?

Verbs	**être**	**avoir**	**prendre**	**descendre**	**finir**
je, j'	suis	ai	prends	descends	finis
tu	es	as	prends	descends	finis
il, elle, on	est	a	prend	descend	finit
nous	sommes	avons	prenons	descendons	finissons
vous	êtes	avez	prenez	descendez	finissez
ils, elles	sont	ont	prennent	descendent	finissent

(ruh-vuh-nOH) (pray-poh-zee-syOH)

Revenons aux prépositions

Let's get back to prepositions

Earlier we saw how the prepositions À ("to," "in") and DE ("of," "from," "about") contract with the definite articles LE and LES to become AU, AUX, and DU, DES. But we practiced them mostly before names of places (Paris, le cinéma, etc.). However,

À is the equivalent of "to" in a statement such as:

Je parle au garçon.	I speak to the boy.

The indefinite article DES (plural of UN, UNE) could be considered a contraction of DE + LES, meaning "about the," "of the," "from the." However,

DE + definite article (or proper name) expresses possession:

Le livre du garçon	The boy's book
Le livre de Paul	Paul's book

and means "about" in sentences such as:

Nous parlons du professeur.	We are talking about the teacher.

A little practice? Try these:

1. Le livre ______ (of the) garçon
2. Le cahier ______ (of the) fille
3. Les amis ______ (of the) étudiant
4. L'ami ______ (of the) étudiante *(ay-tew-dyAHt)* (fem. student)
5. Je parle ______ (about the) étudiant
6. Le professeur parle ______ (about the) livre ______ (to the) étudiants
7. J'ai ______ (some) amis ______ (in) Montréal
8. Je donne *(don)* (give) le livre ______ (to the) garçon
9. Nous téléphonons *(tay-lay-fo-nOH)* ______ (to the) hôtel

ANSWERS

DE 1. du 2. de la 3. de l' 4. de l' 5. de l' 6. du aux 7. des à 8. au 9. à l'

The following brief passage will let you find out how well you have learned to answer questions and to get around town.

Track 10
03:35

Monsieur Legros et sa femme prennent l'autobus et descendent deux arrêts plus loin. Puis ils prennent le métro. Ils descendent à la rue Rousseau. Ils arrivent au marché et achètent beaucoup de choses.

sa (his) · **deux** (two) · **plus** *(plew)* (more) · **Puis** (then) · **rue** *(roo-soh)* · **achètent** *(a-shet)* · **beaucoup** *(boh-koo)* (many) · **choses** *(shohz)* (things)

1. Qu'est-ce que les Legros prennent?

   Les Legros prennent l'autobus et le métro.

2. Où descendent-ils?

   Ils descendent à la rue Rousseau.

3. Et ensuite (then), qu'est-ce qu'ils prennent?

   Ensuite ils prennent le métro.

4. Où est-ce que les Legros arrivent?

   Les Legros arrivent au marché.

5. Qu'est-ce qu'ils achètent?

   Ils achètent beaucoup de choses.

ANSWERS

Questions **1.** (Ils prennent) l'autobus. **2.** (Ils descendent) deux arrêts plus loin. **3.** (Ils prennent) le métro. **4.** (Ils arrivent) au marché. **5.** (Ils achètent) beaucoup de choses.

5 Comment exprimer l'heure et les nombres

(ko-mAH) (lūhr) (nOHbr)

Expressing Time and Numbers

TRACK 11

Tokyo	**Paris**	**Anchorage**	**New York**
Tokyo	Paris	Anchorage	New York

Il est 9 heures du matin. **Il est 1 heure du matin.** **Il est 3 heures de l'après-midi.** **Il est 8 heures du soir.** **Il est 3 heures du matin.**

Expressing time is easy. Simply state the number of the hour, followed by the word heure(s).

You use *du matin* *(ma-tEH)* (A.M.) for the morning and *de l'après midi* *(duh) (la-preh-mee-dee)* (P.M.) for early afternoon; *du soir* *(swar)* (P.M.) is used for later afternoon and evening.

COMMENT COMPTER EN FRANÇAIS

(kOH-tay)

How to Count in French

Les nombres cardinaux 1–1000

(kar-dee-noh)

Cardinal numbers 1–1000

1	2	3	4	5	6	7	8
			(katr)	*(sEHk)*	*(sees)*	*(seht)*	*(weet)*
un	**deux**	**trois**	**quatre**	**cinq**	**six**	**sept**	**huit**

9	10	11	12	13	14	15
		(OHz)	*(dooz)*	*(trehz)*	*(ka-torz)*	*(kehz)*
neuf	**dix**	**onze**	**douze**	**treize**	**quatorze**	**quinze**

16	17	18	19	20
(sehz)	*(dee-set)*	*(dee-zweet)*	*(deez-nuhf)*	*(vEH)*
seize	**dix-sept**	**dix-huit**	**dix-neuf**	**vingt**

Now it's easy . . . until we reach 70.

21 vingt et un
22 vingt-deux
23 vingt-trois etc.
(trAHt)
30 trente
31 trente et un
32 trente-deux
(ka-rAHt)
40 quarante

(sEH-kAHt)
50 cinquante
(swa-sAHt)
60 soixante
70 soixante-dix
71 soixante et onze
72 soixante-douze etc.
80 quatre-vingts
81 quatre-vingt-un
82 quatre-vingt-deux etc.

90 quatre-vingt-dix
91 quatre-vingt-onze
92 quatre-vingt-douze etc.
(sAH)
100 cent
200 deux cents etc.
(meel)
1000 mille

PRONUNCIATION NOTE: Six and ten are pronounced "sees" and "dees" if they are by themselves. When followed by a noun, they become "see" and "dee." Eight is pronounced "weet" by itself, "wee" when followed by a noun:

(see) **six garçons** *(dee)* **dix filles** *(wee)* **huit tables**

When these numbers are followed by a noun that begins with a vowel, one has to link:

(see) (zamee) **six amis** *(dee) (zay-kol)* **dix écoles** schools

And when nine is followed by a vowel sound, the final "F" sounds like a "V": *(nuh) (vuhr)* **il est neuf heures**

(or-dee-noh)

Les nombres ordinaux 1–10

Ordinal numbers 1–10

First (Masculine): *(pruh-myay)* **premier**

First (Feminine): *(pruh-myer)* **première**

Second: *(dūh-zyehm)* **deuxième**

Third: *(trwah-zyehm)* **troisième**

Fourth: *(ka-try-ehm)* **quatrième**

Fifth: *(sEH-kyehm)* **cinquième**

Sixth: *(see-zyehm)* **sixième**

Seventh: *(se-tyehm)* **septième**

Eighth: *(wee-tyehm)* **huitième**

Ninth: *(nuh-vyehm)* **neuvième**

Tenth: *(dee-zyehm)* **dixième**

(rayd) (shoh-say) **rez-de-chaussée**

ALARME **STOP**
9ème **10ème**
7ème **8ème**
5ème **6ème**
3ème **4ème**
1er **2ème**

NOTE: The "rez-de-chaussée" is the ground floor in the U.S.; the "premier *(ay-tahzh)* étage" is the second floor in the U.S.

(ke) (luh) (reh) (teel)

QUELLE HEURE EST-IL?

What Time Is It?

1. To add the minutes, simply add the number:

Il est six heures dix du matin.

(dee) (zuhr)
Il est dix heures cinquante du matin.

(se)
Il est sept
(tuhr) (vEH)
heures vingt.

Il est huit heures
(trAHt) (nuhf)
trente-neuf.

Il est onze heures cinquante-cinq du matin.

2. If the minute hand is close to the next, you can also say the next hour **moins** *(mwEH)* (minus) the number of minutes to go:

(OH) (zuhr) (mwEH) (dees)
Il est onze heures moins dix.

3. Finally, the quarter hours and the half hours (although not in official time) can be replaced by the following expressions:

2:15—deux heures et **quart** *(kar)* (quarter)

3:30—trois heures et **demie** *(duh-mee)* (half—feminine because HEURE is feminine)

2:45—trois heures moins le **quart**

12:30—midi (minuit) et **demi** (half—masculine because MIDI and MINUIT are masculine)

Easy? In France the 24-hour system is often used, especially in travel schedules and performance times; for example, *quatorze heures* (14 hours) is 2 P.M. To understand this system, subtract 12 from any number more than 12 and add P.M.

A few examples:
Le train part à 22 h 13 = The train leaves at 10:13 P.M.
Le concert commence à 20 h 30 = The concert begins at 8:30 P.M.
L'avion arrive à 17 h 35 = The plane arrives at 5:35 P.M.

Un moment. Now give the following times in French:

2:15	1:10
8:30	3:35
9:45	5:25
7:00	4:55

Express these numbers in French:

14	62
23	71
37	89
46	98
55	116

The following dialogue contains some useful expressions related to the telling of time. Read it out loud a few times.

MARC	**Pardon, Monsieur, quelle heure est-il?**	Excuse me, Sir, what time is it?
UN MONSIEUR	**Il est minuit.**	It's midnight.
MARC	*(ehs) (po-seebl) (fay) (tAH-kor) (zhoor)* **Comment est-ce possible? Il fait encore jour.**	How can it be? It is still daytime.
UN MONSIEUR	*(kah)* **Excusez-moi. Dans ce cas il est midi.**	Excuse me. In that case, it is noon.
MARC	*(play-zAH-tay)* **Vous plaisantez?**	Are you joking?
UN MONSIEUR	*(mOHtr) (too-reest)* **Non. Je n'ai pas de montre. Vous êtes touriste?**	No. I don't have a watch. Are you a tourist?

ANSWERS

Time deux heures quinze, huit heures et demie, neuf heures quarante-cinq, sept heures, une heure dix, trois heures trente-cinq, cinq heures vingt-cinq, quatre heures cinquante-cinq

Numbers quatorze, vingt-trois, trente-sept, quarante-six, cinquante-cinq, soixante-deux, soixante et onze, quatre-vingt-neuf, quatre-vingt-dix-huit, cent seize

MARC	**Oui.**	Yes.
UN MONSIEUR	*(voo-lay)* *(ash-tay)* **Voulez-vous acheter une montre? Onze euros.**	Do you want to buy a watch? Eleven euros.
MARC	*(dee)* **Mais vous avez dit que vous n'avez pas de montre!**	But you said that you do not have a watch!
UN MONSIEUR	**Six euros.**	Six euros.
MARC	**Non, merci.**	No, thanks.
UN MONSIEUR	*(ah-tAH-day)* **Attendez! J'ai une très belle montre en or. Vingt euros.**	Wait! I have a very beautiful gold watch. Twenty euros.
MARC	*(eh-gweey)* *(toorn)* **Mais les aiguilles ne tournent pas.**	But the hands aren't turning.
UN MONSIEUR	**C'est vrai. Mais elle est très jolie et elle donne l'heure deux fois** *(fwah)* **par jour, à dix heures dix.**	That's true. But it's very pretty and it tells the time twice a day, at ten after ten.
MARC	*(fee-lay)* **Filez!**	Get lost!

Can you write these phrases in French as they appear in the dialogue?

1. What time is it? Quelle heure est-il?
2. It is midnight. Il est minuit.
3. It is still daytime. Il fait encore jour
4. It is noon. Il est midi.
5. Are you a tourist? Vous êtes touriste?
6. That's true. C'est vrai

ANSWERS

Time 1. Quelle heure est-il? **2.** Il est minuit. **3.** Il fait encore jour. **4.** Il est midi. **5.** Vous êtes touriste? **6.** C'est vrai.

(zh-oor) *(smehn)* LES JOURS DE LA SEMAINE

The Days of the Week

Remember the saying, " If it's Tuesday, I must be in . . . "

(lUH-dee) **lundi** *(mar-dee)* **mardi** *(mer-kruh-dee)* **mercredi** *(zhūh-dee)* **jeudi** *(vAH-druh-dee)* **vendredi** *(sam-dee)* **samedi** *(dee-mAHsh)* **dimanche**

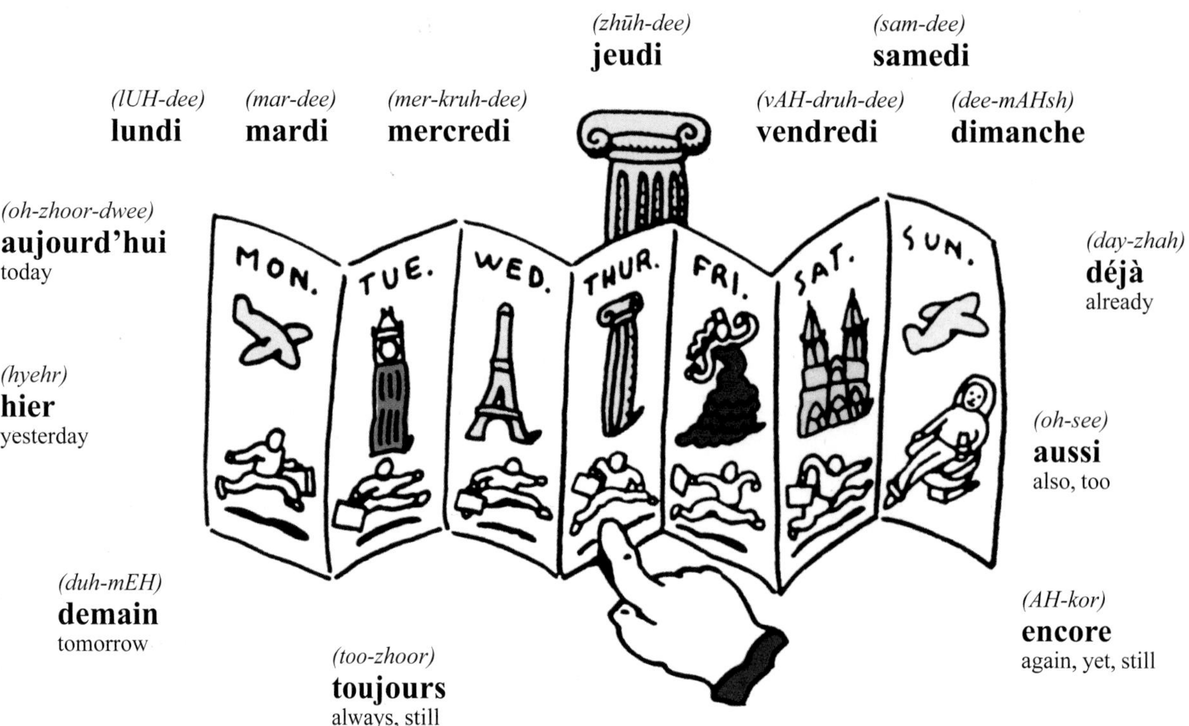

(oh-zhoor-dwee) **aujourd'hui** today

(hyehr) **hier** yesterday

(duh-mEH) **demain** tomorrow

(too-zhoor) **toujours** always, still

(day-zhah) **déjà** already

(oh-see) **aussi** also, too

(AH-kor) **encore** again, yet, still

Now, see if you remember the meaning of the following adverbs by matching them up to their English equivalents.

1. **aujourd'hui**	A. today
2. **hier**	B. yesterday
3. **demain**	C. again
4. **toujours**	D. tomorrow
5. **encore**	E. always
6. **aussi**	F. already
7. **déjà**	G. also

ANSWERS

Matching Adverbs 1. A **2.** B **3.** D **4.** E **5.** C **6.** G **7.** F

(AH-kor) *(vehrb)* *(ee-reh-gew-lyay)*

Encore des verbes irréguliers

More irregular verbs

In a previous unit you learned to conjugate verbs of the second conjugation ending in **-IR**. There is a fairly large group of **-IR** verbs which follow a different pattern and are considered irregular. This table will help you remember these special verbs.

(dor-meer) **DORMIR** (TO SLEEP)		*(par-teer)* **PARTIR** (TO LEAVE)	
je, **tu**	*(dor)* **dor*s***	**je**, **tu**	*(par)* **par*s***
il, **elle**, **on**	*(dor)* **dort**	**il**, **elle**, **on**	*(par)* **part**
nous	*(dor-mOH)* **dorm*ons***	**nous**	*(par-tOH)* **part*ons***
vous	*(dor-may)* **dorm*ez***	**vous**	*(par-tay)* **part*ez***
ils, **elles**	*(dorm)* **dorm*ent***	**ils**, **elles**	*(part)* **part*ent***

Some other verbs in this group are SORTIR *(sor-teer)* to go out, to exit, SERVIR *(ser-veer)* to serve, SENTIR *(sAH-teer)* to smell, to feel, MENTIR *(mAH-teer)* to lie. Unfortunately, you cannot predict which verbs belong to which group.

Add the endings to the verb stems in the following list.

1. Je sor ______
2. Tu dor ______
3. Il par ______
4. Elle ser ______
5. On sen ______
6. Nous men ______
7. Vous dor ______
8. Ils par ______
9. Elles sor ______

ANSWERS

Verbs **1.** Je sors **2.** Tu dors **3.** Il part **4.** Elle sert **5.** On sent **6.** Nous mentons **7.** Vous dormez **8.** Ils partent **9.** Elles sortent

How can you recognize a special "**-IR**" verb that takes these endings? You can't. **Je le regrette.** (I'm sorry!) Let's review all the regular and "semi-regular" verb forms. Now try to put the right endings in the blanks.

a. JE	parl	e	b. TU	parl	es	c. IL/ ELLE/ON	parl	e
	fin	is		fin	is		fin	it
	ven	ds		ven	ds		ven	d
	dor	s		dor	s		dor	t
d. NOUS	parl	ons	e. VOUS	parl	ez	f. ILS/ ELLES	parl	ent
	fin	issons		fin	issez		fin	issent
	ven	dons		ven	dez		ven	dent
	dor	mons		dor	mez		dor	ment

(mOH) (ma) (may)

Mon, ma, mes,

(tOH) (ta) (tay)

Ton, ta, tes

Mine and yours

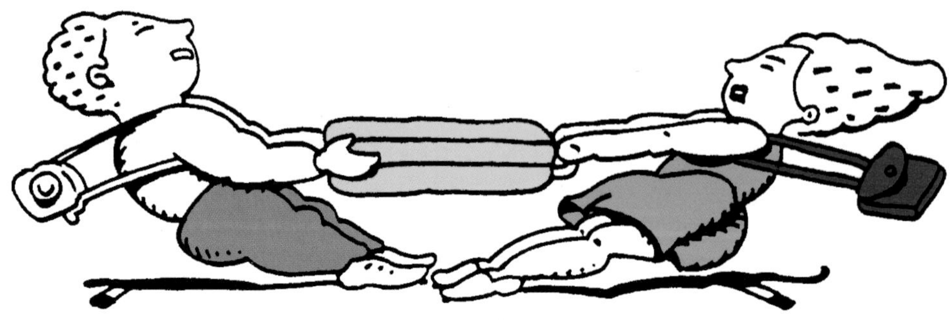

What's "mine" or "yours"? Here's how to tell in French. Note that the forms of these words change, depending on the nouns they describe.

ANSWERS

Regular and Semi-Regular Verbs

a.	**b.**	**c.**	**d.**	**e.**	**f.**
Je parle	Tu parles	Il, Elle, On parle	Nous parlons	Vous parlez	Ils, Elles parlent
Je finis	Tu finis	Il, Elle, On finit	Nous finissons	Vous finissez	Ils, Elles finissent
Je vends	Tu vends	Il, Elle, On vend	Nous vendons	Vous vendez	Ils, Elles vendent
Je dors	Tu dors	Il, Elle, On dort	Nous dormons	Vous dormez	Ils, Elles dorment

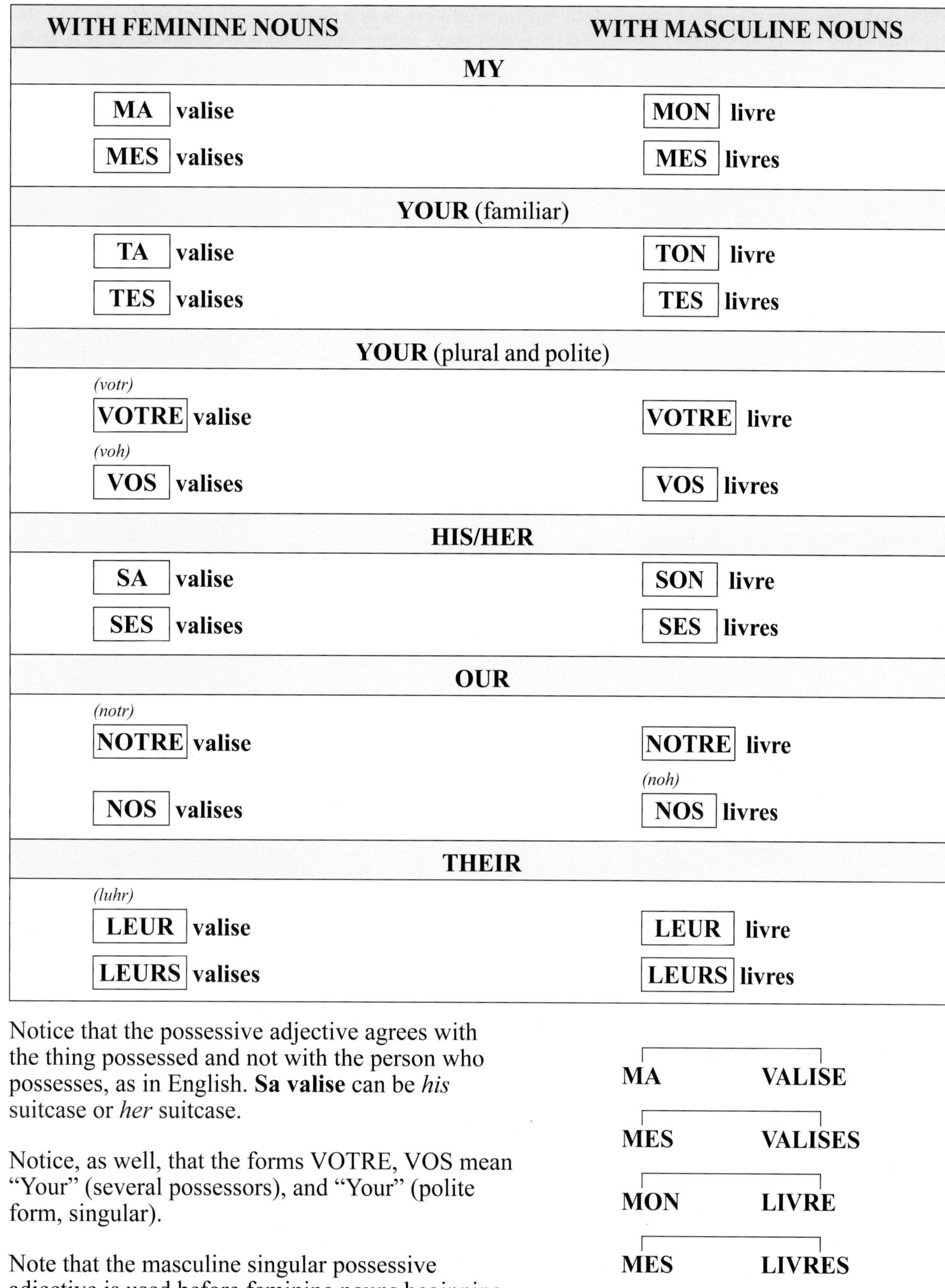

WITH FEMININE NOUNS	WITH MASCULINE NOUNS
MY	
MA valise	**MON** livre
MES valises	**MES** livres
YOUR (familiar)	
TA valise	**TON** livre
TES valises	**TES** livres
YOUR (plural and polite)	
(votr) **VOTRE** valise	**VOTRE** livre
(voh) **VOS** valises	**VOS** livres
HIS/HER	
SA valise	**SON** livre
SES valises	**SES** livres
OUR	
(notr) **NOTRE** valise	**NOTRE** livre
NOS valises	*(noh)* **NOS** livres
THEIR	
(luhr) **LEUR** valise	**LEUR** livre
LEURS valises	**LEURS** livres

Notice that the possessive adjective agrees with the thing possessed and not with the person who possesses, as in English. **Sa valise** can be *his* suitcase or *her* suitcase.

Notice, as well, that the forms VOTRE, VOS mean "Your" (several possessors), and "Your" (polite form, singular).

Note that the masculine singular possessive adjective is used before feminine nouns beginning with a vowel. Example: **mon automobile** (*fem.*).

Now test your knowledge by putting the appropriate possessive adjective in front of the following nouns:

1.	___ma___ (my)	mère	8.	___mes___ (my)	soeurs
2.	___ta___ (your (fam.))	maison	9.	___vos___ (your (fam.))	maisons
3.	___son___ (his)	chat	10.	___ses___ (his)	chats
4.	___son___ (her (BE CAREFUL!!!))	chat	11.	___ses___ (her)	chats
5.	___notre___ (our)	ami (m)	12.	___nos___ (our)	amis
6.	___votre___ (your (polite))	automobile	13.	___vos___ (your (polite))	automobiles
7.	___leur___ (their)	valise	14.	___leurs___ (their)	valises

If someone asks you, can you tell him or her the time in French? Read this passage and then answer the questions that follow.

"Quelle heure est-il?" demande le père à sa fille. "Il est trois heures,"
asks

dit la fille. "À quelle heure pars-tu pour la France?" demande le père. "À dix-sept

(ray-pOH)
heures vingt," répond la fille. "Bon voyage!" "Au revoir, papa."
answers — Goodbye

1. Le père demande à sa fille:
   A. quelle heure il est en France;
   (B.) quelle heure il est;
   C. si elle part en voyage; (*see*) if
   D. quand le train de France arrive.

2. Quelle heure est-il?
   A. Il est deux heures.
   B. Il est six heures et quart.
   (C.) Il est trois heures.
   D. Il est neuf heures moins le quart.

ANSWERS

Possessive Adjectives
1. ma mère
2. ta maison
3. son chat
4. son chat
5. notre ami
6. votre automobile
7. leur valise
8. mes soeurs
9. tes maisons
10. ses chats
11. ses chats
12. nos amis
13. vos automobiles
14. leurs valises

Paragraph. 1. B **2.** C

6 Les trains

(trEH)

Trains

If you need to take the train, the following dialogue might prove useful to you. Don't forget to read it out loud.

MARIE	**Nous voici à la gare.** *(gar)*	Here we are at the train station.
ANNE	**Papa, prenons-nous le TGV** *(tay-zhay-vay)* **pour aller à Cannes?**	Dad, are we taking the TGV to go to Cannes?
MARC	**Bien** *(byEH)* **sûr. C'est très rapide.** *(ra-peed)*	Of course. It's very fast.
ANNE	**Alors, nous allons** *(vwa)* **arriver** *(vew)* **à Cannes ce soir?**	Then we're going to arrive in Cannes this evening?
MARC	**Oui. (à un employé): Pardon.**	Yes. Excuse me,
	Combien coûte un billet aller–retour *(a-lay) (ruh-toor)* **pour Cannes pour quatre personnes?**	how much does a round-trip ticket to Cannes for four people cost?

(Note: **le TGV = le train à grande** *(grAHd)* **vitesse** *(vee-tess)*. This is a high-speed train that connects major French cities.)

(par)

L'EMPLOYÉ **Par le TGV?** — By TGV?

MARC **Oui.** — Yes.

(suh-gOHd)

L'EMPLOYÉ **Première ou seconde classe?** — First or second class?

(Note: We say **seconde classe** instead of **deuxième classe** because there are only two train classes. If there are more than two things, you use **deuxième**: **la deuxième maison à gauche** = the second house on the left—because there are more than two houses.)

MARC **Première.** — First.

L'EMPLOYÉ **Cent quatre-vingt-huit euros par personne.** — 188 euros per person.

MARC **C'est cher . . .** — It's expensive . . .

(suh-gOHd)

L'EMPLOYÉ **Il y a des billets de seconde classe qui coûtent moins cher.** — There are second class tickets that cost less.

MARC **Bon.** — Good.

L'EMPLOYÉ **Quatre cents euros. Voilà vos billets.** — 400 euros. Here are your tickets.

MARC **Merci. À quelle heure est-ce que le train part?** — Thank you. At what time does the train leave?

L'EMPLOYÉ **À quinze heures trente.** — At 3:30 P.M

Match these French words or expressions from the dialogue with their English equivalents.

1. la gare
2. un billet aller-retour
3. première classe
4. des billets de seconde classe
5. le TGV

a. first class
b. second class tickets
c. high-speed train
d. the station
e. a round-trip ticket

If you are traveling between cities in France and you are not in the mood to take the TGV, you can take one of the **Intercités** (*EH-tehr-see-tay*) trains or the **TER** (Transport Express Régional) in the region that you're visiting. The trip will take a bit longer, but you're on vacation!

To help you read **l'horaire** *(uh-rehr)* (schedule) here is the explanation for a few signs:

(zhoor) (oo-vrahbl)
jours ouvrables
weekdays

(va-gOH) (lee)
wagon-lit
sleeper car

(vwa-tewr) (ban)
voiture-bar
bar car

(dee-mAHsh)
dimanches et
Sundays

(feht) (suhl-mAH)
fêtes seulement
holidays only

(rehs-to-rAH)
wagon-restaurant
restaurant car

ANSWERS

Matching 1. d **2.** e **3.** a **4.** b **5.** c

Here is a train schedule. Plan a trip from Paris to Nice. Figure out the cities you would like to visit along the way and the timetable you would follow. (Note: each timetable indicates: (1) in left columns, the departure times from the first station, then arrival time; (2) in right columns, departure times, then arrival times at the end of the line; (3) in italics, the schedule that requires changing trains.)

SUD-EST

×	×	×	×	×	×	×		×	×	×	×	×	×	×
6 55	7 44	10 16	11 42	15 10	17 46	18 40	PARIS-Gare de Lyon*	11 33	12 54	13 54	16 58	18 51	21 43	23 33
|	9 12	|	|	|	|	|	LE CREUSOT TGV*	|	|	12 25	|	|	|	22 04
9 48	10 45	|	14 35	18 05	20 41	21 37	VALENCE*	8 34	9 57	10 51	13 59	|	18 44	20 28
10 46	11 45	14 12	15 33	19 05	21 43	22 37	AVIGNON*	7 34	8 59	9 49	12 59	14 55	17 44	19 28
11 17	12 13	14 39	16 04	19 33	22 11	23 08	NIMES	7 04	8 27	9 20	12 29	14 27	17 14	18 58
11 42	12 39	15 05	16 29	19 59	22 36	23 34	MONTPELLIER*	6 39	8 02	8 55	12 04	14 02	16 49	18 33
12 41	*13 29*	*15 30*	*17 17*	*20 51*	*23 05*	*0 51*	SÈTE*	*6 01*	*7 05*	*8 24*	*11 06*	*12 59*	*16 15*	*17 43*
13 18	*13 55*	*15 58*	*17 21*	*21 19*	*23 35*	*1 21*	BÉZIERS*	*5 29*	*6 31*	*7 59*	*10 41*	*12 25*	*15 45*	*17 12*
13 43	*14 12*	*16 16*	*17 39*	*21 39*	*23 52*	*1 41*	NARBONNE* (A)	*5 12*	*6 16*	*7 42*	*10 24*	*12 10*	*15 27*	*16 50*
...	*14 47*	*17 08*	*18 14*	*22 42*	...	...	PERPIGNAN* (A)	...	*5 35*	*6 40*	*9 22*	*11 22*	*14 24*	*16 03*

×	×	×	×	×	×	×						×	×	×
6 55	7 44	10 10	11 42	12 48	15 10	16 49	PARIS-Gare de Lyon*	6 21	6 25	7 42	8 14	9 29	11 33	12 54
9 48	10 45	13 05	14 35	15 41	18 05	19 52	VALENCE*	|	0 08	|	|	*6a15*	8 34	9 57
10 46	11 45	14 05	15 33	16 39	19 05	20 52	AVIGNON*	|	23 01	23 59	|	*5a14*	7 34	8 59
11 48	12 51	15 07	16 35	17 40	20 11	21 54	MARSEILLE*	|	21 47	22 35	|		6 29	7 58
13 16	*14 00*	*16 03*	*17 29*	*18 37*	*21 13*	*22 45*	TOULON*	21 48	20 48	*21 32*	23 03		*4 35*	*6 52*
14 50	*14 50*	*16 56*	*18 14*	*19 29*	*22 01*	*23 32*	ST-RAPHAEL	20 52	19 25	*20 33*	22 15	...		...
15 17	*15 17*	*17 22*	*18 37*	*19 53*	*22 24*	*23 56*	CANNES	20 26	18 58	*20 08*	21 49	...	...	...
15 31	*15 31*	*17 38*	*18 47*	*20 03*	*22 36*	*0 07*	ANTIBES	20 13	18 40	*19 51*	21 32		...	...
15 48	*15 48*	*18 00*	*19 02*	*20 18*	*22 52*	*0 23*	NICE*	19 55	18 19	*19 30*	21 15	...	...	...

×	×	×						×	×	×	×	×	×	×
17 46	18 40	20 00	20 45	21 46	22 17	22 36	PARIS-Gare de Lyon*	13 54	16 58	18 56	19 50	21 43	22 32	23 33
20 41	21 37	*23a13*	|	|	|	|	VALENCE*	10 51	13 59	|	16 51	18 39	19 33	20 28
21 43	22 37	*0a15*	|	|	|	5 35	AVIGNON*	9 49	12 59	15 00	15 51	17 39	18 29	19 28
22 48	23 40		5 06	|	|	7 20	MARSEILLE*	8 45	11 54	14 00	14 51	16 39	17 29	18 23
	1 22		6 14	|	7 00	*8 33*	TOULON*	*7 47*	*10 53*	*12 59*	*13 55*	*15 31*	*16 21*	*16 46*
...	...	...	7 16	6 50	8 03	*9 27*	ST-RAPHAEL	*6 52*	*9 48*	*12 12*	*13 06*	*14 37*	*15 34*	...
...	...	...	7 42	7 16	8 29	*9 50*	CANNES	*6 27*	*9 21*	*11 49*	*12 43*	*14 13*	*15 10*	...
			8 00	7 35	8 46	*9 59*	ANTIBES	*6 16*	*9 05*	*11 39*	*12 30*	*14 03*	*15 00*	...
...	...	...	8 21	7 55	9 10	*10 14*	NICE*	*6 00*	*8 47*	*11 24*	*12 10*	*13 48*	*14 45*	...

(A) *Voir aussi tableau PARIS-TOULOUSE-BARCELONA.*
(a) *Changement de train à Lyon Part-Dieu.*

Courtesy of S.N.C.F., Paris

(voo-lwar) (poo-vwar)

Vouloir c'est pouvoir

To want is to be able to

"To want" and "to be able to" are very useful verbs when requesting and asking for things. The French verbs are VOULOIR and POUVOIR. They are both irregular, but follow a similar pattern.

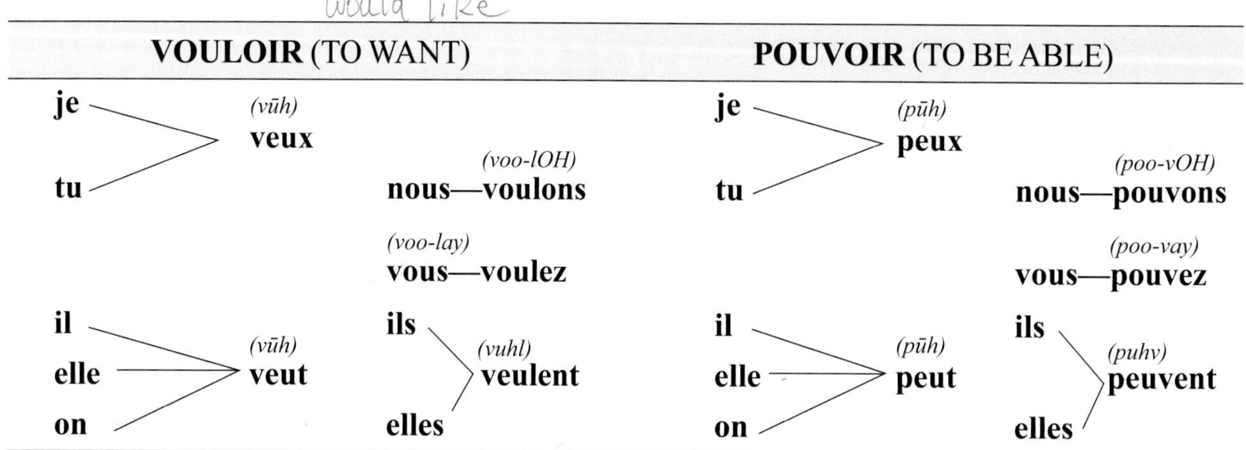

VOULOIR (TO WANT)
je, tu — (vūh) veux
(voo-lOH) nous—voulons
(voo-lay) vous—voulez
il, elle, on — (vūh) veut
ils, elles — (vuhl) veulent
POUVOIR (TO BE ABLE)
je, tu — (pūh) peux
(poo-vOH) nous—pouvons
(poo-vay) vous—pouvez
il, elle, on — (pūh) peut
ils, elles — (puhv) peuvent

If you want to be really polite—"I would like"—"Could you," the forms are:

(voo-dreh)
JE VOUDRAIS ________________________ I would like

Examples: Futur tense

Je voudrais partir. / I would like to leave.

(seel) (voo) (pleh)
Je voudrais un café, s'il vous plaît. I would like a coffee, please.

(poo-ryay)
POURRIEZ-VOUS ________________________ Could you

Example:

Pourriez-vous fermer la fenêtre? Could you close the window?

Now fill in the blanks with the appropriate form of the verb.

1. ___Pouvez___ -vous m'aider? *(meh-day)*
   (could) (help)

2. Je ___veux___ , donc je ___peux___ . *(dOHk)*
   (want) (therefore) (can)

3. ___Voulez___ -vous du café? *(ka-fay)*
   (want)

4. Je ___voudrais___ une omelette, s'il vous plaît. *(om-leht) (seel) (voo) (pleh)*
   (would like)

5. ___Pouvons___ -nous prendre le TGV?
   (can, may)

6. Anne et Jean ne ___peuvent___ pas prendre le TGV.
   (can)

NOTE: You may have noticed that there is only one verb in French for "can" and "may."

ANSWERS

Fill ins

1. Pourriez **2.** veux . . . peux **3.** Voulez **4.** voudrais **5.** Pouvons **6.** peuvent

(AH) (vwa-tewr)

EN VOITURE!

All Aboard!

(pa-sa-zhehr)
une passagère
passenger

(sa-swar)
s'asseoir
to sit down

(suh luh-vay)
se lever
to get up

(sahl) (da-tAHt)
la salle d'attente
waiting room

(o-rehr)
l'horaire (*m.*)
schedule

(kay)
le quai
railway platform

(sha-reht)
la charrette
luggage cart

(por-tuhr)
le porteur
porter

(trEH)
le train
train

(feht) (luh) (voo) (mehm)

Faites-le vous-même

Do it yourself

(ruh-gard) (ta-bloh)
Il regarde le tableau.

Il se regarde.

Reflexive verbs express actions people do "to themselves": to get up, to sit down, to get dressed, to go to bed, to wake up, to get married, to have fun, to be bored. For example, "to get washed" is a reflexive verb because you wash yourself or "reflect back" the action of the verb upon yourself. This is done by means of reflexive pronouns, like "myself" and "yourself." Here are the reflexive pronouns in French.

REFLEXIVE PRONOUNS	
(muh) **ME**, **M'** (before vowel or silent *h*)	myself
(tuh) **TE**, **T'** (before vowel or silent *h*)	yourself (familiar)
SE, **S'** (before vowel or silent *h*)	himself, herself, oneself
NOUS	ourselves
VOUS	yourselves, yourself (polite)
SE, **S'** (before vowel or silent *h*)	themselves

The verb LAVER *(la-vay)* means "to wash": **Madeleine lave la voiture.** Madeleine is washing the car. LAVER can become reflexive "To wash oneself" (SE LAVER) as follows:

JE	**ME**	**LAVE**	I wash myself, I am washing myself, I do wash myself
TU	**TE**	**LAVES**	You wash yourself, etc.
IL, ELLE, ON	**SE**	**LAVE**	He/She/One washes himself/herself/oneself
NOUS	**NOUS**	**LAVONS**	We wash ourselves
VOUS	**VOUS**	**LAVEZ**	You wash yourselves/yourself (polite)
ILS, ELLES	**SE**	**LAVENT**	They wash themselves

Now you try it with the verb AMUSER *(a-mew-zay)*, which in its reflexive form means "To enjoy oneself, to have fun." It begins with a vowel, so the reflexive pronouns (me, te, and se) become m', t', and s'.

1. Je ____m'____ amuse.
2. Tu ____t'____ amuses.
3. Il, Elle ____s'____ amuse.
4. Nous ____nous____ amusons.
5. Vous ____vous____ amusez.
6. Ils, Elles ____s'____ amusent.

* don't pronounce the 't'

ANSWERS

Reflexive verbs

1. je m'amuse
2. tu t'amuses
3. il, elle s'amuse
4. nous nous amusons
5. vous vous amusez
6. ils, elles s'amusent

The following passage is about train travel. Read about Marc and Marie, then answer the questions that follow.

T14 01:50

Marc et Marie vont *(vOH)* **à la gare. Ils achètent** *(eel) (za-sheht)* **deux billets aller-retour Paris-Marseille. Ils voyagent en TGV de Paris à Lyon. Ils partent lundi matin à dix heures. Ils passent** (spend) **deux jours** *(zhoor)* **à Lyon chez leur grand-mère. Ensuite, de Lyon à Marseille, ils prennent le TER. Ils arrivent à Marseille jeudi soir à huit heures.**

1. Où vont Marc et Marie?

   Ils vont à la gare.

2. Qu'est-ce qu'ils achètent?

   Ils achètent un billets aller-retour

3. Qu'est-ce que c'est que le TGV?

   C'est est le Train à Grande Vitesse.

4. Qu'est-ce que c'est que le TER?

   ____

ANSWERS

Reading 1. Ils vont à la gare. **2.** Ils achètent un billet. **3.** C'est le Train à Grande Vitesse.
4. C'est le Train Express Régional (ou le Transport Express Régional)

7 Les pays et les langues

(peh-yee) *(lAHg)*

Countries and Languages

Je parle un peu français. I speak a little French. And so do you ! By now you've learned quite a bit of French. Take a look at the rest of the world, too, and learn how to say the names of other countries in French. Note that in French the article "the" is used with the name of a country, a city, or a language. Also note that, except for Le Mexique, countries ending in E are feminine.

COUNTRIES AND CONTINENTS

Masculine

(AH-tark-teek)
l'Antarctique
Antarctica

(bray-zeel)
le Brésil

(ka-na-dah)
le Canada

(shee-lee)
le Chili

(dan-mark)
le Danemark

(ah-ee-tee)
la République d'Haïti (*m.*)
the Republic of Haiti

(ees-ra-ehl)
Israël (no art.)
Israel

(zha-pOH)
le Japon

(mehk-seek)
le Mexique

(por-tew-gal)
le Portugal

(vay-nay-zew-ay-lah)
le Vénézuéla

Plural

(ay-ta) (zew-nee)
les États-Unis

Feminine

(ah-freek)
l'Afrique
Africa

(al-ma-nyuh)
l'Allemagne
Germany

(a-may-reek) (nor)
l'Amérique du Nord
North America

(a-may-reek) (sewd)
l'Amérique du Sud
South America

(AHn-gluh-tehr)
l' Angleterre
England

(ar-zhAH-teen)
l'Argentine

(ah-zee)
l'Asie
Asia

(ohs-tra-lee)
l'Australie

(oh-treesh)
l'Autriche
Austria

(bel-zheek)
la Belgique
Belgium

(sheen)
la Chine

(ehs-pa-nyuh)
l'Espagne
Spain

(uh-rop)
l'Europe

(frAHs)
la France

(grAHd) (bruh-ta-nyuh)
la Grande Bretagne

(grehs)
la Grèce

(o-lAHd)
la Hollande

(ee-ta-lee)
l'Italie

(po-lo-nyuh)
la Pologne
Poland

(rew-see)
la Russie

(sew-ehd)
la Suède
Sweden

(swees)
la Suisse
Switzerland

(tewr-kee)
la Turquie

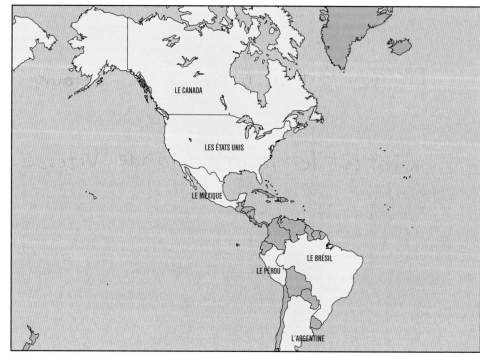

LE CANADA
LES ÉTATS UNIS
LE MEXIQUE
LE BRÉSIL
LE PÉROU
L'ARGENTINE

Je parle

I speak

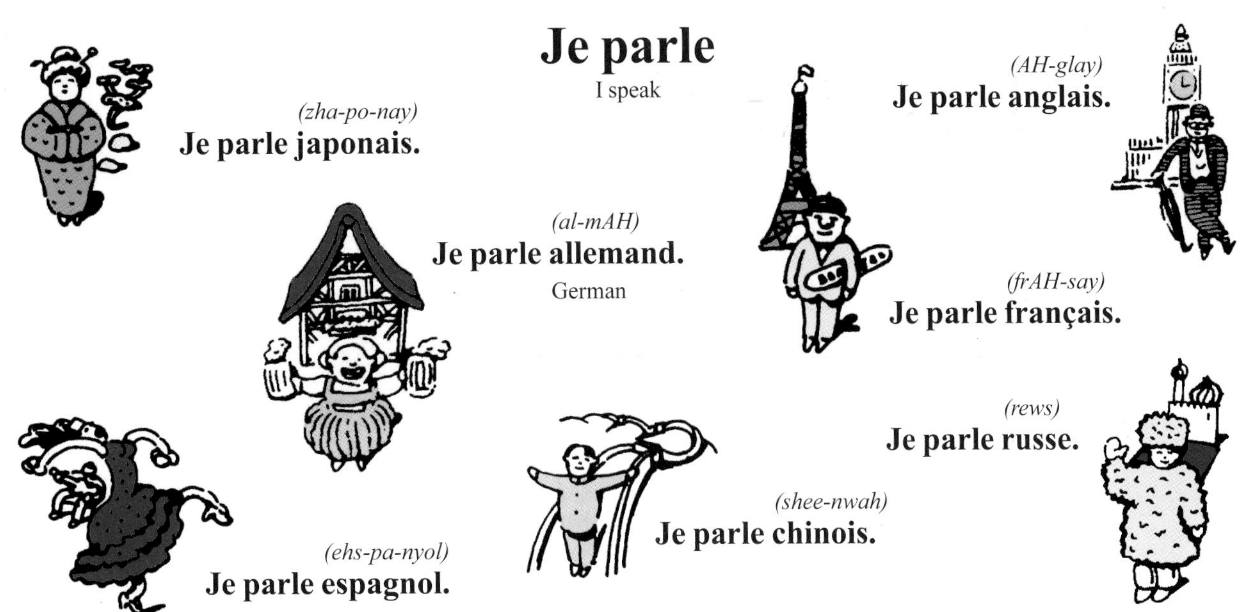

(zha-po-nay)
Je parle japonais.

(al-mAH)
Je parle allemand.
German

(AH-glay)
Je parle anglais.

(frAH-say)
Je parle français.

(rews)
Je parle russe.

(shee-nwah)
Je parle chinois.

(ehs-pa-nyol)
Je parle espagnol.

Names of languages are masculine and are not capitalized. After verbs other than parler (comprendre, apprendre, aimer (eh-may) to like, love, and so on), the definite article LE is used: J'aime le français!

Nationalities are not capitalized when they are used as adjectives. They *are* capitalized when used as nouns. Example: **un homme français arrive**, but **le Français arrive**.

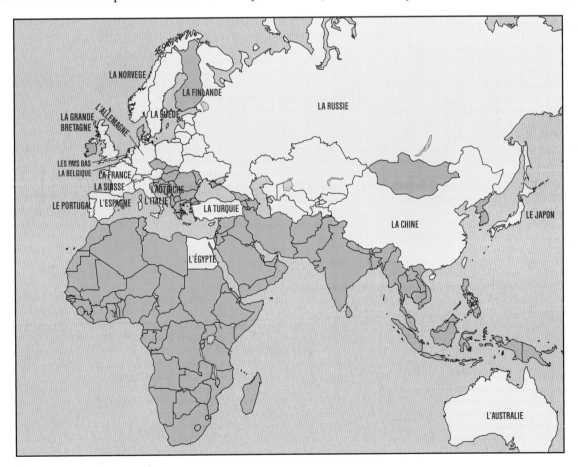

(zhuh) (swee)

Je suis

I am

Many of us are combinations of several nationalities. Which are you? Use **Je suis . . .** (I am . . .)

MASCULIN		FÉMININ
(al-mAH) **Je suis allemand**	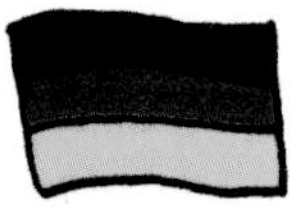	*(al-mahnd)* **allemande**
(a-may-ree-kEH) **américain**		*(a-may-ree-kehn)* **américaine**
(AH-gleh) **anglais**		*(AH-glehz)* **anglaise**
(ohs-tra-lyEH) **australien**		*(ohs-tra-lyehn)* **australienne**
(oh-tree-shyEH) **autrichien**		*(oh-tree-shyehn)* **autrichienne**
(behlzh) **belge**	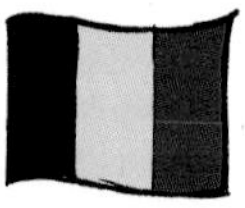	*(behlzh)* **belge**
(ka-na-dyEH) **canadien**		*(ka-na-dyehn)* **canadienne**
(shee-nwah) **chinois**		*(shee-nwahz)* **chinoise**
(da-nwa) **danois**		*(da-nwaz)* **danoise**
(ehs-pa-nyol) **espagnol**	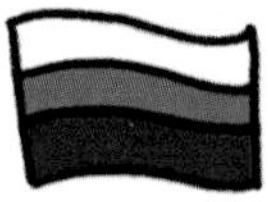	*(ehs-pa-nyol)* **espagnole**
(feen-lAH-deh) **finlandais**	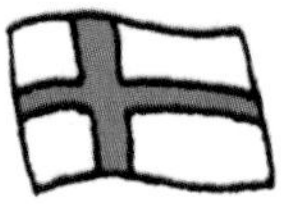	*(feen-lAH-dehz)* **finlandaise**

MASCULIN		FÉMININ
(frAH-seh) **français**		*(frAH-sehz)* **française**
(o-lAH-deh) **hollandais**	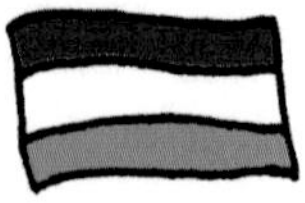	*(o-lAH-dehz)* **hollandaise**
(ee-ta-lyEH) **italien**		*(ee-ta-lyehn)* **italienne**
(zha-po-neh) **japonais**	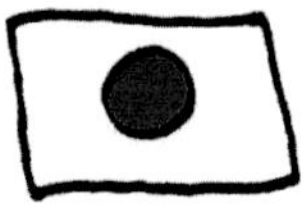	*(zha-po-nehz)* **japonaise**
(mehk-see-kEH) **mexicain**		*(mehk-see-kehn)* **mexicaine**
(nor-vay-zhyEH) **norvégien**		*(nor-vay-zhyehn)* **norvégienne**
(po-lo-neh) **polonais**	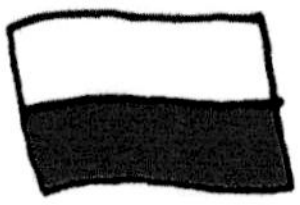	*(po-lo-nehz)* **polonaise**
(rews) **russe**	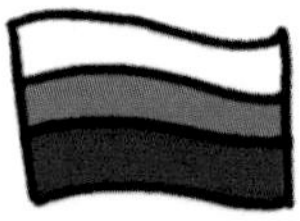	*(rews)* **russe**
(swees) **suisse**		*(swees)* **suisse**
(sew-ah-dwah) **suédois**		*(sew-ay-dwahz)* **suédoise**
(tewrk) **turc**		*(tewrk)* **turque**
(rih-ro-pay-EH) **européen**		*(rih-ro-pay-ehn)* **européene**

TRACK 16

(zhuh) (vay)

Je vais à

I am going to

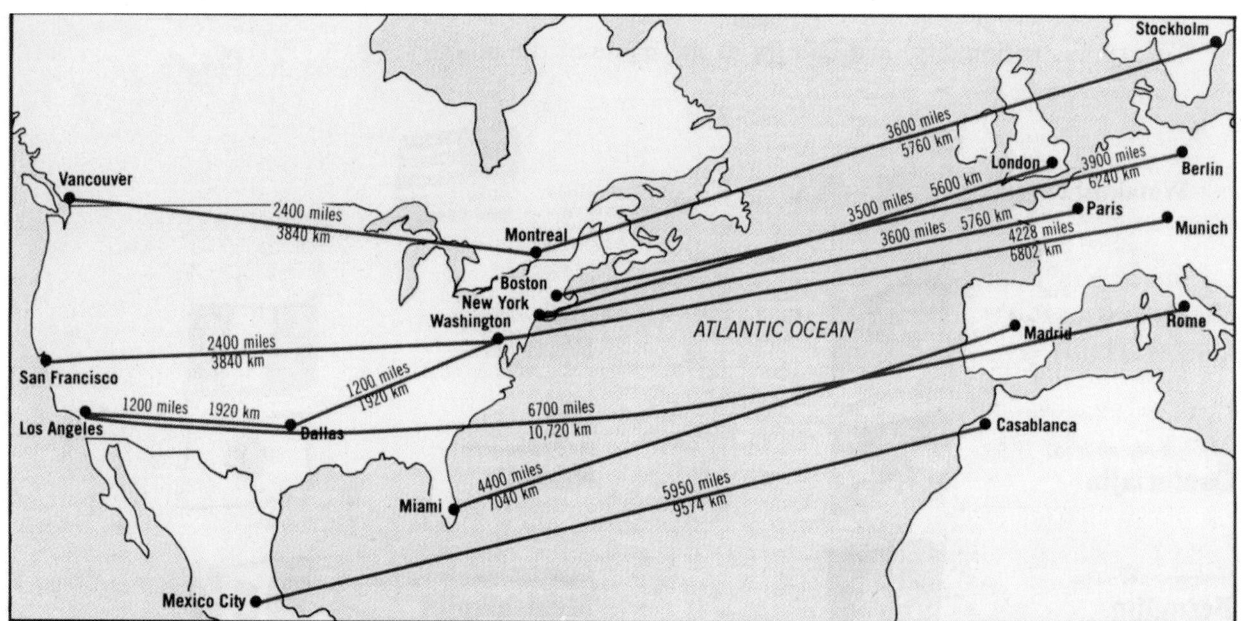

à + CITIES	en + FEMININE COUNTRIES AND REGIONS (AND THOSE STARTING WITH A VOWEL)	au + MASCULINE COUNTRIES AND REGIONS	aux + PLURAL COUNTRIES
(pa-ree) **Paris**	**France**	**Canada**	
(ber-lEH) **Berlin**	**Espagne**	**Portugal**	
(rom) **Rome**	**Allemagne**	**Chili**	**États-Unis**
(brew-sel) **Bruxelles**	**Italie**	**Brésil**	**Pays-Bas**
(zhuh-nehv) **Genève**	**Belgique**	**Mexique**	
(kay-bek) ***Québec**	**Suisse**	**Zaïre**	
	(ee-rAH) **Iran**	***Québec**	
	Europe		

We say "à Québec" when talking about the city and "au Québec" when talking about the Canadian province.

Now, **répondez aux questions**, using the correct **préposition (à, au, aux, en)** as in the following example:

(ark) (duh) (tree-yOHf)
Où est l'Arc de Triomphe? *L'arc de Triomphe est à Paris.*

(toor) (eh-fehl)
1. Où est la Tour Eiffel? (Paris)

____

2. Où est New York? (États-Unis)

____

3. Où est Acapulco? (Mexique)

____

(bah-tOH) (roozh)
4. Où est Bâton Rouge? (Louisiane)
stick red

____

5. Où est Berlin? (Allemagne)

____

(ko-lee-zay)
6. Où est le Colisée? (Rome, Italie)

____

(prah-doh)
7. Où est le Prado? (Madrid, Espagne)

____

(rEH)
8. Où est le Rhin? (Allemagne)

____

ANSWERS

Prepositions **1.** à Paris **2.** aux États-Unis **3.** au Mexique **4.** en Louisiane **5.** en Allemagne **6.** à Rome, en Italie **7.** à Madrid, en Espagne **8.** en Allemagne

(zhuh) (kohn-prAH)

Je comprends

I understand

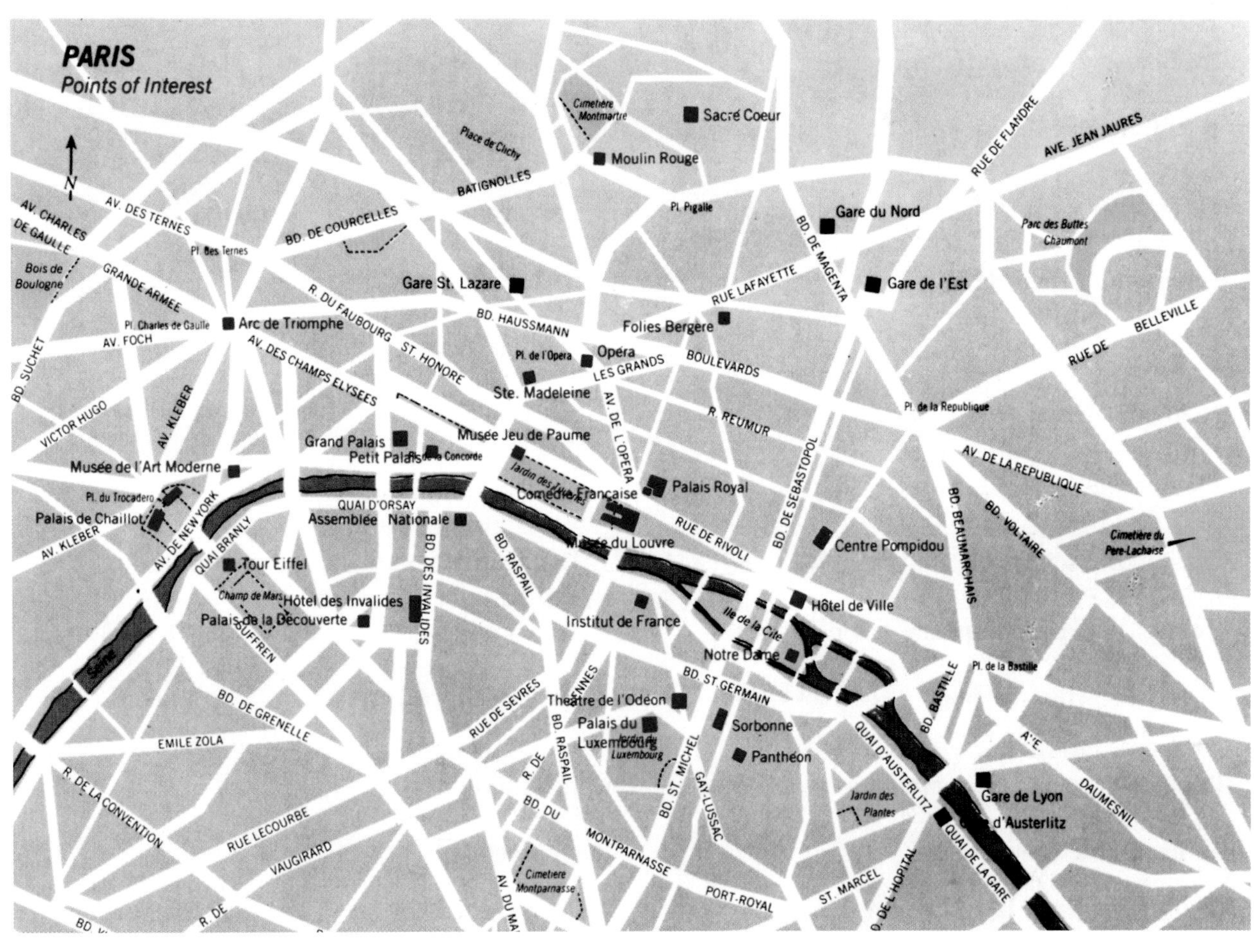

Read the following brief passage and try answering the questions.

(gar) (lyOH) (sAHtr) (pOH-pee-doo)

Anne part de son hôtel près de la Gare de Lyon pour aller au Centre Pompidou, un

(shah-tlay)

musée d'art moderne. A la station du Châtelet, une jeune fille française commence à lui

(a-kOH-pa-nyay) (sor)

parler. Elle dit qu'elle désire l'accompagner voir l'exposition d'art. Quand elle sort du

leaves

(oh) (ahl) (kOH-tAHt) (ofr)

métro aux Halles, Anne est très contente d'avoir une amie. La jeune fille française offre

(seet) (toor-ees-teek)

aussi de lui montrer quelques sites touristiques de la belle capitale et

some

elle l'invite à prendre chez elle un déjeuner typiquement français.

lunch

1. Anne désire
   a. visiter les jardins.
   b. écouter un concert.
   c. aller à un centre d'art.
   d. déjeuner dans un grand restaurant.

2. Anne entre en conversation avec
   a. une Française.
   b. un homme étranger.
   c. un garçon.
   d. une jeune fille américaine.

3. Anne est très contente
   a. d'aller à Nice.
   b. de voyager en métro.
   c. de parler à un garçon.
   d. d'avoir une amie.

4. Anne va prendre
   a. un avion anglais.
   b. un déjeuner français.
   c. une photo de la jeune fille.
   d. une montre française.

ANSWERS

Multiple choice **1.** c **2.** a **3.** d **4.** b

8 Les voitures, grandes et petites

(vwa-tewr) (grAHd) (puh-teet)

Cars, Big and Small

La signalisation routière

(see-nya-lee-za-syOH) (roo-tyehr)

Road Signs

(Le château de Chenonceau. Sixteenth-century castle in the Loire Valley.)

Mark has decided to rent a car and take his family for an excursion into the French countryside. You may want to rent a car and see the country close up yourself!

(a-zhAHs) (lo-ka-syOH)

À L'AGENCE DE LOCATION DE VOITURES

At the Car Rental Office

MARC **Bonjour, Monsieur. Je voudrais** Good morning, Sir. I would like

(loo-ay)

louer une voiture. to rent a car.

rent

(tAH)

L'EMPLOYÉ **Pour combien de temps?** For how long?

(suh-mehn)

MARC **Deux semaines. Ça coûte combien?** Two weeks. How much does that cost?

L'EMPLOYÉ	*(vwa-yOH)* *(pūh-zhoh)* **Voyons . . . Une Peugeot pour deux semaines; trois cent cinq euros,** *(a-sew-rAHs)* *(kOH-preez)* **assurance comprise.** *(pay-yay)* *(plews)* **Vous payez en plus une taxe** *(veerg-ewl)* **de dix-neuf virgule six pour cent.**	Let's see . . . A Peugeot for two weeks; 305 euros, insurance included. You also pay a tax of 19.6%.

Note: In French, a *virgule* (comma) is used instead of a decimal point.

MARC	**C'est cher. Est-ce que vous avez une voiture plus petite?**	That's expensive. Do you have a smaller car?
L'EMPLOYÉ	*(ruh-noh)* **Oui, une Renault: deux cent treize euros.**	Yes, a Renault: 213 euros.
MARC	*(kee-lo-may-trahzh)* *(kOH-pree)* **Est-ce que le kilométrage est compris?**	Is the mileage included?
MARIE (à elle-même) (to herself)	*(mehm)* **Comme il est avare!**	How stingy he is!
L'EMPLOYÉ	*(a-lay)* *(ay-trAH-zhay)* **Oui. Allez-vous à l'étranger?**	Yes. Are you going abroad?
MARC	*(a-lOH)* **Non. Nous allons voir les châteaux de la Loire.**	No, we are going to see the castles of the Loire valley
L'EMPLOYÉ	*(ram-nay)* **Allez-vous ramener la voiture à Paris?**	Are you going to bring the car back to Paris?
MARC	*(pro-bah-bluh-mAH)* *(see-nOH)* **Probablement. Sinon, est-ce que nous pouvons la laisser à votre agence** *(or-lay-AH)* **à Orléans?**	Probably. If not, can we leave it at your agency in Orléans?
L'EMPLOYÉ	*(byEH)* *(sewr)* *(sew-play-mAH)* **Bien sûr. Mais il y a un supplément de soixante-dix-neuf euros.**	Of course. But there is a surcharge of 79 euros.

MARC	*(mOH-tray)* **Pouvez-vous me montrer comment** *(vee-tehs)* **marchent le changement de vitesse et** *(far)* **les phares?**	Can you show me how the gear shift and the lights work?
L'EMPLOYÉ	*(na-tew-rehl-mAH)* **Naturellement. Voilà la clé et les papiers de la voiture. Je** *(vyan)* **viens avec vous.**	Of course. Here are the key and the car's papers. I'm coming with you.
PAUL	*(dyūh)* **Mon Dieu! Il va** *(kOH-dweer)* **conduire une voiture à transmission manuelle!** *(koo-rahzh)* **Courage, Anne!**	My God! He is going to drive a car with a manual transmission! Be brave, Anne!

Pretend that you wish to rent a car. How would you respond to these questions and statements based on the dialogue?

Vous: Je voudrais louer une voiture.
L'employé: Pour combien de temps?

1. Vous: Pour deux semaines.
   L'employé: Quelle voiture prenez-vous? which care
2. Vous: Une Peugeot
   L'employé: Ça coûte trois cent cinq euros.
3. Vous: C'est cher.
   L'employé: Allez-vous à l'étranger?
4. Vous: Non. Nous allons voir les châteaux de la Loire
   L'employé: Où allez-vous ramener la voiture?
5. Vous: Probablement. Nous pouvons la laisser à Orléans?
   L'employé: Bon. Merci. Voici les clés de la voiture.

ANSWERS

Dialogue 1. Pour deux semaines. **2.** Une Peugeot. **3.** C'est cher. **4.** Non. Nous allons voir les châteaux de la Loire. **5.** à Orléans.

The procedure for renting a car in France and other European countries is the same as in the U.S. You can rent a car on a daily, weekly, two-week, or monthly basis. There is a fee for insurance and there is a 19.6% tax. If you want to drop off your car at another location, there is usually a fee. As in the U.S., smaller cars are less expensive. Unlike the U.S., many rental cars have a manual transmission. However, you can also find a car with an automatic transmission. Be clear about the cities and countries that you will want to visit because you may need an emissions sticker for some cities or you may need to make other arrangements to drive in certain countries. Always discuss this with the rental agency to avoid unpleasant situations or fines. In spite of all these considerations, driving is a wonderful way to go sightseeing. **Bonne route!** (Have a nice trip!)

(a-lay) *(vu-neer)*

Aller et venir

To go and to come

While traveling, you will do a lot of "coming" and "going." Study carefully these two very important irregular verbs.

ALLER		VENIR	
je	*(vay)* **vais**	**je**	*(vyEH)* **viens**
tu	*(va)* **vas**	**tu**	*(vyEH)* **viens**
il, elle, on	*(va)* **va**	**il, elle, on**	*(vyEH)* **vient**
nous	*(a-lOH)* **allons**	**nous**	*(vuh-nOH)* **venons**
vous	*(a-lay)* **allez**	**vous**	*(vuh-nay)* **venez**
ils, elles	*(vOH)* **vont**	**ils, elles**	*(vyehn)* **viennent**

Examples:

Nous allons à l'aéroport. We are going to the airport.
Tu viens avec moi? Are you coming with me?

ALLER is also used when inquiring about somebody's health:

(ko-mAH) *(ta-lay) (voo)*
Comment allez-vous? — How are you? How do you feel?

Je vais
- **très bien, merci.** — Very well, thank you.
- **pas mal, merci.** — Not bad, thank you.
- **assez bien, merci.** — Fairly well, thank you.
- *(kom)* *(see)* *(kom)* *(sa)* **comme-ci comme-ça, merci.** — So-so, thank you.
- **mal, merci.** — Not well, thank you.

Et vous? — And you?

Note that the subject and verb are inverted in the following questions.

1. Comment allez-vous?

   Je vais bien, merci.

2. Comment va votre mère?

   Elle va bien, merci.

3. Comment va votre mari?

   Il va mal, merci.

4. Comment vont vos enfants? *(AH-fAH)* children

   Ils vont assez bien, merci.

A simple way of expressing an idea in the future is to use **ALLER** + infinitive:

Je vais prendre un bateau-mouche. I'm going to take a bateau-mouche.

A *bateau-mouche* is a sightseeing boat.

In the negative, **NE** and **PAS** are around the conjugated form of **ALLER**:

Je ne vais pas prendre de bateau-mouche. I'm not going to take a bateau-mouche.

With reflexive verbs, the reflexive pronoun comes before the infinitive:

Je vais me lever. I'm going to get up.

And with negative reflexive constructions, **NE** and **PAS** are around the conjugated form of **ALLER**:

Je ne vais pas me lever. I'm not going to get up.

ANSWERS

Verb ALLER (for health) **1.** Je vais bien, merci, (et vous?) **2.** (Example) Elle va bien, merci. **3.** (Example) Il va très bien, merci. **4.** (Example) Ils vont assez bien, merci.

(e-sAH-syehl)

Quelques expressions essentielles

Some essential expressions

(pehr-dew) **Je suis perdu(e).**	I am lost.
(ga-rahzh) **Est-ce qu'il y a un garage près d'ici?**	Is there a garage near here?
Qu'est-ce qu'il y a?	What's the matter?
(seer-kew-la-syOH) **Il y a beaucoup de circulation.**	There is a lot of traffic.
(ray-zOH) **Vouz avez raison.**	You are right.
(tor) **Vous avez tort.**	You are wrong.
(deesk) **le disque***	the disk
(pehr-mee) (kOH-dweer) **le permis de conduire**	driver's license
(eh-sAHs) **l'essence**	gasoline
(kwEH) **au coin de**	at the corner of
(boo) **au bout de**	at the end of
(nor) **le nord**	north
(sewd) **le sud**	south
(lehst) **l'est**	east
(loo-ehst) **l'ouest**	west
(no) (rehst) **le nord-est, etc.**	northeast, etc.
(fūh) **les feux**	traffic lights
*(zohn) (blūh)** **la zone bleue**	the blue zone

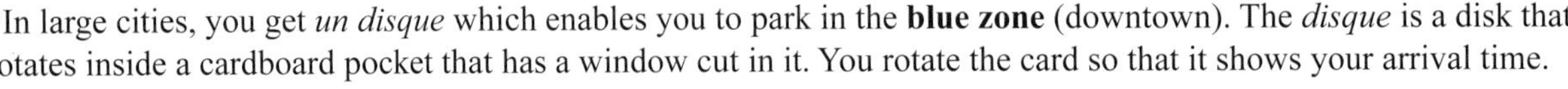

*In large cities, you get *un disque* which enables you to park in the **blue zone** (downtown). The *disque* is a disk that rotates inside a cardboard pocket that has a window cut in it. You rotate the card so that it shows your arrival time.

(see-nya-lee-za-syOH) *(roo-tyehr)*

LA SIGNALISATION ROUTIÈRE

Road Signs

If you're planning to drive while you're abroad, spend some time memorizing the meanings of these signs.

Dangerous intersection
Yield right-of-way to
vehicle on right

Danger!

Stop

Speed Limit
(in km/hr)

Minimum
Speed

End of Limited
Speed

No Entry

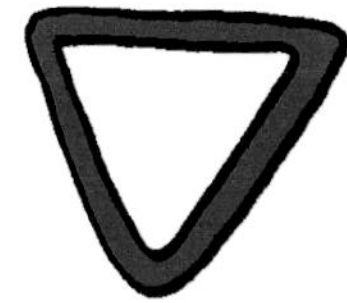

Yield right-of-way

Oncoming traffic
has right-of-way

Dangerous curve

Entrance to expressway

Expressway Ends
(road narrows)

Customs

No Passing

End of
No Passing Zone

Hospital

Detour

Road Closed

Parking

No Parking
(or waiting)

Roundabout

No Parking

No Parking
(or waiting)

No Cyclists

Pedestrian Crossing

Railroad Crossing
(no gate)

Guarded Railroad
Crossing

(sta-syOH) *(sehr-vees)*

À LA STATION SERVICE

At the Service Station

Marc and Suzanne take their rental car on a trip to the cathedral at Chartres. They have a few minor problems . . .

(fehr) (plEH) MARC **J'ai besoin de faire le plein.**	I have to get a fill-up.
(ess-kuh) SUZANNE **Est-ce que cette voiture prend** *(ess-AHs) (gahz-uhl)* **de l'essence ou du gazole?**	Does this car take gas or diesel?
(duh-mAH-day) MARC **Je ne sais pas. Je vais demander** *(zhay-rAH)* **au gérant.**	I don't know. I'm going to ask the manager.

Mark talks to the station manager.

(pahr-duh-nay mwa) **Pardonnez-moi, monsieur. Est-ce que ma voiture prend de l'essence ou du gazole?**	Excuse me, sir. Does my car take gasoline or diesel fuel?

(EH-stAH)
GÉRANT **Un instant, s'il vous plaît . . . C'est marqué** — Just a moment, please . . . It's marked

(boo-shOH) (ray-zehr-vwahr)
sur le bouchon du réservoir d'essence. — on the filler cap.

(vwa-la)
Voilà. Votre voiture prend du gazole. — That's it. Your car takes diesel fuel.

MARC **Excellent. Merci, monsieur.** — Excellent. Thank you, sir.

(vay-ree-fyay) (preh-syOH) (pnūh)
Et pour vérifier la pression des pneus? — And to check the tire pressure?

(pOHp) (la-bah)
GÉRANT **Il y a une pompe à air là-bas.** — There's an air pump over there.

(ka-tay-drahl) (shahrtr)
MARC **Nous allons à la Cathédrale de Chartres.** — We are going to the Chartres Cathedral.

(koort)
Quelle est la route la plus courte? — Which is the shortest way?

GÉRANT (showing Mark on his map)

(drwah)
Regardez. Vous êtes ici. Allez tout droit, — Look. You are here. Go straight

(gohsh)
tournez à gauche, puis à droite. Ensuite — ahead, turn left, then right. Then

(swee-vay) (pah-noh) (seen-yal-eez-a-syOH)
suivez les panneaux de signalisation. — follow the road signs.

(bo-koo)
MARC **Merci beaucoup!** — Thank you very much!

Now write these important words and phrases from the dialogue.

1. I have to get a fill-up. J'ai besoin de faire le plein
2. Excuse me, sir. Pardonnez-moi, monsieur.
3. There's an air pump over there. Il y a une pompe à air lá-bas.
4. Which is the shortest way? Quelle est la route la plus courte?
5. To the left à gauche
6. To the right à droite
7. Follow the road signs. Suivez les panneux de signalisation

ANSWERS

Dialogue 1. J'ai besoin de faire le plein. **2.** Pardonnez-moi, monsieur. **3.** Il y a une pompe à air là-bas. **4.** Quelle est la route la plus courte. **5.** À gauche **6.** À droite **7.** Suivez les panneaux de signalisation.

(vwa-tewr)

LA VOITURE (L'AUTOMOBILE)

The Car

(klak-sOH)
le klaxon
horn

(vo-lAH)
le volant
steering wheel

(AH-bray-yahzh)
l'embrayage
clutch pedal

(frEH)
le frein
brake pedal

(eh -swee)(glas)
les essuie-glaces
windshield wipers

(ta-bloh) (bor)
le tableau de bord
dashboard

(lev-yay) (vee-tehs)
le levier de vitesse
gearshift

(ak-say-lay-ra-tuhr)
l' accélérateur
accelerator

(par) (breez)
le pare-brise
windshield

(mo-tuhr)
le moteur
engine

(ra-dya-tuhr)
le radiateur
radiator

(ka-poh)
le capot
hood

(ba-tree)
la batterie
battery

(fahr)
les phares
headlights

(ruh-kewl)
le phare de recul
backup light

(klee-nyo-tAH)
le clignotant
directional signal

(stop)
le feu de stop
brake light

(kofr)
le coffre
trunk

(lew-neht) (ar-yehr)
la lunette arrière
rear window

(fũh) (a-ryehr)
le feu arrière
rear light

(plak) (ee-ma-tree-kew-la-syOH)
la plaque d'immatriculation
license plate

(pOH) (pa) (eh-sAHs)
la pompe à essence
gas pump

(veetr)
la vitre
window

(por-tyehr)
la portière
door

(twa)
le toit
roof

(ka-ros-ree)
la carrosserie
body (of car)

(el)
l'aile
fender

(par) (shok)
le pare-chocs
bumper

(ray-zehr-vwar) (ay-sAHss)
le réservoir à essence
tank

(roo)
la roue
wheel

(pnūh)
les pneus
tires

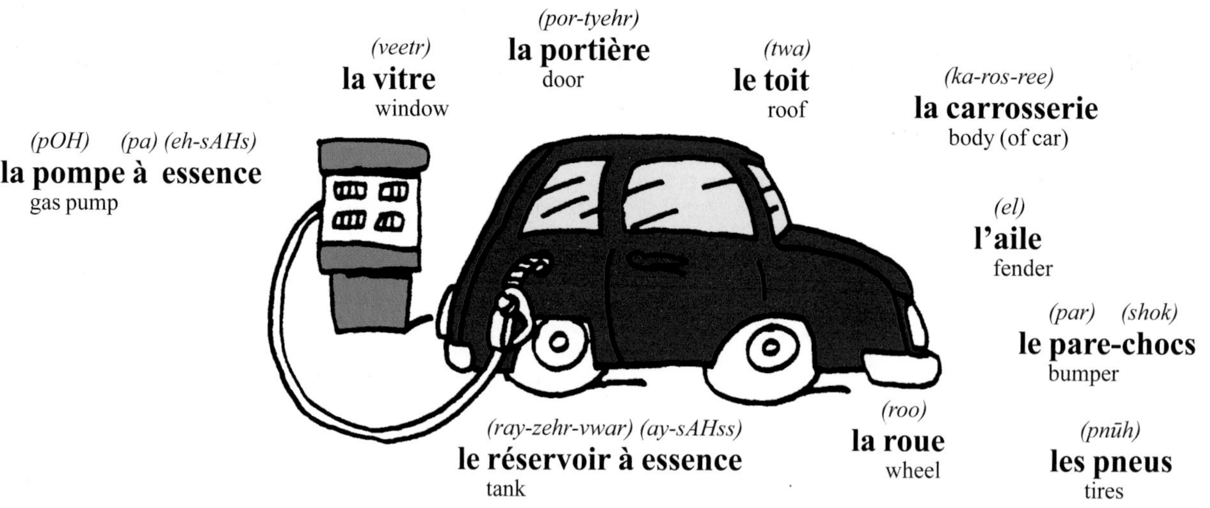

Now fill in the names for the following auto parts.

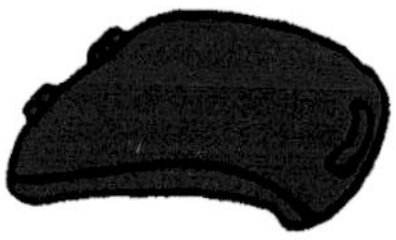

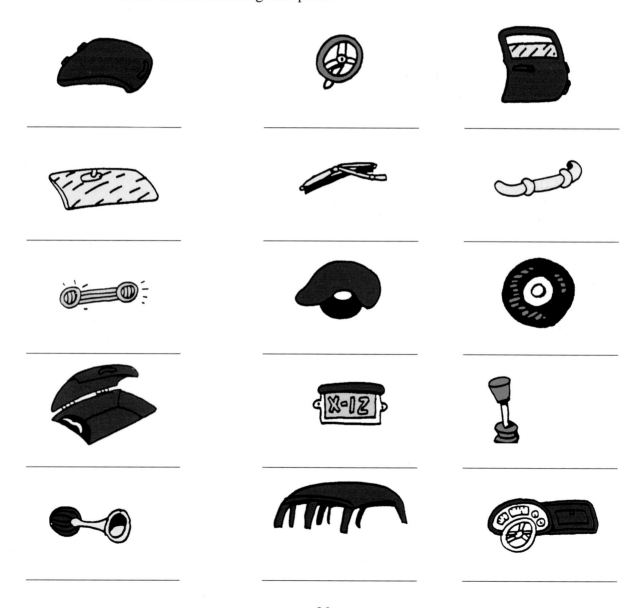

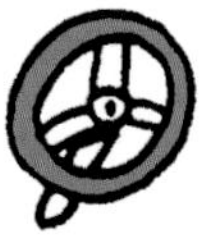

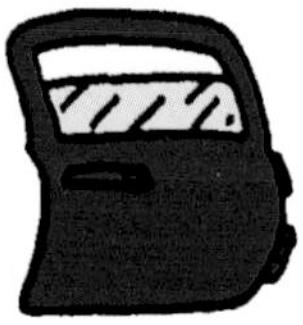

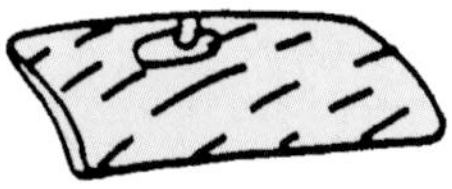

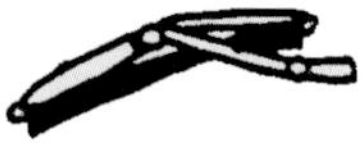

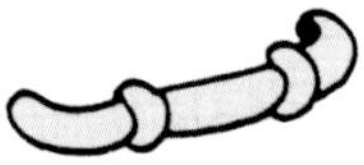

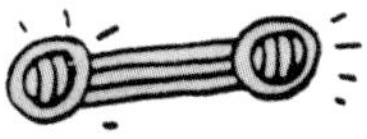

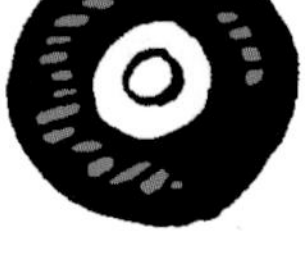

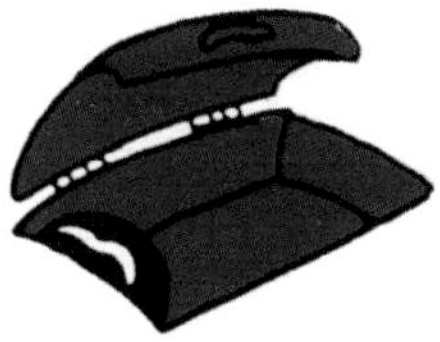

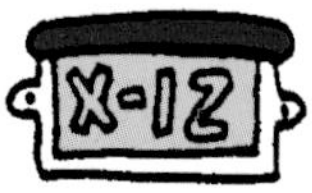

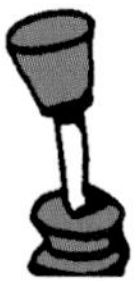

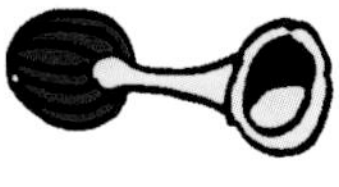

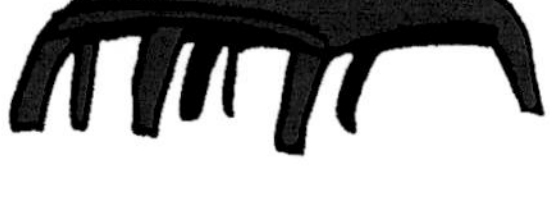

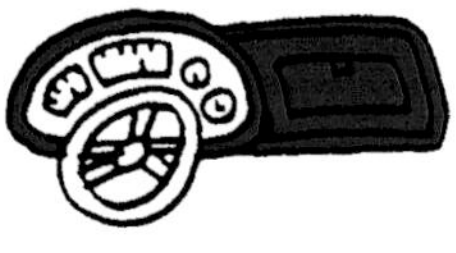

Quelques expressions utiles en cas de difficulté
(ew-teel) (kah) (dee-fee-kewl-tay)

Some useful phrases in case of problems

(meh-day) **Pouvez-vous m'aider?**	Can you help me?
(kruh-vay) **J'ai un pneu crevé.**	I have a flat tire.
(pan) **Ma voiture est en panne.**	My car has broken down.
(day-mar) **Ma voiture ne démarre pas.**	My car won't start.
Je suis en panne d'essence.	I've run out of gas.
(marsh) **Mes freins ne marchent pas.**	My brakes don't work.
Ma voiture chauffe.	My car is overheating.
(ra-tay) **Mon moteur a des ratés.**	My engine is misfiring.
(day-pah-nūhz) **J'ai besoin d'une dépanneuse.**	I need a tow truck.
(fweet) **Le radiateur a une fuite.**	The radiator is leaking.
(trAHs-mee-syOH) (kah-say) **La transmission est cassée.**	The transmission is broken.
(pla) **La batterie est à plat.**	The battery is dead.
(klee-nyo-tAH) **Les clignotants ne marchent pas.**	The signal lights don't work.
(fweet) (weel) **Ma voiture a une fuite d'huile.**	The oil is leaking.
(klee-ma-tee-za-syOH) **La climatisation (le chauffage) ne marche pas.**	The air conditioning (heater) doesn't work.

Fill in the blanks by referring to the dialogue and these new expressions.

1. Je voudrais ____________________ une voiture.
   to rent
2. Pourriez-vous ______________ ______________ ______________, s'il vous plaît?
   fill 'er up
3. Mes freins ne ____________________ pas.
   work
4. Quelle est la route la plus ____________________ ?
   short
5. Est-ce qu'il y a un ____________________ près d'ici?
   garage

(fehr)

Faire

To do, to make

Now, here is another common—and irregular—verb:

FAIRE			
je / **tu**	*(feh)* **fais**	I / you	do, make / do, make
il, elle, on	*(feh)* **fait**	he, she, it	does, makes
nous	*(fuh-zOH)* **faisons**	we	do, make
vous	*(feht)* **faites**	you	do, make
ils, elles	*(fOH)* **font**	they	do, make

Expressions with *faire*:

faire du ski to ski **faire la lessive** *(less-eev)* to do the laundry **faire un appel** *(ap-ehl)* to make a call

Fill in the correct form of the verb FAIRE.

1. Je ____________________ la liste.
2. Que ____________________ -vous?
3. Nous ____________________ une promenade.
4. Qu'est-ce qu'il ____________________ ?
5. Elles ____________________ la queue .
   line

ANSWERS

Fill in the blanks 1. louer **2.** faire le plein **3.** marchent **4.** courte **5.** garage

FAIRE 1. fais **2.** faites **3.** faisons **4.** fait **5.** font

(see) (voo) (voo-lay) (ordr)

Si vous voulez donner des ordres . . .

If you want to give orders . . . Impératif

In order to get people to do things for you, you will have to know how to use verbs in a "command" or "imperative" way. The following chart shows you how to form the imperative of regular verbs. Just keep in mind that the subject of a command is "YOU" (understood). So, simply use the **TU** form of the verb to be familiar and the **VOUS** form to be polite, without using the subject pronouns.

THE IMPERATIVE

	Parler		**Finir**
Familiar	**Tu parles → Parle!**	Familiar	**Tu finis → Finis!**
Polite or Plural	**Vous parlez → Parlez!**	Polite or Plural	**Vous finissez → Finissez!**

(Drop the final **-s** from the **tu** form for **-er** verbs only.)

	Attendre
Familiar	**Tu attends → Attends!**
Polite or Plural	**Vous attendez → Attendez!**

To say "Let's," use the **NOUS** form and drop the subject pronoun:

Parlons! Let's speak!
Finissons! Let's finish!
Attendons! Let's wait!

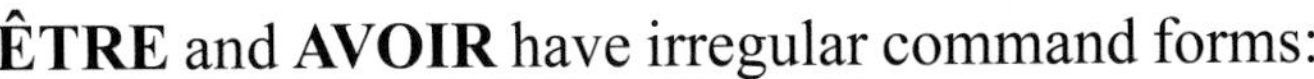

ÊTRE and **AVOIR** have irregular command forms:

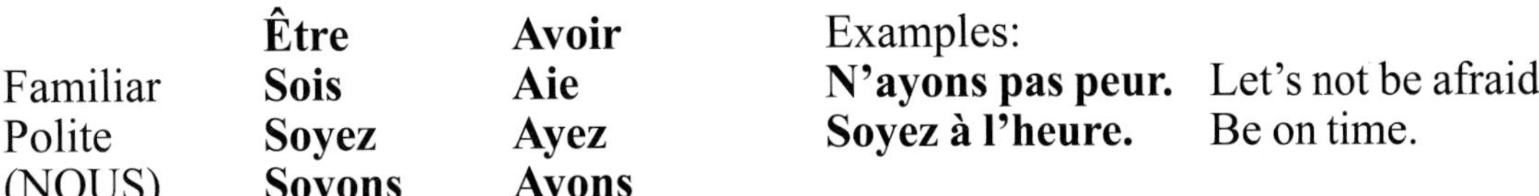

	Être	**Avoir**
Familiar	**Sois**	**Aie**
Polite	**Soyez**	**Ayez**
(NOUS)	**Soyons**	**Ayons**

Examples:
N'ayons pas peur. Let's not be afraid.
Soyez à l'heure. Be on time.

Don't get discouraged. With a little practice, you will become familiar and quite proficient with these verb forms. To make a command negative, put **NE** before the verb and **PAS** after the verb. Remember that **ne** becomes **n'** before a vowel or silent **h**.

Ne parlez pas! Don't speak!
Ne finis pas! Don't finish!
N'attendons pas. Let's not wait.

Now try the following. You are speaking to a person you meet in your travels. Tell him the following:

1. (wait for) Attendez -moi.
2. (finish) Finissez vite. (quickly)
3. (speak) Parlez lentement *(lAH-tem-AH)* (slowly), s'il vous plaît.
4. (be) Soyez prudent.
5. (have) Ayez du courage.

ANSWERS

Commands **1.** Attendez **2.** Finissez **3.** Parlez **4.** Soyez **5.** Ayez

Attention! (Watch out!) Driving in a foreign country means watching the road even when the scenery is breathtaking. **Très beau!** Yes, very beautiful! Read the following passage and determine what happened on the trip. Then answer the questions.

(ak-see-dAH)

UN ACCIDENT

An Accident

PREMIER CHAUFFEUR **Vous ne pouvez pas faire attention?** *(a-tAH-syOH)* **Vous êtes dingue?** *(dEHg)* **J'ai** *(ay)* **la priorité!** — Can't you be careful? Are you nuts? I have the right of way!

DEUXIÈME CHAUFFEUR **Je le sais!** *(say)* **Mais vous faites du 150 kilomètres à l'heure et la limite de vitesse** (speed) **est 60 kilomètres à l'heure!** — I know! But you are driving at 150 km per hour and the speed limit is 60 km per hour!

TROISIÈME CHAUFFEUR **Est-ce que je peux vous aider?** — May I help you?

PREMIER CHAUFFEUR **Oui. Demandez à l'agent là-bas de venir examiner** *(ehg-za-mee-nay)* **les dégâts.** *(day-gah)* — Yes. Ask the policeman over there to come and look at the damage.

L'AGENT **Qu'est-ce qui se passe?** — What's happening?

(ee-dyoh) (ūhr-tay)
PREMIER CHAUFFEUR **Cet idiot a heurté ma voiture. Il a tort.** — This idiot hit my car. He is in the wrong.

(vreh)
DEUXIÈME CHAUFFEUR **Ce n'est pas vrai.** — It's not true.
(teep) (foo)
Ce type conduit comme un fou. — This guy drives like a madman.
(krwa) (pee-lot) (koors)
Il se croit pilote de course. — He thinks he's a race car driver.

(pehr-son) (bleh-say)
L'AGENT **Personne n'est blessé? Bon. Vos permis de conduire, s'il vous plaît.** — Nobody is hurt? Good. Your driver's licenses, please.
(au deuxième chauffeur): Est-ce que c'est une voiture de location? — (To the second driver): Is this a rented car?

DEUXIÈME CHAUFFEUR **Oui.** — Yes.

(foh) (prayv-neer)
L'AGENT **Alors il faut prévenir l'agence et**
(kOH-pa-nyee) (a-sew-rAH)
aussi votre compagnie d'assurance. — Then it's necessary to notify the agency and also your insurance company.

DEUXIÈME CHAUFFEUR **Est-ce qu'il y a un garage près d'ici?** — Is there a garage near here?

(pro-shen)
L'AGENT **Oui, au coin de la prochaine**
(ee)
route. Vous pouvez y aller à pied. — Yes, at the corner of the next road. You can walk there.

(Au garage)

DEUXIÈME CHAUFFEUR **Est-ce que vous**
(ray-pa-ray)
pourriez réparer ma voiture? — Could you repair my car quickly?

(may-ka-nee-syEH) (shAHs)
LE MÉCANICIEN **Vous avez de la chance.** — You are lucky.
(vwah-lay)
La roue arrière est voilée et le
(ka-bo-say)
pare-choc est cabossé, c'est tout. — The rear wheel is bent and the bumper is dented, that's all.
Téléphonez demain après-midi. — Telephone tomorrow afternoon.

Mon numéro de téléphone est le quarante-quatre cinquante-et-un dix-sept. My number is 44-51-17.

DEUXIÈME CHAUFFEUR **Merci mille fois.** Many thanks.

Circle the statements that might be appropriate if you had a car accident in France:

1. Je voudrais faire le plein.
2. Demandez à l'agent de venir examiner les dégâts.
3. Je voudrais louer une voiture.
4. Votre permis de conduire, s'il vous plaît.
5. Est-ce qu'il y a un garage près d'ici?
6. Je cherche une agence de location.

If you get into an accident, do the same things you would do in this country: get the name, address, and telephone number of the other person. If you are traveling in a rented car, notify the rental agency. Ask someone to notify the police and, if necessary, to call an ambulance. If it's a minor accident and both persons can drive away, be especially careful to have all the information needed by the insurance company. And try to keep calm!

ANSWERS

Circle statements 2. 4. 5.

9	*(kAH-peng)* **Le camping** Camping

(nay-seh-sehr)
LE NÉCESSAIRE
Essentials

(mat-la) (pnūh-ma-teek)
le matelas pneumatique
air mattress

(a-bee)
les habits
clothes

(bwaht) (kOH-sehrv)
les boîtes de conserve
cans

(pa-gay)
les pagaies
paddles

(koo-vehr-tewr)
la couverture
blanket

(tAHt)
la tente
tent

(arbr)
un arbre
tree

(soh-leh-y)
le soleil
sun

(rwee-soh)
le ruisseau
brook

(sak) (duh) (koo-shahzh)
le sac de couchage
sleeping bag

(lAHp) (duh) (posh)
la lampe de poche
flashlight

(pa-nyay)
un panier
basket

(bwaht)
une boîte
box

(ka-noh-ay)
le canoë
canoe

(soh)
un seau
bucket

(kan) (pehsh)
une canne à pêche
rod fishing

(teer) (boo-shOH)
le tire-bouchon
corkscrew

(ews-tAH-seel) (kwee-zeen)
les ustensiles de cuisine
cooking utensils

(bot)
des bottes
boots

(ar-teekl) (twa-leht)
les articles de toilette
toilet articles

(tehr-mohs)
le thermos

(ra-dyoh) (por-ta-teev)
la radio portative
portable radio

(a-lew-meht)
des allumettes
matches

(sEH-dee-ka) (dee-nee-sya-teev)

In many cities, a good source of information is the Syndicat d'Initiative, the local tourism office. You can look for a local site on the Internet as you prepare for your trip by searching for the place you are visiting and adding the words "office du tourisme" or "syndicat d'initiative." Most sites have options to choose among several languages. For camping information, you can visit the web site of the Fédération Française de Camping et de Caravaning (www.ffcc.fr).

(root) (teh-rEH)

EN ROUTE POUR LE TERRAIN DE CAMPING

On the Way to the Campground

Now read the following dialogues, which contain some useful words, expressions, and information on camping. Read them aloud, repeating each line several times, so you know how to pronounce the new words.

MARC **Excusez-moi, Monsieur. Est-ce que** — Excuse me, Sir.

(poo-ryOH) (kAH-pay)

nous pourrions peut-être camper sur — Could we perhaps camp on

(pro-pree-yay-tay)

votre propriété? — your property?

(fehr-myay) (seh)

LE FERMIER (farmer) **Je suis désolé, mais c'est** — I am sorry, but it's

(tEH-po-seebl) (kAH-puhr)

impossible. Les campeurs font trop — impossible. Campers make

de cochonneries. — too much of a mess.

MARC **Je comprends. Est-ce qu'il y a un** — I understand. Is there a

terrain de camping près d'ici? — campground near here?

LE FERMIER **Oui. À vingt kilomètres.** — Yes. Twenty kilometers from here.

(pa-noh) (see-nya-lee-za-syOH)

Suivez les panneaux de signalisation. — Follow the signs.

(mee-lyūh)

Il y a une tente au milieu. — There is a tent in the middle (of the signs).

MARC **Savez-vous s'il y a des douches?** — Do you know if there are showers?

(mwEHdr) (ee-day)

LE FERMIER **Pas la moindre idée.** — Not the slightest idea.

On va vous le dire au camping. — They'll tell you at the campground.

(pray-fay-ray)

Ou si vous préférez, vous pouvez vous — Or if you prefer, you can

(a-reh-tay) (san-dee-ka) (dee-nee-sya-teev)

arrêter au Syndicat d'Initiative au — stop at the Tourist Office in

(mee-lyūh) (vee-lahzh)

milieu du village. — the middle of the village.

(teh-rEH)

SUR LE TERRAIN DE CAMPING

At the Campground

MARC **Est-ce que vous avez de la place** *(plas)* **pour nous?** — Do you have room for us?

LE DIRECTEUR *(dee-rek-tūhr)* (manager) **Oui. Combien de temps** *(tAH)* **comptez-vous** *(kOH-tay)* **rester?** *(rehs-tay)* — Yes. How long are you planning to stay?

MARC **Deux ou trois nuits.** *(nwee)* **Est-ce qu'il y a des douches?** — Two or three nights. Are there any showers?

LE DIRECTEUR **Oui.** — Yes.

ANNE **Ouf!** *(oof)* **Je vais pouvoir me laver la tête.** *(teht)* — Oh! I am going to be able to wash my hair!

> You can also say: "se laver les cheveux" *(shūh-vūh)* (hair)

MARC **C'est combien par jour?** — How much is it per day?

LE DIRECTEUR **Pour quatre personnes, vingt-cinq euros. Il y a l'électricité** *(ay-lehk-tree-see-tay)* **dans le bâtiment principal.** *(prEH-see-pal)* **Le soir,** *(swar)* **nous regardons** *(re-gar-dOH)* **un film à** *(a)* **partir de** *(par-teer)* **vingt heures.** — For four people, 25 euros. There is electricity in the main building. In the evening, we watch a movie from 8 P.M. on.

Fill in the missing word in French:

1. Est-ce qu'il y a ______________ (a campground) près d'ici?
2. Savez-vous s'il y a des ______________ (showers)?
3. Vous pouvez vous arrêter au ______________ (tourist office).
4. Combien de temps comptez-vous ______________ (to stay)?

ANSWERS

Fill in **1.** un terrain de camping **2.** douches **3.** syndicat d'initiative **4.** rester

(buh-zwEH)

J'ai besoin de . . .

I need

Study the vocabulary on page 99, then make a list of items you need to go camping.

EX.: **Pour aller camper, j'ai besoin d'une tente, d'un matelas pneumatique, d'allumettes, etc.** (If the noun is plural, you don't need to use an article; only DE or D'.)

The following puzzle contains seven camping terms in addition to the one circled. Try to find the French equivalents for: boots, bucket, stream, sun, basket, tree, blankets.

T	S	C	O	U	V	E	R	T	U	R	E	S
B	E	A	R	B	R	E	U	X	E	T	I	L
O	R	N	I	A	C	O	I	N	S	T	S	I
T	D	T	T	H	S	U	S	V	U	E	N	T
T	R	O	A	E	E	L	S	O	L	E	I	L
E	X	U	N	O	A	A	E	U	Z	N	U	E
S	D	A	V	O	U	I	A	I	N	N	E	M
P	A	N	I	E	R	S	U	R	E	S	O	N

(ay -pees-ree)

At the Grocery Store

MARIE **Je voudrais une livre** *(leevr)* **de nouilles,** *(noo-y)*	I would like a pound of noodles,
cent grammes *(gram)* **de beurre,** *(buhr)* **quatre**	100 grams of butter, four
tranches *(trAHsh)* **de jambon,** *(zhAH-bOH)* **un litre** *(leetr)* **de lait,** *(leh)*	slices of ham, one liter of milk,
du sel *(sel)* **et une bouteille** *(boo-teh-y)* **de vin** *(vEH)* **rouge**	some salt, and a bottle of ordinary red wine . . .
ordinaire . . . et aussi une boîte	and also a box
d'allumettes.	of matches.

ANSWERS

Puzzle (Camping) BOTTES SEAU RUISSEAU SOLEIL PANIER ARBRE COUVERTURES

L'ÉPICIÈRE *(lay-pee-syehr)* fem. grocer	**Vous êtes campeurs? Vous savez qu'il est interdit de faire du feu?** *(kAH-pühr)* *(füh)*	You are campers? You know it's forbidden to light fires?
MARC	**Oui, nous avons un réchaud à gaz.** *(gahz)*	Yes. We have a gas heater.
MARIE	**Je vous dois combien?** *(dwa)*	How much do I owe you?
L'ÉPICIÈRE	**Quatorze euros.**	14 euros.
	Vous avez un filet? *(fee-leh)*	Do you have a string bag?
MARIE	**Non.**	No.
L'ÉPICIÈRE	**Pas de problème! Je vais vous trouver un sac en papier.** *(pahd-prub-lehm)*	No problem! I'm going to find a paper bag for you.
MARC (à l'épicière)	**Merci. Au revoir, Madame. Bonne journée!**	Thank you. Good-bye, Madam! Have a good day!

Match these French expressions with their English equivalents.

1. une livre	a. a slice
2. cent grammes	b. a bottle
3. une tranche	c. a liter
4. un litre	d. 100 grams
5. une bouteille	e. a pound

ANSWERS

Matching 1. e 2. d 3. a 4. c 5. b

(sa-vwar) *(ko-nehtr)*

Les verbes *savoir* et *connaître*

to know to know

SAVOIR implies acquired knowledge; to know how to do something; to know a fact.

Je sais où se trouve Paris.	I know where Paris is.
Je sais nager.	I know how to swim.
Je ne sais pas.	I don't know.

(meh)
Mais
But

CONNAÎTRE—to know, to be acquainted with, a person, place, or thing.

Je connais Paris.	I know Paris (because I was there).
Je connais Robert.	I know Robert (I have met him).

SAVOIR		CONNAÎTRE	
je / **tu**	*(seh)* **sais**	**je** / **tu**	*(ko-neh)* **connais**
il / **elle** / **on**	*(seh)* **sait**	**il** / **elle** / **on**	*(ko-neh)* **connaît**
nous	*(sa-vOH)* **savons**	**nous**	*(ko-neh-sOH)* **connaissons**
vous	*(sa-vay)* **savez**	**vous**	*(ko-neh-say)* **connaissez**
ils / **elles**	*(sahv)* **savent**	**ils** / **elles**	*(ko-nehs)* **connaissent**

To practice the new verbs, fill in the blanks:

1. Je ________________ Londres.
   know
2. Tu ________________ qui est le
   know
   Président de la République française.
3. Il ________________ Brigitte Bardot.
   knows
4. Nous ________________ parler français.
   know (how)

ANSWERS

New Verbs **1.** connais **2.** sais **3.** connaît **4.** savons

(ko-mAH) (dee) (tOH)

Comment dit-on

How do you say

In English, you say: I am hot, you are hungry, she is cold, he is afraid, we are thirsty, they are sleepy. In French, the tendency is to use the verb **avoir** (to have) and say I have heat, you have hunger, and so on.

Ils ont chaud.

They are hot.

(frwah)

Nous avons froid.

We are cold.

(pūhr)

Les garçons ont peur.

The boys are afraid.

(fEH)

Le chien a faim.

The dog is hungry.

(OHt)

Le garçon a honte.

The boy is ashamed.

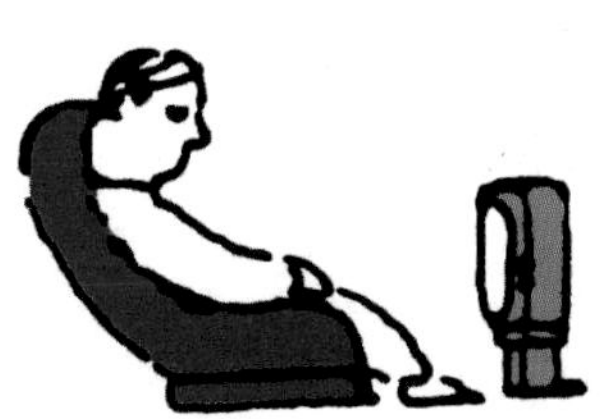

(so-meh-y)

L'homme a sommeil.

The man is sleepy.

Can you match up the pictures and sentences below?

1. Ils ont froid.
2. La dame a chaud.
3. Il a sommeil.
4. Les enfants ont peur.
5. Le garçon a faim.
6. La fille a honte.

ANSWERS

Match up sentences **1.** d **2.** a **3.** f **4.** e **5.** b **6.** c

Très bien! (Very good!) Now practice your irregular verbs, some old, some new, and adjective agreement.

1. Je suis ici.

   Tu ______________________ ici.

   Elle ______________________ ici.

   On ______________________ ici.

   Nous ______________________ ici.

   Vous ______________________ ici.

   Ils ______________________ ici.

2. Je ne sais pas.

   Ils ne ______________________ pas.

   Nous ne ______________________ pas.

   Vous ne ______________________ pas.

   On ne ______________________ pas.

   Il ne ______________________ pas.

   Tu ne ______________________ pas.

3. Nous pouvons aller à Paris.

   Je ______________________ aller à Paris.

   On ______________________ aller à Paris.

   Vous ______________________ aller à Paris.

   Elles ______________________ aller à Paris.

   Il ______________________ aller à Paris.

4. Vous avez faim.

   J' ______________________ faim.

   Il ______________________ faim.

   On ______________________ faim.

   Nous ______________________ faim.

   Ils ______________________ faim.

ANSWERS

Irregular Verbs

1. Tu es
Elle est
On est
Nous sommes
Vous êtes
Ils sont

2. Ils ne savent pas
Nous ne savons pas
Vous ne savez pas
On ne sait pas
Il ne sait pas
Tu ne sais pas

3. Je peux
On peut
Vous pouvez
Elles peuvent
Il peut

4. J'ai
Il a
On a
Nous avons
Ils ont

10 Le temps, les saisons, les mois, et les jours

(tAH) Le temps, *(seh-zOH)* les saisons,
The Weather, The Seasons

(mwah) les mois, et les *(zhoor)* jours
Months and Days

(lee-vehr)
C'EST L'HIVER.
winter

(frwah)
Il fait froid.
cold

(nehzh)
Il neige.
It's snowing.

(vAH)
Il fait du vent.
windy

(prEH-tAH)
C'EST LE PRINTEMPS.
spring

(freh)
Il fait frais.
cool

(boh)
Il fait beau.
beautiful

(so-leh-y)
Il fait du soleil.
sunny

(ay-tay)
C'EST LE L'ÉTÉ.
summer

(shoh)
Il fait chaud.
warm

Il fait très chaud.
very hot

(or-azh)
Il fait des orages.
thunderstorms

(oh-ton)
C'EST L'AUTOMNE.
autumn

(broo-yar)
Il fait du brouillard.
fog

(plūh)
Il peut.
It's raining.

(zhel)
Il gèle.
It's freezing.

(kehl) (tAH) (feh) (teel)

QUEL TEMPS FAIT-IL?

How Is the Weather?

As you noticed, the French don't say "It IS cold." They say "It MAKES cold," "*Il fait froid.*"

Il fait

. . . beau

(sew-pehrb)
. . . un temps superbe

. . . chaud

(o-reebl)
. . . un temps horrible

(mehr-veh-yūh)
. . . un temps merveilleux
marvelous

(frwah)
. . . froid
cold

(a-frūh)
. . . un temps affreux
awful

(ew-meed) *(loor)*
Il fait humide, lourd, It is humid, heavy,
(o-ra-zhūh)
orageux. stormy.
(vAH)
Il fait du vent. It is windy.

Note these exceptions:

Il neige.	It is snowing.
Il pleut.	It is raining.
(vers) **Il pleut à verse.**	It is pouring.

Can you describe the weather in the pictures below?

1. Il fait beau

2. Il fait chaud.

3. Il neige

4. Il fait un temps horrible

ANSWERS

Weather **1.** un temps merveilleux **2.** Il fait chaud. **3.** Il neige. **4.** Il fait un temps horrible.

(klehr)
Il fait clair.
light

(ma-tEH)
C'est le matin.
morning

Il fait jour.
day

(sOHbr)
Il fait un peu sombre.

(a-preh -mee-dee)
C'est l'après-midi.
afternoon

Il fait sombre.

(swar)
C'est le soir.
evening

(nwee)
Il fait nuit.
dark

C'est la nuit.
night

Track 21 03:20

ANNE	**Quelle heure est-il?**	What time is it?
SUZANNE	**Sept heures et demie.**	7:30.
ANNE	**Déjà? Quel temps fait-il?**	Already? What's the weather like?
SUZANNE	*(ma-nee-feek)* **Magnifique!**	Magnificent!
	(luh-vay) **Quel lever du soleil!**	What a sunrise!
	(may-tay-oh) **La météo** (weather) *(a-nOHs)* **annonce:** (reports)	The weather forecast is:
	"Cet après-midi, temps beau et *(doo)* **doux.** (mild)	"Beautiful, mild weather this afternoon.

(AHtr) **Temperature entre quinze et dix-huit** between	Temperature between 15 and 18°C.
(duh-gray) *(new-a-zhūh)* **degrés centigrades. Ce soir, nuageux** cloudy	This evening, cloudy
(behs) *(tAH-pay-ra-tewr)* **à couvert avec baisse de température.** lowering	and overcast with temperatures dropping.
(par-syehl-mAH) **Mercredi, partiellement couvert.** partially	Wednesday, partly cloudy.
Température entre dix-sept	Temperatures between 17
et vingt degrés centigrades."	and 20°C."
ANNE **Levons-nous! J'ai faim!**	Let's get up! I am hungry!

Choose the correct answer:

1. Cet après-midi, il va faire
   A. très chaud B. très froid
   C. mauvais D. beau

2. C'est la météo pour un jour
   A. d'août B. de janvier
   C. de février D. d'avril

Temperature conversions

Centigrade Degrés Fahrenheit

Thermomètre

To change Fahrenheit to Centigrade: Subtract 32 and multiply by $\frac{5}{9}$.

To change Centigrade to Fahrenheit: Multiply by $\frac{9}{5}$ and add 32.

ANSWERS

Multiple choice 1. D 2. D

(ka-lAH-dree-yay)

LE CALENDRIER

The Calendar

(mwah)

THE MONTHS OF THE YEAR—LES MOIS DE L'ANNEE

(zhAH-vyay) **janvier** January	*(ah-vreel)* **avril** April	*(zhwee-yeh)* **juillet** July	*(ok-tobr)* **octobre** October
(fay-vree-yay) **février** February	*(meh)* **mai** May	*(oot)* or *(oo)* **août** August	*(no-vAHbr)* **novembre** November
(mars) **mars** March	*(zhwEH)* **juin** June	*(sehp-tAHbr)* **septembre** September	*(day-sAHbr)* **décembre** December

(suh -men)

THE DAYS OF THE WEEK—LES JOURS DE LA SEMAINE

(dee-mAHsh) **dimanche** Sunday	*(lUH-dee)* **lundi** Monday	*(mar-dee)* **mardi** Tuesday	*(mehr-kruh-dee)* **mercredi** Wednesday	*(zhuh-dee)* **jeudi** Thursday	*(vAH-druh-dee)* **vendredi** Friday	*(sam-dee)* **samedi** Saturday

Si c' est mardi, je dois — If it's Tuesday, I must

(vee-zeet)
rendre visite à ma mère, parce que — pay a visit to my mother, because
pay a visit

***le mardi*, je vais toujours visiter ma mère.** — I always go to visit my mother on Tuesdays.

Use LE with days of the week when describing a habit or a customary practice that takes place on a day of the week, but if you want to say, "On Tuesday, (this particular Tuesday) I am going to visit my mother," it is **Mardi, je vais rendre visite à ma mère**.

(ehk-spree-may) *(dat)*

Comment exprimer la date

How to express the date

To express the date in French use:

LE + number + month + year

C'est le six avril deux mille quatorze (2014).
It is

Use this formula to express all dates, except for the first of the month:

C'est le premier mai.
first

(feht)
La fête nationale américaine est le 4 juillet.

La fête nationale française est le 14 juillet.

(noh-ehl)
Noël est le 25 décembre.

Pâques est en avril.

La Saint-Sylvestre est le trente-et-un décembre.

La fête nationale suisse est le premier août. **La fête nationale belge est le 21 juillet.**

Comment exprimer les mois

How to express the months

Use EN with months to express "in":

En janvier, je fais du ski. In January, I ski.

With seasons, use AU before a consonant. Use EN before a vowel to express "in the":

au printemps, en été, en automne, en hiver.

Complete the following sentences, using the correct form:

1. Quel jour est-ce aujourd'hui? *(oh-zhoor-dwee)* today

   C'est aujourd'hue mercredi

2. Quelle est la date?

   C'est aujourd'hue le vingt-six avril.

3. Quelle est la date de votre anniversaire? *(a-nee-vehr-sehr)*

   C'est le trente mars.

4. Quand est la fête nationale française?

   C'est le quatorze juillet.

5. Quand est la fête nationale américaine?

   C'est le quatre juillet.

ANSWERS

Date 1. C'est aujourd'hui lundi. (example) **2.** C'est aujourd'hui le onze juillet. (example) **3.** C'est le douze janvier. (example) **4.** C'est le quatorze juillet. **5.** C'est le quatre juillet.

(ad-zhehk-teef)
Les adjectifs
Adjectives

Throughout your trip you will notice many wonderful things that you will want to describe. In order to do this, you will have to know how to use French adjectives. Adjectives agree in gender (masculine or feminine) and number (singular or plural) with the nouns they modify.

In most instances, add -E to the masculine form of the adjective to obtain the corresponding feminine form:

un garçon intelligent — **une fille intelligente**
un dîner parfait — **une maison parfaite**

Masculine	Feminine
(preh) **prêt** ready	*(preht)* **prête**
(loor) **lourd** heavy	*(loord)* **lourde**
(par-feh) **parfait** perfect	*(par-feht)* **parfaite**

More examples.

(shAHbr)		
MON HÔTEL EST . . . My Hotel Is . . .		**MA CHAMBRE EST . . .** My Room Is . . .
Masculine		**Feminine**
(brwee-yAH) **bruyant** noisy		*(brwee-yahnt)* **bruyante**
(klehr) **clair** bright		*(klehr)* **claire**
(grAH) **grand** big		*(grAHd)* **grande**
(puh-tee) **petit** small		*(puh-teet)* **petite**

BUT

If the masculine form of the adjective already ends in -E, add nothing to obtain the feminine form.

(sahl) **sale** dirty		*(sahl)* **sale**
(pūh) (kOH-for-tahbl) **peu confortable** not very comfortable		*(pūh) (kOH-for-tahbl)* **peu confortable**

JE SUIS
I am . . .

Masculine		Feminine
(sa-tees-feh) **satisfait** satisfied		*(sa-tees-feht)* **satisfaite**
(kOH-tAH) **content** pleased, glad		*(kOH-tAHt)* **contente**
(puh-tee) **petit** small		*(puh-teet)* **petite**
(zho-lee) **joli** pretty, handsome		*(zho-lee)* **jolie** pretty

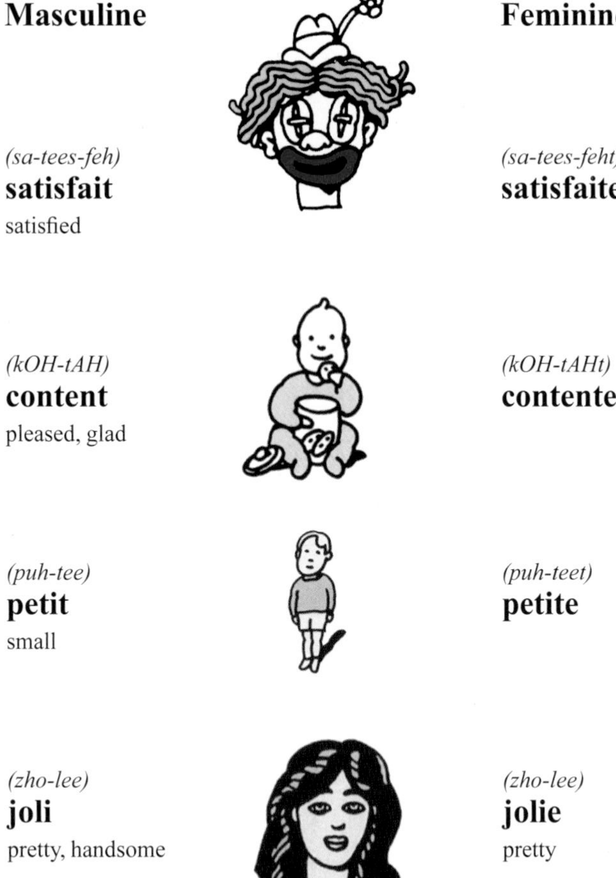

When a masculine adjective ends in -É, the adjective is considered regular. The feminine form, therefore, is simply obtained by adding another -E: *(AH-shAH-tay)* **enchanté**, **enchantée**. delighted

(fa-tee-gay) **fatigué** tired	**fatiguée**
(fa-shay) **fâché** angry	**fâchée**

Masculine	Feminine
(a-zhay) **âgé** old	**âgée**
(ee-ree-tay) **irrité** annoyed	**irritée**

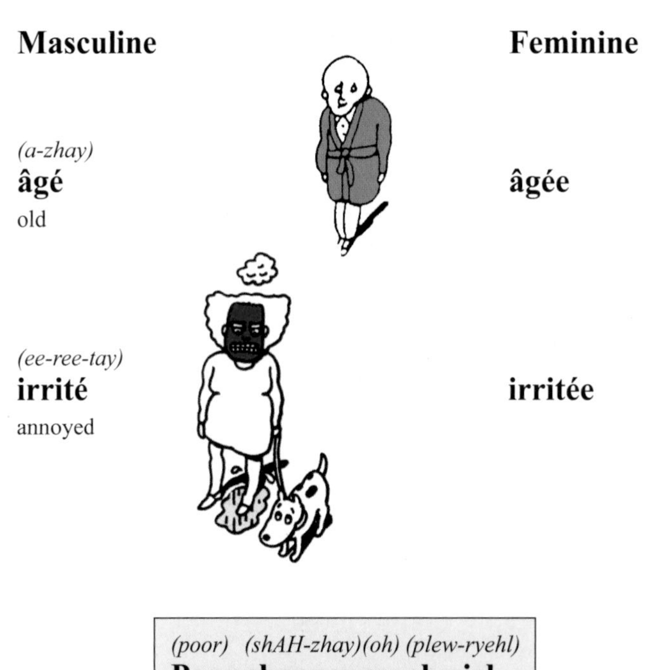

(poor) (shAH-zhay)(oh) (plew-ryehl)
Pour changer au pluriel
To change to the plural

Add -S to the masculine or feminine singular form of the adjective to obtain the corresponding plural forms of most adjectives. Add nothing to form the plural of an adjective that ends in -S or -X. The -AL ending of a masculine singular adjective becomes -AUX in the plural;

Masculine Forms

un garçon intelligent	**des garçons intelligents**
un dîner parfait	**des dîners parfaits**
un garçon surpris	**des garçons surpris**
un problème national	**des problèmes nationaux**

Feminine Forms

une fille intelligente	**des filles intelligentes**
une maison parfaite	**des maisons parfaites**
une fille surprise	**des filles surprises**
une fête nationale holiday	**des fêtes nationales**

Fill in the correct form of the adjective in parentheses:

1. (content) Les garçons ____contents____
2. (parfait) La voiture ____parfaite____
3. (satisfait) La mère ____satisfaite____
4. (prêt) L'homme ____prêt____
5. (lourd) Les livres ____lourds____
6. (intelligent) Les filles ____intelligente____
7. (général) Les problèmes (m.) ____généralaux____
8. (surpris) Les pères ____surpris____

(oo) (lay) (mehtr)
Où les mettre
Where to put them

Adjectives are usually placed after the nouns they modify except when they are short, common, and express **Beauty**, **Age**, **Goodness**, and **Size** (**BAGS**): **beau**, **joli**, **jeune**, **vieux**,
young old

nouveau, **bon**, **petit**, **grand**
new good big

le garçon intelligent

les femmes importantes

but

le petit garçon

les jolies femmes

ANSWERS

Adjectives **1.** contents, **2.** parfaite, **3.** satisfaite, **4.** prêt, **5.** lourds, **6.** intelligentes, **7.** généraux, **8.** surpris

11

(vwa-yahzh) (a-vyOH)

Voyages en avion

Plane Trips

(too-reesm)

Le tourisme

Sightseeing

A plane trip within a country is often an easy and enjoyable way to travel. Note that in France, *(la -ay-ro-por) (sharl) (gohl)* **l'Aéroport Charles de Gaulle** is for international flights; Le Bourget *(boor-zheh)* is mostly for domestic flights; Orly *(or-lee)* is for medium-length domestic and international flights. Study the following vocabulary and then follow the tourist as he goes to one of France's most popular resorts, Cannes.

Pouvez-vous trouver ...

(lee-ny) (a-ay-ryehn)
la ligne aérienne
airline

(kOH-twar) (bee-yay)
le comptoir des billets
ticket counter

(or-lozh)
l'horloge (f.)
clock

(ehs-ka-lyay) (roo-lAH)
l'escalier roulant
escalator

(tro-twar)
le trottoir roulant
moving sidewalk

(dwah-nyeh) (dwah-nyehr)
le douanier, la douanière
customs officer

(kOH-trohl) (pas-por)
le contrôle des passeports
passport control

(EH-pehk-tuhr)
l'inspecteur (m.), **l'inspectrice** (f.)
inspector

(sor-tee)
la sortie
gate, exit

(ba-gahzh)
les bagages
luggage

(pee-lot) (koh-pee-lot)
la pilote, la copilote
le pilote, le copilote

(oh-tehs) (ehr)
l'hôtesse de l'air
stewardess

(stee-wart)
le steward
steward

(toor)
la tour de contrôle
control tower

(ka-myOH)
le camion
truck

L'HÔTESSE *(AH-bar-kuh-mAH)* **Votre carte d'embarquement, s'il vous plaît.**	Your boarding pass, please.
LE TOURISTE **Oui . . . Je l'ai . . . Mais où est-elle?**	Yes . . . I have it . . . but where is it?
L'HÔTESSE *(day-pay-shay)* **Dépêchez-vous, s'il vous plaît.**	Hurry up, please.
Il y a une longue *(lOHg)* **queue** *(kuh)* **derrière vous.**	There is a long line behind you.
LE TOURISTE (Il fouille *(foo-y)* dans toutes ses poches.)	(He searches through all his pockets.)
L'HÔTESSE **Monsieur, l'avion part dans quelques minutes.** *(mee-newt)*	Sir, the plane is leaving in a few minutes.
LE TOURISTE **Ça y est! La voilà enfin!**	There we are! Here it is at last!

L'AVION

The Plane

(day-ko-lazh)
le décollage

(ay-kee-pahzh)
l'équipage
crew

(ewr-zhAHs)
la sortie d'urgence
emergency exit

(ew-bloh)
le hublot
window

(ka-been)
la cabine
cabin

(pla-toh)
le plateau
tray

(fewz-lahzh)
le fuselage

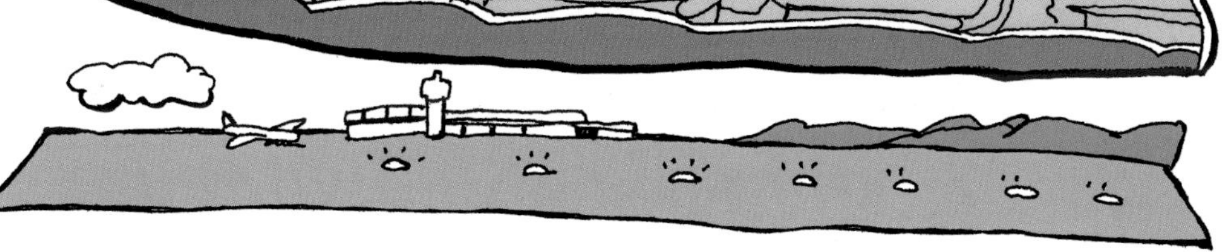

la piste
runway

l'atterrissage
landing

la ceinture de sécurité
safety-belt

le passager, la passagère

(syehzh)
le siège
seat

LE PILOTE **Nous allons décoller** *(day-ko-lay)* **dans quelques minutes. Veuillez** *(vuh-yay)* **attacher vos ceintures de sécurité et redresser le dossier de votre siège.**	We are going to take off in a few minutes. Please fasten your seat belts and straighten the back of your seat.
(Later)	
LE PILOTE **Nous allons atterrir à Cannes à quatorze heures trente. Nous volons à une altitude** *(al-tee-tewd)* **de dix mille mètres. Le temps à Cannes est nuageux et pluvieux** *(plew-vyūh)* **et la température est trente-et-un degrés centigrade** *(sAH-tee-grad)***.**	We are going to land in Cannes at 2:30 P.M. We are flying at an altitude of 10,000 meters. The weather in Cannes is cloudy and rainy. And the temperature is 31 degrees Celsius.
PREMIER PASSAGER **Madame, est-ce que vous servez un déjeuner** *(day-zhūh-nay)***?**	Ma'am, do you serve lunch?
L'HÔTESSE **Je vous l'apporte** *(a-port)* **dans un instant.**	I'll bring it to you in a moment.
DEUXIÈME PASSAGER **Chic!** *(sheek)* **J'adore manger en avion. Ça fait passer** *(pah-say)* **le temps.**	Good! I love eating on the plane. It makes the time pass quickly.
PREMIER PASSAGER **Madame! Je voudrais une boisson** *(bwa-SOH)***, s'il vous plaît.**	Ma'am! I would like a drink please.
L'HÔTESSE **Tout** *(toot)* **de suite** *(sweet)***.**	Right away.

(Later)

PREMIER PASSAGER	**J'ai sommeil.**	I'm sleepy.
	Madame, pouvez-vous me	Ma'am, can you give me
	(koo-vehr-tewr) (sew-play-mAH-tehr) **donner une couverture supplémentaire?**	an extra blanket?
	(day-rAHzh) (ay-tEH) (lew-myehr) **Ça vous dérange si j'éteins la lumière?**	Does it bother you if I turn off the light?
DEUXIÈME PASSAGER	*(rOHfl)* **Zut! Il ronfle**	Darn! He is already snoring!
	déjà! Et moi qui ne peux jamais	And I can never
	dormir en avion!	sleep on planes!

Can you give the French equivalent for these expressions?

1. Your boarding pass, please. Votre carte d'embarquement, s'il vous plaît.
2. I have it. Je l'ai.
3. Hurry up. Dépêchez-vous!
4. Right away. Tout de suite!
5. I'm sleepy. J'ai sommeil.

Encore des verbes

More verbs

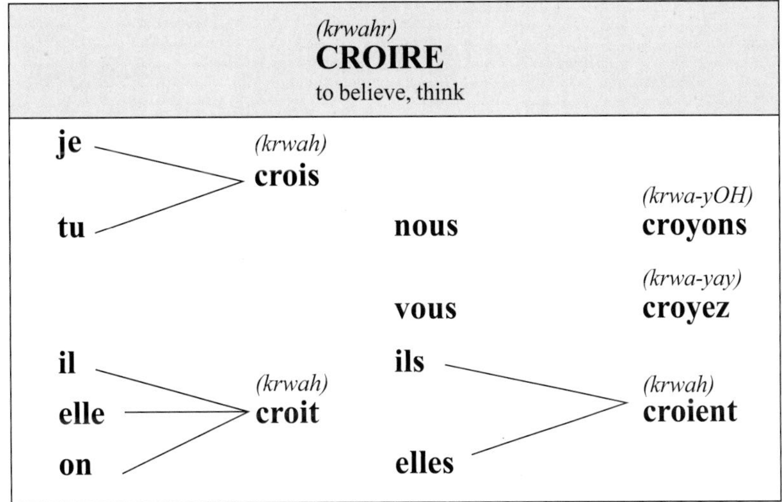

(krwahr)
CROIRE
to believe, think

je, **tu**	*(krwah)* **crois**	**nous**	*(krwa-yOH)* **croyons**
		vous	*(krwa-yay)* **croyez**
il, **elle**, **on**	*(krwah)* **croit**	**ils**, **elles**	*(krwah)* **croient**

ANSWERS

Equivalents **1.** Votre carte d'embarquement, s'il vous plaît. **2.** Je l'ai. **3.** Dépêchez-vous. **4.** Tout de suite. **5.** J'ai sommeil.

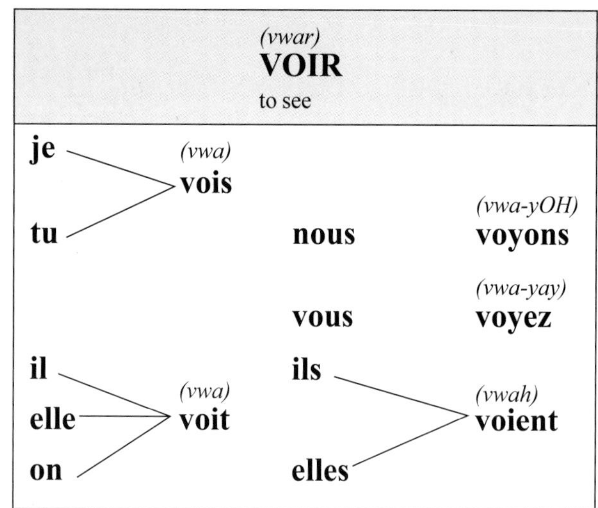

(vwar) **VOIR** to see			
je, **tu**	*(vwa)* **vois**	**nous**	*(vwa-yOH)* **voyons**
		vous	*(vwa-yay)* **voyez**
il, **elle**, **on**	*(vwa)* **voit**	**ils**, **elles**	*(vwah)* **voient**

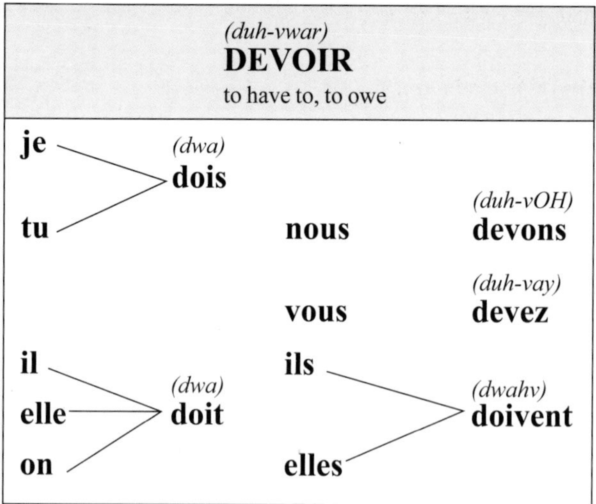

(duh-vwar) **DEVOIR** to have to, to owe			
je, **tu**	*(dwa)* **dois**	**nous**	*(duh-vOH)* **devons**
		vous	*(duh-vay)* **devez**
il, **elle**, **on**	*(dwa)* **doit**	**ils**, **elles**	*(dwahv)* **doivent**

How about practicing these verbs in sentences:

1. Je ________________ (believe) qu'il va faire beau temps demain.
2. ________________ (see) -vous ce beau lever du soleil?
3. Nous ________________ (believe) le garçon.
4. Marc ________________ (believes) qu'il y a un terrain de camping près d'ici.
5. En France, on ________________ (sees) la Tour Eiffel.
6. Madeleine ________________ (has to) se brosser *(bruss-ay)* les cheveux.

(gra-mehr)

Un peu de grammaire

Some grammar

The direct object pronouns are:

***me, m'**	me	**nous**	us
***te, t'** (before a vowel)	you (fam.)	**vous**	you (polite, plural)
le, l' (before a vowel)	it, him	**les**	them
la, l' (before a vowel)	it, her		

*__Me__ becomes **moi** in affirmative commands. **Te** becomes **toi** in affirmative commands.

ANSWERS

Verbs (fill ins) **1.** crois **2.** Voyez **3.** croyons. **4.** croit **5.** voit **6.** doit

They are placed before the verb:

Paul me voit. Paul sees me.

Paul m'aime. Paul loves me.

Paul te voit. Paul sees you.

Paul t'aime. Paul loves you.

Paul le (la) voit. Paul sees him (her).

Direct object pronouns replace direct object nouns. Note that the direct object pronoun precedes the verb.

Je regarde le film. I watch the film.

Je le regarde. I watch it.

Il cherche Anne. He looks for Anne.

Il la cherche. He looks for her.

Direct object pronouns are placed before the verb except in an affirmative command:

Vous me regardez. You look at me.

Regardez-moi. Look at me.

Vous le prenez. You take it.

Prenez-le. Take it.

In negative sentences, the word order is:

Je ne le regarde pas. I don't watch it.

Il ne la cherche pas. He does not look for it.

In negative commands, the word order is:

Ne me regardez pas. Don't look at me.

Ne le prenez pas. Don't take it.

Replace the noun by a pronoun as in the example that follows:

Je prends le livre. **Je le prends.**

Nous regardons la télévision. 1. **Nous** ________________ **regardons.**

J'aime les films. 2. **Je** ________________ **aime.**

ANSWERS

Pronouns **1.** la **2.** les

J'apporte le dîner. 3. **Je** ______________ **apporte.**

Tu connais Jean Reno? 4. **Tu** ______________ **connais?**

Il n'aime pas ce film. 5. **Il ne** ______________ **aime pas.**

Je ne comprends pas les exercices. 6. **Je ne** ______________ **comprends pas.**

Regardez les garçons! 7. **Regardez-** ______________ **!**

(foh-toh)
Prenez la photo! 8. **Prenez-** ______________ **!**

(ad-mee-ray) *(mOH-ta-nyuh)*
Admirez les montagnes! 9. **Admirez-** ______________ **!**

(veel)

En ville

In the city

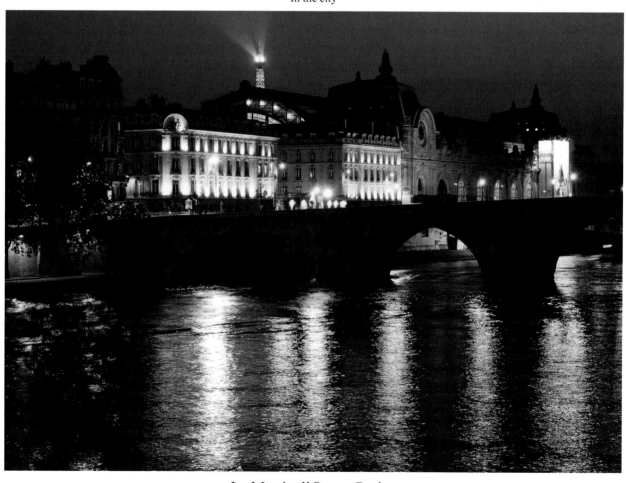

Le Musée d'Orsay. Paris.

ANSWERS

Pronouns **3.** l' **4.** le **5.** l' **6.** les **7.** les **8.** la **9.** les

Back in Paris, our tourist decides to do some sightseeing.

LE TOURISTE	**Pardon, Monsieur.**	Excuse me, Sir.
	Pouvez-vous me dire où se trouve le (se trouve: is found)	Can you tell me where the
	(zhew) (pom) **"Jus de Pomme"?**	"Apple Juice" is?

The tourist is confused because the impressionist collection of the Musée du Jeu de Paume was moved to the Musée d'Orsay.

LE PARISIEN *(pa-ree-zyan)*	*(kwa)* **Le quoi?**	The what?
LE TOURISTE	*(say-lehbr) (mew-zay)* **Le célèbre musée qui**	The famous museum that
	(ta-bloh) (an-preh-syo-neest) **a tous les tableaux impressionnistes.**	has all the Impressionist paintings.
LE PARISIEN	*(mew-zay)* **Vous voulez dire le Musée**	You mean the Musée
	(dor-say) (zhews-tuh-mAH) **d'Orsay? Je vais justement dans cette**	d'Orsay? I happen to be going in that
	(dee-rehk-syOH) (mOH-tray) **direction. Je vais vous montrer.**	direction. I'll show you.
LE TOURISTE	*(eh-mahbl)* **Vous êtes très aimable.**	You are very kind.
LE PARISIEN	*(dohtr)* **Avez-vous visité d'autres**	Have you visited other
	(mo-new-mAH) **monuments?**	monuments?
LE TOURISTE	**Oui. La magnifique**	Yes. The magnificent
	Cathédrale de Notre-Dame et la Sainte-	Notre Dame and Sainte
	Chapelle. Demain matin je vais faire	Chapelle. Tomorrow morning I'll tour
	(oh-toh-kar) **le tour de la ville en autocar et**	the city by bus and
	demain après-midi je vais prendre un	tomorrow afternoon I'll take a
	(ba-toh) (moosh) (sehn) **bateau-mouche sur la Seine.**	bateau-mouche on the Seine. (bateau-mouche: sightseeing barge)
	(kOHt) **Je compte aussi aller**	I also intend to go to
	au Louvre, naturellement.	the Louvre, of course.

LE PARISIEN **Avez-vous vu des** *(plahzh)* **plages et des montagnes?**

Have you seen any beaches and mountains?

LE TOURISTE **Je suis allé à Cannes et à Nice.** **J'espère** *(ruh-vuh-neer)* **revenir une autre fois pour voyager dans les Alpes. Je voudrais prendre le** *(tay-lay-fay-reek)* **téléphérique de** *(ay-gwee-y)* **l'Aiguille du** *(mee-dee)* **Midi.**

I have been to Cannes and Nice. I hope to come back another time to travel in the Alps. I would like to take the Aiguille du Midi cable car.

LE PARISIEN **Voilà le Musée d'Orsay.** **Au revoir et bon** *(say-zhoor)* **séjour!**

Here is the Musée d'Orsay! Good-bye, have a pleasant stay!

LE TOURISTE (à lui-même) **Que les Parisiens sont aimables!**

How friendly the Parisians are!

Can you match the questions in the left column with the answers in the right column?

1. Avez-vous visité d'autres monuments?
2. Avez-vous vu des plages?
3. Comment aller au Musée d'Orsay?
4. Qu-est-ce que vous allez faire demain matin?
5. Quel musée a des tableaux impressionnistes?

A. Je suis allé à Cannes et à Nice.
B. Le Musée d'Orsay a des tableaux impressionnistes.
C. Oui, la Cathédrale de Notre-Dame et la Sainte Chapelle.
D. Demain matin je vais faire le tour de la ville en autocar.
E. Je vais justement dans cette direction.

ANSWERS

Matching 1. C 2. A 3. E 4. D 5. B

ENTERTAINMENT

(dee-vehr-tees-mAH)
Les divertissements

12 Le théâtre, le cinéma et les jours de fête

(kAH-peng) (see-nay-ma) (feht)

Theater Movies Holidays

Jack and Suzanne are a middle-aged couple from Portland, Maine, who take a trip to France for the first time. They like the theater. It is their second day in Paris. Being of French descent, they both speak French quite well. "Not one word of English during our vacation," they decide.

LE THÉÂTRE

Theater

À L'HÔTEL

JACQUES	**Qu'est-ce que tu as envie (AH-vee) de faire ce soir?**	What do you feel like doing tonight?
SUZANNE	**On pourrait aller au théâtre?**	We could go to the theater.
	Il paraît qu'il y a plus de 55 salles à Paris.	It seems there are more than 55 theaters in Paris.
JACQUES	**On donne *Phèdre* (fehdr) de Racine (ra-seen) à la Comédie (ko-may-dee) Française. Mais c'est samedi et il ne reste probablement que des places (plas) au poulailler (poo-la-yay).**	*Phèdre* by Racine is playing at the Comédie-Fraçaise. But it's Saturday and the only seats left are probably in the chicken coop.

SUZANNE	**Qu'est-ce que c'est que ça?**	What's that?
	(bal-kOH) (AH) (oh)	
JACQUES	**Le quatrième balcon, tout en haut.**	The 4th balcony, way up.
	(fo-lee) (ber-zhehr)	
	Est-ce que tu veux aller aux Folies-Bergère?	Do you want to go to the Folies-Bergère?
SUZANNE	**Ah non! C'est pour les touristes.**	No no! That's for tourists.
	(shahn -so-nyay)	
	On pourrait aller voir un chansonnier	We could go and see a cabaret artist
	à Pigalle.	at Pigalle.
	(shoo)	
JACQUES	**Mais, mon chou, ces gens-là parlent**	But, my darling, those people speak
	(vee-tehs)	
	à toute vitesse!	horribly fast!
SUZANNE	**Dans ce cas, peut-être un bon**	In that case, maybe a good
	(feelm)	
	film français. . . .	French film. . . .
	(ee-day)	
JACQUES	**Bonne idée!**	Good idea!
	(prom-nOH)	
	Promenons-nous sur les Champs-Elysées.	Let's walk on the Champs-Elysées.
	Et s'il n'y a pas de bon film,	
	(sEH-pluh-mAH)	
	nous allons simplement	And if there is no good film, we'll simply
	(vehr)	
	prendre un verre dans un café.	have a drink in a café.

Answer these questions based on the dialogue:

1. Qu'est-ce que Marie a envie de faire ce soir?

____

2. Qu'est-ce qu'on donne?

____

3. Qu'est-ce que c'est que "le poulailler"?

____

4. Pourquoi Marc, n'a-t-il pas envie d'aller voir un chansonnier?

____

5. Quelle est la bonne idée de Marie?

____

ANSWERS

Dialogue 1. Marie a envie d'aller au théâtre. **2.** On donne *Phèdre* de Racine. **3.** C'est le quatrième balcon, tout en haut. **4.** Ces gens-là parlent à toute vitesse. **5.** La bonne idée est de voir un bon film.

See how similar these words are:

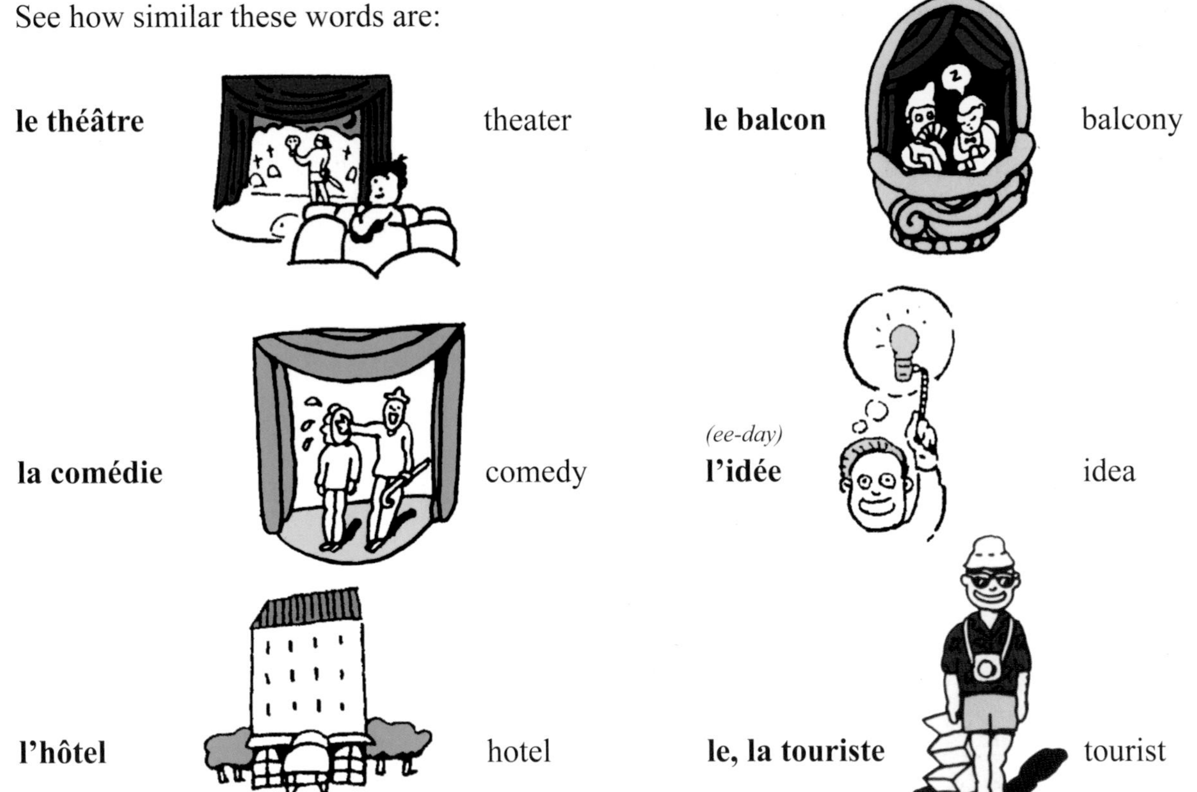

le théâtre — theater

le balcon — balcony

la comédie — comedy

(ee-day)
l'idée — idea

l'hôtel — hotel

le, la touriste — tourist

If you go to the theater or the movies in France (and other European countries), be prepared to give a small **pourboire** *(poor-bwar)* to the **ouvreuse** *(oo-vrūhz)* (woman usher) after she has led you to your seat. At the movies, there is usually an **entracte** *(AH-trakt)* (intermission) during which advertisements are projected on the screen. In French, a **comédie** is not only a comedy, as we think of it in English. It is also used to refer to the theater. The **Comédie-Française** is the French national theater.

(pūh) (tew) (muh) (do-nay) (UH) (pūh) (dahr-zhAH)

Peux-tu me donner un peu d'argent?

Can you give a little money . . . to me?

Indirect Object Pronouns			
***me, m'**	to me	**nous**	to us
***te, t'**	to you (fam.)	**vous**	to you (polite, plur.)
lui	to him, to her	**leur**	to them
se, s'	to himself, to herself	**se**	to themselves

***Me** becomes **moi** in an affirmative command. **Te** becomes **toi** in an affirmative command.

The chart below will show you how the direct and indirect pronouns are placed in sentences:

DIRECT or INDIRECT	DIRECT	INDIRECT

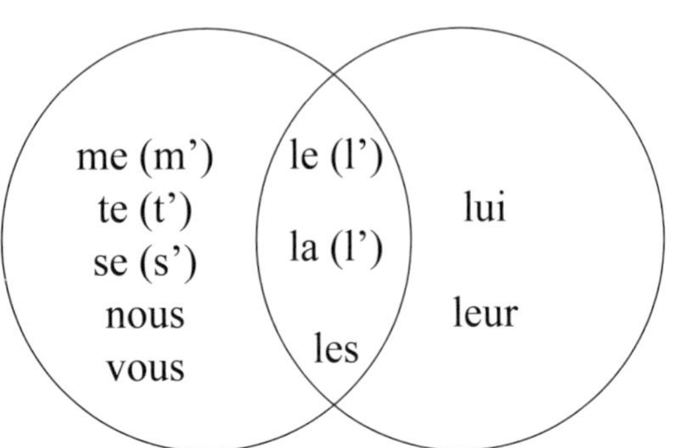

Indirect object nouns are preceded by a form of à (TO): (à, à la, à l', au, aux). Indirect object pronouns may replace indirect object nouns:

Je parle à Anne . I speak to Anne.	**Je lui parle.** I speak to her.
Il parle au garçon . He speaks to the boy.	**Il lui parle.** He speaks to him.
Vous parlez aux hommes . You speak to the men.	**Vous leur parlez.** You speak to them.

Indirect object pronouns are usually placed before the verb.

Vous lui parlez. You speak to him.	**Vous me parlez.** You speak to me.
Vous ne lui parlez pas. You don't speak to him.	**Vous ne me parlez pas.** You don't speak to me.
Ne lui parlez pas! Don't speak to him!	**Ne me parlez pas!** Don't speak to me!

However, in the affirmative command, the indirect object pronoun follows the verb.

Parlez- lui ! Speak to him!	**Parlez- moi !** Speak to me!

Replace the indirect object noun with the correct pronoun and then write the sentence.

1. Je parle *à Georges*. ______________________
2. Il n'écrit pas *au garçon*. ______________________
   writes
3. Ne lisez pas *aux enfants*. ______________________
   reads
4. Elle parle *à Henri et à Michel*. ______________________
5. Parlez *au docteur*. ______________________

Since ME, TE, NOUS, VOUS may be direct object pronouns, indirect object pronouns or reflexive pronouns, their use is relatively easy. For the other pronouns just remember:

le—him, it	lui—to him, to her	se—(to) himself
la—her, it	leur—to them	herself
les—them		itself
		oneself
		themselves

TRACK 26

LES JOURS DE FÊTE

Holidays.

JACQUES **C'est intéressant** *(EH-tay-reh -sAH)* **de comparer les** *(kOH-pa-ray)* **fêtes françaises avec les fêtes américaines. Six jours après le Nouvel An, les** *(noo-vehl) (AH)* **Français célèbrent l'Épiphanie, la fête** *(ay-pee-fa-nee)* **des rois mages.** *(rwah) (mahzh)*	It's interesting to compare the French holidays with the American ones. Six days after New Year's Day, the French celebrate the Epiphany, the feast of the three kings.
SUZANNE **Peut-être qu'ils ont besoin d'un jour de congé après le** *(kOH-zhay)* **réveillon . . .** *(ray-veh-yOH)*	Maybe they need a holiday after the holiday meal . . .

ANSWERS

Dialogue **1.** Je lui parle. **2.** Il ne lui écrit pas. **3.** Ne leur lisez pas. **4.** Elle leur parle. **5.** Parlez-lui.

JACQUES **Et à Pâques, ils ont congé le Jeudi Saint, le Vendredi Saint et le Lundi de Pâques. Ils font le pont et ont presque une semaine de vacances! Ensuite il y a l'Ascension puis la Pentecôte . . .**
(pahk) *(pOH)* *(a-sAH-syOH)* *(pAH-koht)*

And at Easter time, they have days off on Good Thursday, Good Friday and Easter Monday. They take a long weekend and have almost a week's vacation! Then there is Ascension Day, then Pentecost Day . . .

un pont = a bridge; **faire le pont** means to take a long weekend

SUZANNE **. . . et c'est presque l'été et les grandes vacances.**
(prehsk)

. . . and it's almost summer and the big vacation.

JACQUES **Exactement. Au mois d'août.**

Exactly. In August.

SUZANNE **Est-ce qu'on célèbre la Journée du Travail?**
(tra-vah-y)

Do they celebrate Labor Day?

JACQUES **Oui, le premier mai.**

Yes, on May 1st.

SUZANNE **Et en automne?**

And in the fall?

JACQUES **Il y a la fête de l'Armistice le 11 novembre et la Toussaint le premier novembre. À propos, sais-tu pourquoi nous ne devons pas apporter de chrysanthèmes à ta tante Sophie demain?**
(ahr-mees-tees) *(too-sEH)* *(pro-poh)* *(kry-zahn-tehm)*

There is Armistice Day on November 11 and All Saints Day on November 1. By the way, do you know why we mustn't take mums to your Aunt Sophie tomorrow?

SUZANNE **Pourquoi?**

Why?

JACQUES **Parce que la Toussaint est une journée solennelle pour les morts et les gens apportent des chrysanthèmes au cimetière.**
(so-la-nehl) *(mor)* *(seem-tyehr)*

Because All Saints Day is a solemn day for the dead and people take mums to the cemetery.

SUZANNE **Vraiment?**
(vreh-mAH)

Really?

JACQUES **De toute manière, peu après la Toussaint, il y a Noël, et un autre réveillon!**
(toot) *(ma-nyehr)* *(no-ehl)*

Anyway, shortly after All Saints Day there is Christmas, and another big feast!

Fill in the correct French word:

1. À Paris, il y a plus de ________________ théâtres.
   55

2. C'est ________________ de comparer les fêtes
   interesting
   françaises avec les fêtes américaines.

3. Jacques et Suzanne vont voir un film ________________ .
   French

4. Qui est-ce que Jacques et Suzanne vont voir demain?
   Il vont voir ________________ .
   Aunt Sophie

5. Si vous êtes invités à dîner chez une famille
   (shay) at the home of
   française, il ne faut pas apporter de ________________ .
   Chrysanthemums

6. La fête de l'Armistice est ________________ .
   November 11

7. La Toussaint est une ________________
   day
   solennelle.

8. Les Français ont beaucoup de jours de ________________ .
   off

9. Jacques et Suzanne ________________ le théâtre.
   like

10. Noël ________________ .
    is December 25

ANSWERS

Fill in blanks **1.** cinquante-cinq **2.** intéressant **3.** français **4.** Tante Sophie **5.** chrysanthèmes **6.** le onze novembre **7.** journée **8.** congé **9.** aiment **10.** est le vingt-cinq décembre

13 Les sports

(spor)

Sports

(marsh) *(zho-geen)*

LA MARCHE ET LE JOGGING

Hiking and Jogging

(ruh-por-tehr) *(luh-for)* UN REPORTER **Monsieur Lefort?**	Mr. Lefort?
LEFORT **Oui, c'est moi.**	Yes, that's me.
(sharl) *(la-plewm)* LE REPORTER **Je suis Charles Laplume.**	I am Charles Laplume.
(ay-kree) *(zhoor-nal)* **J'écris pour le journal**	I write for the paper
France-Amérique.	*France-Amérique.*
(AH-shAH-tay) LEFORT **Enchanté!**	Delighted!
(mwa) *(mehm)* LE REPORTER **Moi de même.**	Me too.
(EH-tehr-vyoo) LEFORT **Vous voulez une interview?**	You want an interview?
LE REPORTER **Exactement.**	Exactly.
(sew-zheh) LEFORT **À quel sujet?**	About what?
(pray-zee-dAH) LE REPORTER **Comme président de la**	As president of the
(leeg) *(a-ma-tuhr)* **Ligue Française des amateurs de**	French Amateur Sport League,
(sehr-tehn-mAH) **sport, vous êtes certainement très**	you are certainly very

(koo-rAH) *(kOH-sehrn)*	
au courant de tout ce qui concerne le	well informed about everything concerning
(see-kleesm)	
jogging, la marche, le cyclisme et la	jogging, hiking, cycling and
(na-ta-syOH)	
natation.	swimming.
(fla-tay)	
LEFORT **Vous me flattez.**	You flatter me.
LE REPORTER **Je voudrais écrire un article**	I would like to write an article
(lad-sew)	
là-dessus.	about that.
(a-lay) *(zee)* *(swee-vay)*	
LEFORT **Allez-y! Et suivez-moi!**	Go ahead! And follow me!
LE REPORTER **D'abord, le jogging.**	First, jogging.
(po-pew-lehr)	
LEFORT **Oui, c'est très populaire ici.**	Yes, it's very popular here.
Comme beaucoup d'autres choses, ça	Like many other things, it
vient naturellement d'Amérique et	comes from America, and
(mEHt-nAH)	
maintenant les Européens en sont	now the Europeans are
(foo)	
fous.	crazy about it.
(EH-por-tAH) *(moh)*	
Nous importons même le mot. On ne	We even import the word.
(koor)	
court plus, on fait du jogging.	One doesn't run any more, one jogs.
LE REPORTER **Vous aussi, Monsieur?**	You too, Sir?
LEFORT **Et comment! Le jogging est un**	And how! Jogging is a
(sEH) *(mar-shay)* *(suhl)*	
sport sain et bon marché. Les seuls	healthy and inexpensive sport. The only
(EH-vehs-tees-mAH) *(sweht-shūhrt)*	
investissements sont un sweat-shirt	investments are a sweat shirt
(shoh-sewr)	
et des chaussures	and a pair of
de jogging	comfortable
confortables.	jogging shoes.
LE REPORTER **Et que pensez-vous de la**	And what do you think
marche?*	about hiking?

(rAH-do-nay)

*Another useful expression is **faire une randonnée**, which is to go for a hike in the woods or mountains.

LEFORT **Un sport merveilleux, et très** *(ray-pAH-dew)* **répandu ici en France. Tous nos** *(sAH-tyay)* *(mar-kay)* **sentiers sont bien marqués. Impossible de se perdre.**

A marvelous sport, and very widespread here in France. All our footpaths are well marked. Impossible to lose one's way.

LE REPORTER **De quoi a-t-on besoin pour ce sport?**

What does one need for this sport?

LEFORT *(sas-ka-doh)* **D'un sac à dos et d'une paire** *(zhAH)* **de bonnes jambes et de bonnes** *(shoh-sewr)* **chaussures de marche. Si vous êtes** *(AH-bee-syūh)* **ambitieux, peut-être un sac de couchage, des ustensiles de cuisine et une gourde.**

A backpack and a pair of good legs with good walking (hiking) shoes. If you are ambitious, maybe a sleeping bag, cooking utensils, and a canteen.

1. Qu'est-ce que c'est (what is it)?

C'est un ____________

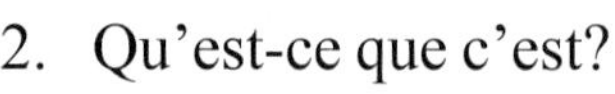

2. Qu'est-ce que c'est?

C'est un ____________

3. Qu'est-ce que c'est?

C'est un ____________

4. Qu'est-ce que c'est?

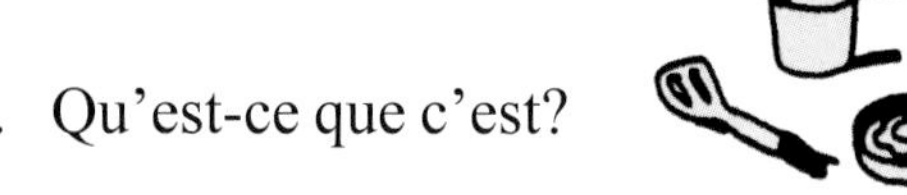

C'est un ____________

5. Qu'est-ce que c'est?

C'est une ____________

There are many American expressions used as French words, such as *jogging* for *courir*, *interview* for *entrevue*. This new language is called "franglais" *(frAH-glay)* and its usage is controversial.

ANSWERS

Qu'est-ce que c'est? **1.** sweat-shirt **2.** sac de couchage **3.** sac à dos **4.** ustensiles de cuisine **5.** gourde

Retenez

Remember

Que pensez-vous de la marche? — **QUE, QU'** (before a vowel) What — What do you think about hiking?

refers to a thing, but is not preceded by a preposition.

De quoi a-t-on besoin? — **QUOI** What — What does one need? (*lit*: of What does one have need?)

refers to a thing, and is preceded by a preposition.
(de quoi, à quoi, avec quoi, sur quoi)

À quoi est-ce que tu penses? — What are you thinking about? (*lit*: About what are you thinking?)

Encore des verbs

More verbs

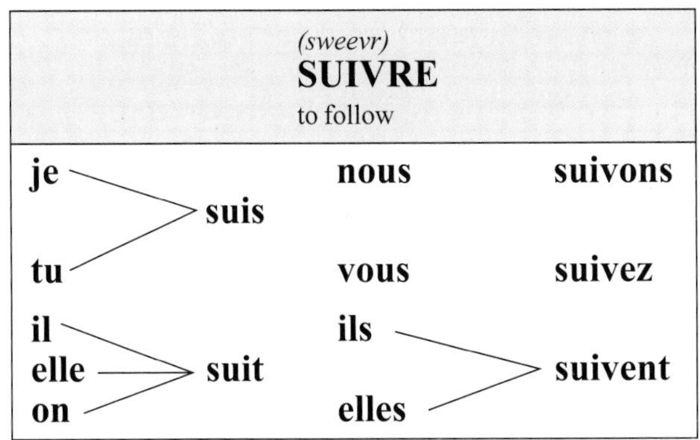

(sweevr) **SUIVRE** to follow			
je	**suis**	**nous**	**suivons**
tu	**suis**	**vous**	**suivez**
il / **elle** / **on**	**suit**	**ils** / **elles**	**suivent**

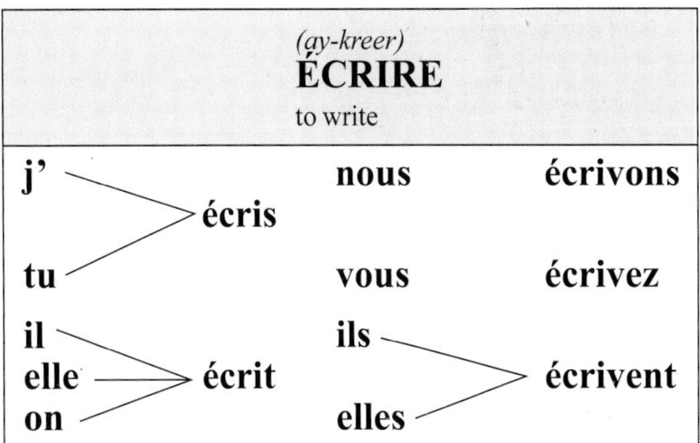

(ay-kreer) **ÉCRIRE** to write			
j'	**écris**	**nous**	**écrivons**
tu	**écris**	**vous**	**écrivez**
il / **elle** / **on**	**écrit**	**ils** / **elles**	**écrivent**

Fill in the blanks with the appropriate form of the verb:

1. Le lundi, j' ____________ (write) toujours à ma mère.
2. ____________ (follow) -moi, je vais vous montrer le Musée d'Orsay.
3. Vous ____________ (write) bien en français.
4. Charles Laplume ____________ (writes) pour *France-Amérique*.
5. Est-ce que tu vas ____________ (write) à ton frère?
6. Nous ____________ (write) des cartes postales. *(kart) (pos-tahl)*

ANSWERS

Fill in blanks **1.** écris **2.** Suivez **3.** écrivez **4.** écrit **5.** écrire **6.** écrivons

TRACK 28

(see-kleesm) *(na-ta-syOH)*

LE CYCLISME ET LA NATATION

Bicycling and Swimming

LE REPORTER	**Que pensez-vous du cyclisme, Monsieur?**	What do you think of bicycle riding, Sir?
LEFORT	*(stew-peed) (mwa-yEH)* **Un sport stupide, un moyen de** *(trAHs-por) (EH-sa-tees-fuh-zAH)* **transport insatisfaisant.** *(sAH)* **C'est sans** *(zEH-tay·reh)* **intérêt. Pas de vitesse, rien. Et à la montée, il faut pousser le machin.** *(ma-shEH)* **Et les règlements sont tellement stricts!** *(reh -gluh-mAH) (tehl-mAH) (streekt)* **Est-ce qu'en Amérique vous devez avoir des phares devant et derrière?** *(far)*	A stupid sport, unsatisfactory means of transportation. It's without interest. No speed, nothing. And up hill you have to push the thing. And the rules are so strict! In America, do you have to have lights in front and in the rear?
LE REPORTER	**Non. Que pensez-vous de la natation?**	No. What do you think of swimming?
LEFORT	**Ah! La natation! Là, je suis** *(AH-too-zyast)* **enthousiaste. Mon docteur me dit que** *(dok-tūhr) (dee)* **c'est le meilleur et le plus sain des sports. Et c'est un autre sport bon marché: un maillot de bain, c'est tout ce qu'il faut.**	Ah! Swimming! There, I am enthusiastic. My doctor tells me it's the best and the healthiest of sports. And it's another inexpensive sport: a bathing suit, that's all you need.
LE REPORTER	*(pūh-tehtr) (bee-kee-nee)* **Peut-être un bikini.**	Perhaps a bikini.
LEFORT	**C'est tout . . . Peut-être des** *(lew-neht) (plOH-zhay)* **lunettes de plongée.**	That's all . . . Maybe diving goggles.
LE REPORTER	**Comment un débutant** *(day-bew-tAH)* **commence-t-il ici?**	How does a beginner start here?
LEFORT	**Avec la brasse.** *(bras)*	With the breaststroke.

Ensuite viennent le crawl et le dos crawlé. — Then come the crawl and the backstroke.

LE REPORTER **Vous avez des épreuves** *(ay-prūhhv)* **régulièrement?** *(ray-gew-lyehr-mAH)* — Do you have tests regularly?

LEFORT **Absolument. Si on passe l'épreuve de nage libre, on peut fièrement** *(fyehr-mAH)* **porter** *(port-tay)* **un petit insigne** *(EH-seen-y)* **sur son maillot de bain.** — Absolutely . If someone passes the free-style swimming test, one can proudly wear a little badge on one's bathing suit.

LE REPORTER **Monsieur, je vous remercie pour l'interview.** — Sir, I thank you for the interview.

Now let's see if you can remember the adjectives that describe M. Lefort's opinion about these sports:

Selon M. Lefort, le cyclisme est: 1. ______________________
according to

2. ______________________

3. ______________________

4. ______________________

Selon M. Lefort, la natation est: 5. ______________________

6. ______________________

Retenez
Remember

Éventuellement. Watch this word, and how you use it. In French it means *possibly* or *perhaps*. **Actuellement** is another traitor: it means *now*, *at the present time*, not *in fact* or *actually*.

ANSWERS

Opinion **1.** un sport stupide. **2.** un moyen de transport insatisfaisant. **3.** sans intérêt. **4.** sans vitesse. **5.** le meilleur et le plus sain des sports. **6.** un autre sport bon marché.

Il faut, an expression you have encountered a few times before, is very common and very useful. It means: *It is necessary*, *one must*, *you have to*, *one needs to*, and may be followed by an infinitive:

C'est tout ce qu'il faut.	That's all that's required.
Il faut pousser le machin.	It's necessary to push the thing.

In the negative, put NE and PAS around FAUT:

Il ne faut pas partir.	It's not necessary to leave. You don't need to leave.

Encore des verbs

More verbs

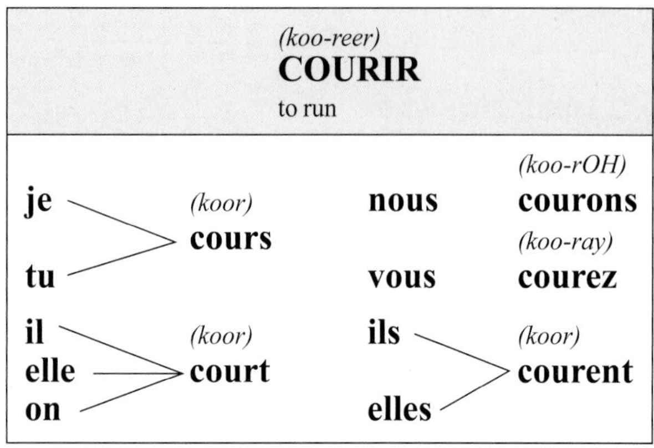

(koo-reer)
COURIR
to run

je / **tu**	*(koor)* **cours**	**nous**	*(koo-rOH)* **courons**
		vous	*(koo-ray)* **courez**
il / **elle** / **on**	*(koor)* **court**	**ils** / **elles**	*(koor)* **courent**

(deer)
DIRE
to say

je / **tu**	*(dee)* **dis**	**nous**	*(dee-zOH)* **disons**
		vous	*(deet)* **dites**
il / **elle** / **on**	*(dee)* **dit**	**ils** / **elles**	*(deez)* **disent**

Give the correct form of the verb.

COURIR

1. Nous ____________________ à l'école.
2. Il ____________________ vite.
3. ____________________ -tu au cinéma?
4. Vous ne ____________________ pas au marché.

DIRE

1. Que ____________________-vous?
2. Je ____________________ la vérité.
3. Elles ____________________ "Non".
4. Paul ne ____________________ pas "Bonjour".

ANSWERS

Verbs COURIR: 1. courons **2.** court **3.** Cours **4.** courez
DIRE: 1. dites **2.** dis **3.** disent **4.** dit

ORDERING FOOD

(ko-mAH) (ko-mAH-day) (ruh-pah)
Comment commander un repas

14 Les repas / la nourriture

(noo-ree-tewr)
Meals / Food

J'aime manger
I like to eat

You're going to want to taste some French specialties on your trip, whether it's **Pâté de foie gras**, or **coq au vin de Bourgogne**, or **framboises**. So be sure to learn how to request what you'd like. Note below, that you can request some items by saying you'd like *the* or *some* of it, just like in English.

THE

(sohs)
J'aime [la] sauce.

(loh) (vee-shee)
J'aime [l'] eau de Vichy.
Vichy water

SOME

Je mange [de la] sauce.

Après le déjeuner, je vais boire [de l'] eau de Vichy.

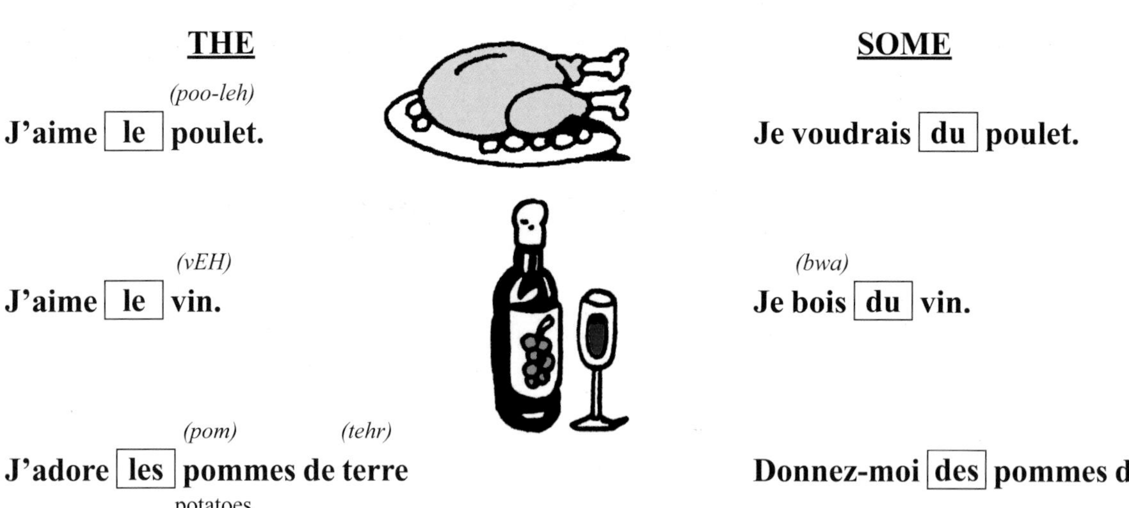

THE	**SOME**
(poo-leh) **J'aime** **le** **poulet.**	**Je voudrais** **du** **poulet.**
(vEH) **J'aime** **le** **vin.**	*(bwa)* **Je bois** **du** **vin.**
(pom) *(tehr)* **J'adore** **les** **pommes de terre** (potatoes) *(freet)* **frites.** (fried)	**Donnez-moi** **des** **pommes de terre frites, s'il vous plaît.**

SOME, ANY

Sometimes you just can't eat the whole thing, but you can eat a part of it. Refer to the following chart to choose the form of "SOME" or "ANY" that you use before the noun.

	Singular	Plural
masculine noun (starting with a consonant)	DU	DES
feminine noun (starting with a consonant)	DE LA	DES
masculine or feminine noun (starting with a vowel)	DE L'	DES

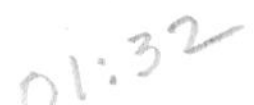

Je mange le gâteau.

Je mange du gâteau.

When talking about something you like or dislike in general, use LE, LA, L' or LES.

J'aime **la** **glace.**
I like ice cream.

When talking about something you would like a part of, use DE LA, DU or DE L', DES.

Je mange [de la] glace.
I eat some ice cream.

When the item is countable (potatoes, string beans, strawberries, and so forth—in English, you use the plural), use LES or DES, and UN or UNE if you want one item.

Je n'aime pas [les] légumes.
I don't like vegetables.

(frehz)
J'aimerais une fraise au chocolat.
I'd like a chocolate-covered strawberry.

In the negative, simply use DE or D', and no article. (DE means "any" in a negative sentence.)

Je ne veux pas [de] légumes.
I don't want any vegetables.

> Try to remember that whenever SOME or ANY is implied, you must use DE LA, DU, DE L' in affirmative sentences, and DE (D') in negative sentences and after expressions of quantity.

Try this:

1. Je fais ____du____ sport.
2. J'adore ____la____ musique *(mew-zeek)* (fem.)
3. Je déteste ____les____ épinards. *(ay-pee-nar)* spinach
4. Les chiens sont ____des____ animaux. *(a-nee-moh)* animals

A little practice? See the pictures of food items and the French words for them.
Then decide whether to use LE, LA, L', DU, DE LA, DES , or DE (D' before a vowel).

1. **fromage** (masc.)

   J'adore __le__ **fromage**.

2. *(gah-toh)* *(sho-ko-lah)*
   gâteau au chocolat (masc.)

   J'aime __la__ **gâteau au chocolat**.

3. **vin rouge** (masc.)

   Je voudrais __du__ **vin rouge**.

4. *(pwa-sOH)*
   poisson (masc.)

   __Du__ **poisson**, s'il vous plaît!

ANSWERS

Some, Any 1. du 2. la 3. les 4. des

Food 1. le 2. le 3. du 4. Du

(sa-lad)
5. **salade** (fem.)

6. **eau** (fem.)

J'aimerais _____ **salade**.

J'ai soif! Donnez-moi _____ **eau**, s'il vous plaît.

(lay) (zad-vehrb) (kAH-tee-tay)

Les adverbes de quantité

Adverbs of quantity

(sha)
Les Martin ont beaucoup de chats.
The Martins a lot of

(troh)

En fait, les Martin ont trop de chats.
As a matter of fact too much

(fro-mahzh)
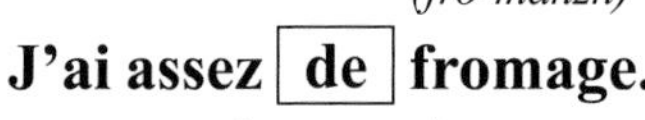
J'ai assez de fromage.
enough cheese

(soh-see-sOH)
Je voudrais un peu de saucisson.
a little salami

(em-reh) (an) (toop) (tee) (pūh)
J'aimerais un tout petit peu d' eau.
would like a tiny little bit

After expressions of quantity, use DE or D' (before a vowel).

Fill in the blanks:

1. Je mange beaucoup de poulet.
   a lot of
2. Il boit assez de vin.
   enough
3. Je voudrais un peu d' eau.
   a little
4. Elle a trop de gâteau.
   too much
5. Aimerais-tu un tout petit peu de sauce?
   a tiny little bit of

ANSWERS

Food **5.** de la **6.** de l'

Fill in the blanks **1.** beaucoup de **2.** assez de **3.** un peu d' **4.** trop de **5.** un tout petit peu de

Un nouveau verbe

A new verb

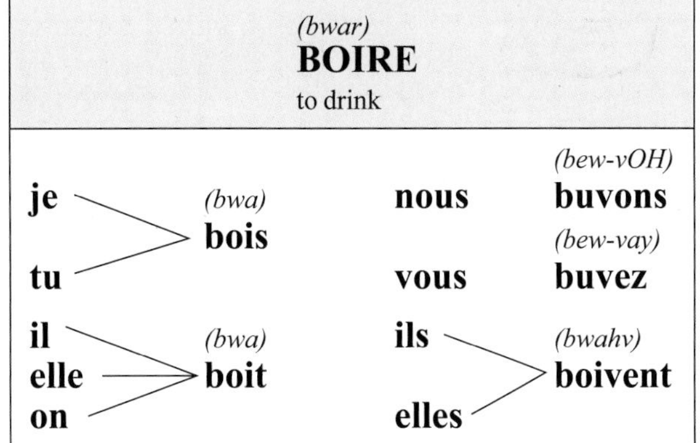

(bwar) **BOIRE** to drink			
je	*(bwa)* **bois**	**nous**	*(bew-vOH)* **buvons**
tu		**vous**	*(bew-vay)* **buvez**
il	*(bwa)* **boit**	**ils**	*(bwahv)* **boivent**
elle		**elles**	
on			

AMÉRIQUE

FRANCE

Fill in the blanks with the correct form: DE, DU, DE LA, DE L', DES.

1. Les Américains boivent ______ jus d'orange (masc.) et ______ café (masc.) avec ______ lait *(leh)* (masc.) milk froid.

2. Les Français boivent ______ café avec beaucoup ______ lait chaud.

3. Les Américains boivent ______ lait, ______ Coca-Cola ou ______ café.

4. Les Français boivent ______ vin et ______ Perrier *(peh-ryay)* (masc.).

ANSWERS

Fill in the blanks **1.** du du du **2.** du de **3.** du du du **4.** du du

Verbes avec des changements orthographiques

(shAHzh-mAH) (or-to-gra-feek)

Verbs with spelling changes

to eat

To keep the ZH sound in verbs that end in -GER (MANGER, CHANGER), it is necessary to add an E before an A, O, or U. To remember the hard and soft sounds, think of the word **garage**. The first **g** is a hard **g** and the second is a soft **g**.

(mAH-zhay) **MANGER**			
je	(mAHzh) **mange**	**nous**	(mAH-zhOH) **mangEons**
tu	(mAHzh) **manges**	**vous**	(mAH-zhay) **mangez**
il / elle / on	(mAHzh) **mange**	**ils / elles**	(mAHzh) **mangent**

pp mangé

to start, to begin

(ko-mAH-say) **COMMENCER**			
je	(ko-mAHs) **commence**	**nous**	(ko-mAH-sOH) **commençons**
tu	**commences**	**vous**	(ko-mAH-say) **commencez**
il / elle / on	**commence**	**ils / elles**	(ko-mAH) **commencent**

pp commencé

To keep the S sound in verbs that end in -CER (COMMENCER), it is necessary to add a Ç before A, O, or U. The squiggle under the **c** is called a **cedilla**. Think of it as the bottom half of the letter **s**.

to like, to prefer

Something happens also with verbs ending in É or E + consonant + ER, such as PRÉFÉRER:

pp préféré

(pray-fay-ray) **PRÉFÉRER**			
je	(pray-fehr) **préfère**	**nous**	(pray-fay-rOH) **préférons**
tu	(pray-fehr) **préfères**	**vous**	(pray-fay-ray) **préférez**
il / elle / on	(pray-fehr) **préfère**	**ils / elles**	(pray-fehr) **préfèrent**

(ak-sAH) (tay-gew) (grahv)

Note: ´ is called **accent aigu**; ` is called **accent grave**.

Now, let's practice some of the phrases you're going to use as you dine.

1. Les Américains ___mangent___ (eat) *(vyAHd)* de la viande. (meat)

2. Les Français ___préférent___ (prefer) des omelettes.

In France *(day-zhūh-nay)* **le déjeuner** (lunch) is still the most important meal in most places. In large cities, however, many people **mangent sur le** *(poos)* **pouce** (literally, on the thumb) that is, lightly and quickly, at a McDonald's or other fast food place. Breakfast (**le** *(puh-tee)* **petit déjeuner**) consists simply of bread, small croissants, or rolls, butter and jam and **café au lait**, and supper (**le** *(dee-nay)* **dîner**) is more like lunch in the U.S. But there are many exceptions to the rule.

LE PETIT DÉJEUNER

Breakfast

(tas) **une tasse de** *(leh)* **café au lait**
a cup of coffee with milk

SIMON **À quelle heure aimes-tu manger ton petit déjeuner?**

LUCIE **À huit heures.**

SIMON **Je préfère le manger à huit heures moins le quart.**

(poh) **un pot** *(kOH-fee-tewr)* **de confiture**
a jar of jam

ANSWERS

Fill in blanks **1.** mangent **2.** préfèrent

(sa-sheh)
un sachet
(tay)
de thé
a tea bag

(tas)
une tasse
a cup
de thé
of tea

(pEH)
du pain
(gree-yay)
grillé
toast

(bree-yuhsh)
les brioches
breakfast rolls

(būhr)
le beurre
butter

(vehr) *(zhew)*
un verre de jus
(o-rAHzh)
d'orange
a glass of orange juice

(toh-maht)
le jus de tomate
tomato juice

LUCIE **Est-ce que tu prends du café au lait ou du café noir?**
black

SIMON **Je n'aime pas le café. Je préfère le thé. Ma mère sert toujours du thé.**
tea serves always

LUCIE **Est-ce que tu aimes le pain grillé avec du beurre et de la confiture?**

SIMON **Quelle idée! Dans ma famille, nous mangeons des croissants.**
What an idea

LUCIE **Aimes-tu le jus d'orange?**

(zha-meh)
SIMON **Oui, mais je ne bois jamais de jus de fruit le matin.**
never

(vrehm-AH)
LUCIE **Vraiment? Comment allons-nous voyager ensemble?**
Really? together

Imagining that you are in France, how would you answer these questions from the dialogue?

1. À quelle heure aimez-vous manger le petit déjeuner?
   J'aime manger le petit déjeuner à sept heures
2. Est-ce que vous prenez du café au lait ou du café noir?
   Je préfere café au lait
3. Est-ce que vous aimez le pain grillé avec du beurre ou de la confiture?
   J'aime mon pain grillé avec du beurre et de la confiture.
4. Aimez-vous le jus d'orange?
   Oui, j'aime le jus d'orange.

ANSWERS

Dialogue **1.** J'aime manger le petit déjeuner à huit heures. **2.** Je n'aime pas le café. Je prends du thé. **3.** J'aime le pain grillé avec du beurre. **4.** Je n'aime pas le jus d'orange.

(tah-bl)

LA TABLE

The Table

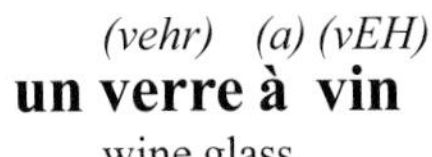

(vehr) (a) (vEH)
un verre à vin
wine glass

(vehr)
un verre
glass

(tahs)
une tasse
cup

(sewkr)
le sucre
sugar

(sel) (pwahvr)
le sel et le poivre
salt and pepper

(soo-koop)
une soucoupe
saucer

(sehr-vyeht)
une serviette
napkin

(a-syeht)
une assiette
plate

(for-sheht)
une fourchette
fork

(kwee-yehr)
une cuillère
spoon

(koo-toh)
un couteau
knife

(vo-ka-bew-lehr)

Encore du vocabulaire

More vocabulary

(bwa-sOH) **une boisson**	a beverage	*(shAH-pee-nyOH)* **des champignons**	mushrooms
(see-trOH) (preh-say) **un citron pressé**	a lemonade	*(ehs-kar-goh)* **des escargots**	snails
(byehr) **une bière**	a beer	*(pah-tay)* **du pâté**	pate
(ka-raf) (frehsh) **une carafe d'eau fraîche**	a carafe of water	*(ra-dee)* **des radis** (masc.)	radishes
(soop) **une soupe**	a soup	*(soh-see-sOH)* **du saucisson**	sausage
(day) (or) (duhvr) **des hors-d'oeuvre**	appetizers	**de la viande**	meat
(ar-tee-shoh) **des artichauts**	artichokes	*(zhAH-bOH)* **du jambon**	ham
(as-pehrzh) **des asperges**	asparagus	*(la-pEH)* **du lapin**	rabbit

(pwa-sOH)	**du poisson**	fish
(poo-leh)	**du poulet**	chicken
(ros-beef)	**du rosbif**	roast beef
(voh)	**du veau**	veal
	des légumes	vegetables
(ka-rot)	**des carottes**	carrots
(shoo) (fluhr)	**du chou-fleur**	cauliflower
(kOH-kOHbr)	**du concombre**	cucumber
	des épinards	spinach
(day) (a-ree-koh) (vehr)	**des haricots verts**	string beans
(o-nyOH)	**des oignons**	onions
(ptee) (pwah)	**des petits pois**	peas
(ree)	**du riz**	rice
(to-mat)	**des tomates**	tomatoes
(a-bree-koh)	**des abricots**	apricots
(ba-nan)	**des bananes**	bananas
(suh-reez)	**des cerises**	cherries
(frehz)	**des fraises**	strawberries
(frAH-bwahz)	**des framboises**	raspberries
(muh-lOH)	**du melon**	melon
(o-rAHzh)	**des oranges**	oranges
(pAH-pluh-moos)	**des pamplemousses**	grapefruit
(pehsh)	**des pêches**	peaches
(pwar)	**des poires**	pears
(pom)	**des pommes**	apples
(reh-zEH)	**des raisins**	grapes
(sek)	**des raisins secs** (secs = dry)	raisins
(dee-zhes-teef)	**un digestif**	an after-dinner drink
(lee-kuhr)	**une liqueur**	a sweet after-dinner drink (Grand Marnier, etc.)
(ehks-prehs)	**un express**	an espresso
(sho-ko-la)	**du chocolat**	hot chocolate
(say-ray-ahl)	**des céréales**	cereal
(ya-oort)	**du yaourt**	yogurt

(ruh-pah) (prEH-see-pal)

LE REPAS PRINCIPAL (LE DÉJEUNER)

The Main Meal Lunch

Note that cheese is not served as an appetizer and green salad is not served as a first course.

UN REPAS FRANÇAIS

A French Meal

1. **les hors-d'oeuvre**
2. **la soupe**
3. *(AH-tray)* **l'entrée (viande ou poisson avec légumes)**
4. **la salade**
5. **le fromage**
6. *(deh-sehr)* **le dessert**
7. *(lee-kuhr)* **le café et la liqueur ou le digestif**

Following are pictures of the courses of a French meal, but they are out of order, and the diner doesn't know where to start. Help him by writing numbers above each to show the right order. Of course, he can start the wine when he likes.

Now can you say the courses aloud, in order and from memory?

ANSWERS

Courses **1.** hors-d'oeuvre **2.** soupe **3.** viande/poisson/légumes **4.** salade **5.** fromage **6.** dessert **7.** café

15 Les restaurants (rehs-toh-rAH) — Les pourboires (poor-bwar)

Restaurants — Tipping

"A LA CUISSE DE GRENOUILLE"

42 RUE DES GOURMETS
Paris 6e

CUISINE RAFFINÉE
P. Lebon, Propriétaire

HORS-D'OEUVRE

MENU TOURISTIQUE—€24

(va-ryay)
Hors-d'oeuvre variés
assorted

(ko-kee-y) (frwee) (mehr)
Coquille de fruits de mer
shell fruit sea

(teh-reen) (shehf)
Terrine du Chef

(kwees) (gruh-noo-y)
Cuisses de grenouille
legs frog

Soupe du jour

CARTE

Hors-d'oeuvre variés €4

(shar-kew-tree)
Assiette de charcuterie €5
cold cuts

(ko-kee-y) (sEH) (zhank)
Coquille St. Jacques €5, 50

Terrine Maison €6

(grah) (trew-fay)
Pâté de foie gras truffé €12
goose liver with truffles

(cok-tehl) (kruh-veht)
Cocktail de crevettes €7
shrimps

Soupe du jour €3

PLATS DU JOUR

MENU TOURISTIQUE

Steak, frites
French fried potatoes

(ro-nyOH) (voh) (ma-dehr) (ree)
Rognons de veau, sauce madère, riz
kidneys veal madeira

(kok) (rees-leen) (va-puhr)
Coq au Riesling, pommes vapeur
capon potatoes steam

CARTE

(boor-gon-y)
Coq au vin de Bourgogne €11
Burgundy

Coq au Riesling €11

(foh) (fee-leh) (ree-so-lay)
Faux-filet et pommes rissolées €13
Sirloin potatoes sautéed

(toor-nuh-doh) (bay-ar-nehz)
Tournedos sauce à la béarnaise €17

(ro-tee) *(ree-so-lay)*
Poulet rôti, pommes rissolées
roasted sautéed

Salade verte

(fee-leh) *(sol)* *(mũh-nyehr)*
Filet de sole à la meunière **€10**

(vehrt)
Salade verte **€3**
green

DESSERTS

Au choix:
choice of

(pla-toh)
Plateau de fromages
tray cheese

(krehm) *(ka-ra-mehl)*
Crème caramel
flan

(tart) *(ta-tEH)*
Tarte Tatin maison
tart

(trAHsh) *(na-po-lee-tehn)*
Tranche napolitaine
slice

(pla-toh)
Plateau de fromages **€4**

(pro-fee-trol)
Profiterolles **€5,50**

(par-feh) *(mees-tehr)*
Parfait-Mystère **€4,25**
goose liver with truffles

(soo-flay) *(grAH)* *(mar-nyay)*
Soufflé au Grand Marnier **€12**
(2 pers.)

(oh) *(mee-nay-rahl)* *(ay-vyAH)*
BOISSONS—Eaux minérales (Vichy, Évian)

(roh-zay) *(blAH)*
Vins (rouge, rosé, blanc):

(ka-ra-fOH)
carafon (4 dl) **€4**

(ka-raf)
carafe (8 dl) **€7,50**

(mews-ka-deh) *(lee)*
Muscadet sur lie **€8,50**
lees

(boh-zho-leh)
Beaujolais **€7,75**

(bor-doh) *(blAH)*
Bordeaux blanc **€8,50**

(shah-toh-nuhf) *(pap)*
Châteauneuf du Pape **€16**
pope

Service 15% en sus—Boissons non comprises

Note: **SERVICE COMPRIS** on the menu means that the service is included. If service is **EN SUS**, pay a **pourboire** of 15%.

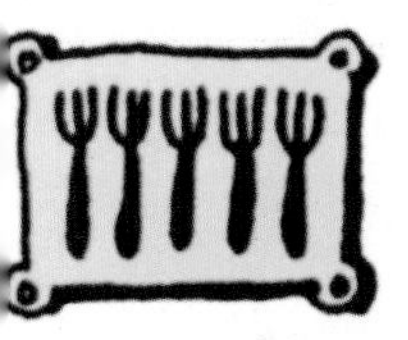

François et Pierre go to a fine restaurant in Paris, one rated with three forks and two stars. (Five forks indicate extremely expensive and posh places, three stars indicate the highest possible quality according to the *Guide Michelin*). The waiter arrives and brings them the menu. They order the dishes they are going to have.

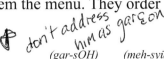

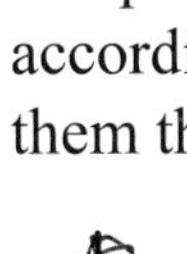

LE GARÇON *(gar-sOH)* **Messieurs, voici la carte.** *(meh-syūh)* *(kart)* (menu)

Nos spécialités sont les cuisses de grenouille et le coq au Riesling. *(spay-sya-lee-tay)* (legs; frog; capon)

FRANÇOIS **Apportez-nous des hors-d'oeuvre et une assiette de charcuterie.**

PIERRE **Ensuite je vais prendre un coq au Riesling avec des pommes rissolées.**

FRANÇOIS **Pour moi, du poisson: un filet de sole à la meunière s'il vous plaît.** *(fee-leh)* *(sol)* *(mūh-nyehr)*

LE GARÇON **De la salade?**

PIERRE **Oui, deux salades vertes. Ensuite, apportez-nous le plateau de fromages, s'il vous plaît.** (Then; bring)

LE GARÇON **Et comme boisson?**

FRANÇOIS **Du vin de la maison—un carafon de blanc, un de rouge.** *(meh-zOH)*

LE GARÇON **Vous prendrez un dessert?** *(prAH-dray)* (will take)

PIERRE **Un soufflé au Grand Marnier pour deux personnes. Et ensuite deux express et deux cognacs. Et l'addition, s'il vous plaît.** *(pehr-son)* *(ko-nyak)* *(a-dee-syOH)* (check)

FRANÇOIS (À Pierre) **N'oublions pas le pourboire!** *(poor-bwar)* (Let's not forget; tip)

(or) *(dūhvr)*
les hors-d'oeuvre
appetizers

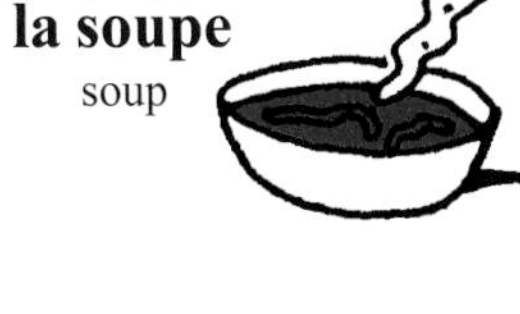

(soop)
la soupe
soup

(poo-leh)
le poulet
chicken

(pom) *(freet)*
les pommes frites
french fried potatoes

(pEH)
le pain
bread

(reh-zEH)
les raisins
grapes

(ka-fay)
le café
coffee

(shar-kew-tree)
la charcuterie
cold cuts

(sa-lad)
la salade
salad

(sehl) *(pwahvr)*
le sel et le poivre
salt and pepper

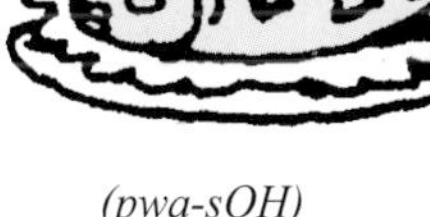

(pwa-sOH)
le poisson
fish

(fro-mahzh)
le fromage
cheese

(ko-nyak)
le cognac
brandy

Using the menu, the pictures, and the conversation, try filling in the blanks:

1. Le garçon (The waiter) apporte le menu aux clients *(klee-yAH)* customers.

2. La spécialité (specialty) de la maison est les cuisses de grenouille (frog's legs).

3. François demande des hors-d'oeuvre (appetizers).

4. Le garçon apporte (brings) des haricots verts.

5. Pierre commande *(ko-mAHd)* orders de la salade (some salad).

6. Ils vont boire une bouteille *(boo-teh-y)* bottle de vin rouge (red wine).

ANSWERS

Menu **1.** Le garçon **2.** spécialité, cuisses de grenouilles **3.** hors-d'oeuvre **4.** apporte
5. de la salade **6.** vin rouge

HOW'RE YOU DOING?

(ko-mAH) (sa) (va)
Comment ça va?

This section is designed to help you see where you are at this point. We have covered a lot of ground so far. The following activities and games may help you define your strengths and weaknesses.

Can you match the questions on the left with the answers on the right?

1. Comment vous appelez-vous?
2. Quelle heure est-il?
3. Pouvez-vous nous donner une chambre pour une semaine?
4. Combien coûte un billet aller–retour?
5. À quelle heure aimes-tu prendre ton petit déjeuner? (at what)
6. Qu'est-ce que vous allez prendre?
7. Quel temps fait-il?
8. Qu'est-ce qui se passe?
9. Comment allez-vous?
10. Pouvez-vous nous dire où se trouve le musée?

A. Je vais très bien merci, et vous?
B. Il fait un temps superbe.
C. Continuez tout droit jusqu'à la rue Molière.
D. Je m'appelle Mark Smith.
E. Il est midi.
F. Impossible, il n'y a plus de chambres.
G. Quatre-vingt-dix euros.
H. Je vais prendre un coq au Riesling.
I. À huit heures.
J. Cet idiot a heurté ma voiture.

Would you use **TU** or **VOUS** when speaking to the following people?

1. votre mari ________
2. votre soeur ________
3. un agent de police ________
4. vos parents ________
5. un pompiste ________

ANSWERS

TU or VOUS **1.** tu **2.** tu **3.** vous **4.** vous **5.** vous

Match questions-answers **1.** D **2.** E **3.** F **4.** G **5.** I **6.** H **7.** B **8.** J **9.** A **10.** C

Can you fill in the correct French word below?

1. sa mère
   His

2. ses parents
   Her

3. mon automobile
   My

4. leur hôtel
   Their

5. votre dîner
   Your (polite)

Can you make five questions from the five following statements using EST-CE QUE? Two examples:

Il aime les épinards. Est-ce qu'il aime les épinards ?

Vous aimez manger (quand). Quand est-ce que vous aimez manger ?

1. François et Pierre vont manger (quand). Quand est-ce que ?
2. Vous allez en France (pourquoi?). Pourquoi est-ce que ?
3. Il y a un terrain de camping près d'ici (où). Où est-ce qu'il y a ?
4. Tu aimes manger ton petit déjeuner (à quelle heure?). à quelle heure est-ce que ?
5. Ils voyagent à Paris (comment). Comment est-ce qu'ils voyagent ?

Magnifique! See how it's all making sense? Now form questions using inversion, for instance:

Vous parlez français (quand?). Quand parlez-vous français ?

Vous allez à Paris (pourquoi?). Pourquoi allez-vous à Paris ?

1. Vous aimez voyager (quand?). Quand aimez-vous voyager? ?
2. Vous allez (comment?) Comment allez-vous? ?

ANSWERS

Fill in **1.** sa **2.** ses **3.** mon **4.** leur **5.** votre

Make five questions **1.** Quand est-ce que François et Pierre vont manger? **2.** Pourquoi est-ce que vous allez en France? **3.** Où est-ce qu'il y a un terrain de camping près d'ici? **4.** À quelle heure est-ce que tu aimes manger ton petit déjeuner? **5.** Comment est-ce qu'ils voyagent à Paris?

Inverted questions **1.** Quand aimez-vous voyager? **2.** Comment allez-vous?

Amusez-vous as you continue your review.

(moh) (krwah-zay)

Mots croisés

Crossword puzzle

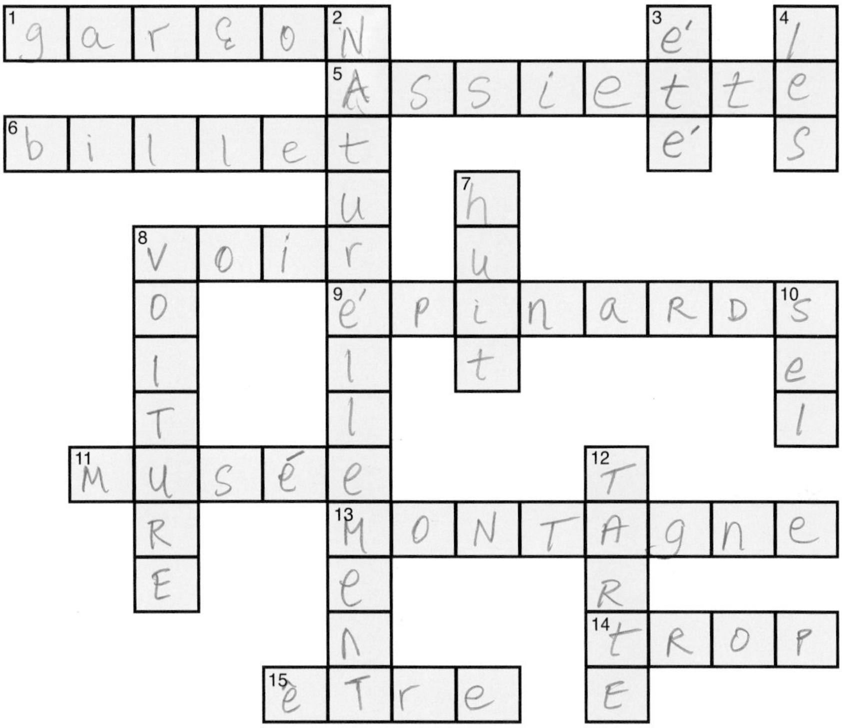

ACROSS

1. Boy, waiter
5. Plate
6. Ticket
8. To see
9. Spinach
11. Museum
13. Mountain
14. Too much
15. To be

DOWN

2. Naturally
3. Summer
4. The (pl.)
7. Eight
8. Car
10. Salt
12. Pie

ANSWERS

Crossword puzzle ACROSS **1.** garçon **5.** assiette **6.** billet **8.** voir **9.** épinards **11.** musée **13.** montagne **14.** trop **15.** être

DOWN **2.** naturellement **3.** été **4.** les **7.** huit **8.** voiture **10.** sel **12.** tarte

Can you make the following sentences negative?

Example: Je prends du poisson. Je ne prends pas de poisson.

1. Je suis très fatigué. ______
2. Vous avez soif. ______
3. Je me sens très bien. ______
4. J'aime les haricots verts. ______
5. La banque est loin d'ici. ______

Describe the pictures in simple sentences.

Example:

Le chat est sous la table.

1. Le garçon ______

2. M. Smith ______

3. Le chien ______

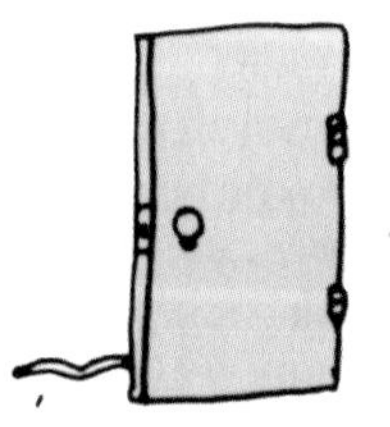

4. La souris ______

ANSWERS

Negative sentences **1.** Je ne suis pas très fatigué. **2.** Vous n'avez pas soif. **3.** Je ne me sens pas très bien. **4.** Je n'aime pas les haricots verts. **5.** La banque n'est pas loin d'ici.

Describe pictures **1.** Le garçon est à côté de la porte. **2.** M. Smith est dans la cuisine. **3.** Le chien est devant le garage. **4.** La souris est derrière la porte.

Can you order your **déjeuner** at the TROIS CANARDS?

(ka-nar)
AUX TROIS CANARDS
ducks

Plat du Jour:
Menu à 20 euros

Lapin au vin blanc
ou
Steak/pommes frites
Salade verte

Plat du Jour:
Menu à €22

(ehs-ka-lop)
Escalopes de veau au madère
ou
(kan-tOH)
Caneton rôti
Salade verte

Desserts—
Crème caramel
(moos)
Mousse au chocolat
Parfait
(sa-ba-yOH)
Sabayon (€3 supplément)

Boissons—eaux minérales (Évian, Vichy)
vins de la maison (rouge, blanc, rosé)
café, thé
(Boissons non comprises)

4 RUE LECOQ
MONBOUDIN

JEAN LAPOULE,
PROPRIÉTAIRE

You don't know what **caneton** and **sabayon** mean, so you ask the waiter.

1. ______________________________?

You find this meal delicious, so you tell the waiter.

2. ______________________________!

At the end of the meal, you ask if the service is included.

3. ______________________________?

Check please!

4. ______________________________!

ANSWERS

Conversation with waiter (sample answers)

1. Qu'est-ce que c'est que ça? (A **caneton rôti** is roast duckling; **sabayon** is a sauce.)
2. C'est délicieux! **3.** Est-ce-que le service est compris? **4.** L'addition, s'il vous plaît!

AT THE STORE

(ma-ga-zEH)
Au Magasin

16 Les magasins de confection

(ma-ga-zEH) *(kOH-fek-syOH)*
Les magasins de confection
Clothing Stores

(ta-y) *(muh-zewr)* *(koo-luhr)* *(prEH-see-pal)*
Tailles et mesures/Couleurs principales
Sizes and Measurements / Basic Colors

(veht-mAH)
Vons essayez des vêtements
Trying on clothes

METTRE — To put (on)

ESSAYER — To try, to try on

S'HABILLER — To get dressed

ENLEVER — To take off

IL ME FAUT — I need

(por-tay)
PORTER — to wear, to carry

(preht)
PRÊT-À-PORTER — ready-to-wear

Here are some verbs that will come in very handy if you want to purchase clothing.

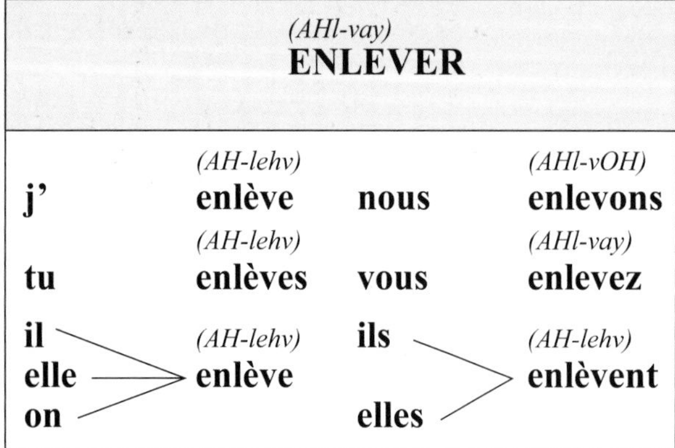

(AHl-vay)
ENLEVER

j'	*(AH-lehv)* **enlève**	**nous**	*(AHl-vOH)* **enlevons**
tu	*(AH-lehv)* **enlèves**	**vous**	*(AHl-vay)* **enlevez**
il / elle / on	*(AH-lehv)* **enlève**	**ils / elles**	*(AH-lehv)* **enlèvent**

(ash-tay)
ACHETER
to buy

j'	*(a-sheht)* **achète**	**nous**	*(ash-tOH)* **achetons**
tu	*(a-sheht)* **achètes**	**vous**	*(ash-tay)* **achetez**
il / elle / on	*(a-sheht)* **achète**	**ils / elles**	*(a-sheht)* **achètent**

NOTE: **Enlever** and **Acheter** (to buy) undergo spelling changes, like **Préférer**.

The verbs **enlever** and **acheter** (as well as other French verbs whose infinitives end in E + CONSONANT + ER) take an accent grave over the E that precedes a silent E in the **je**, **tu**, **il**, **elle**, **on**, **ils**, **elles** forms.

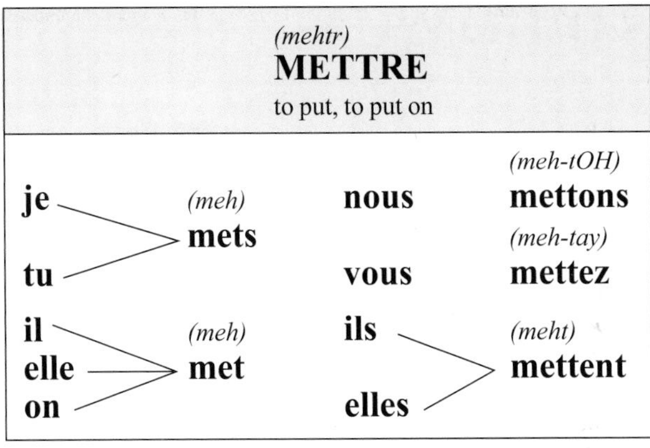

(mehtr)
METTRE
to put, to put on

je	*(meh)* **mets**	**nous**	*(meh-tOH)* **mettons**
tu	*(meh)* **mets**	**vous**	*(meh-tay)* **mettez**
il / elle / on	*(meh)* **met**	**ils / elles**	*(meht)* **mettent**

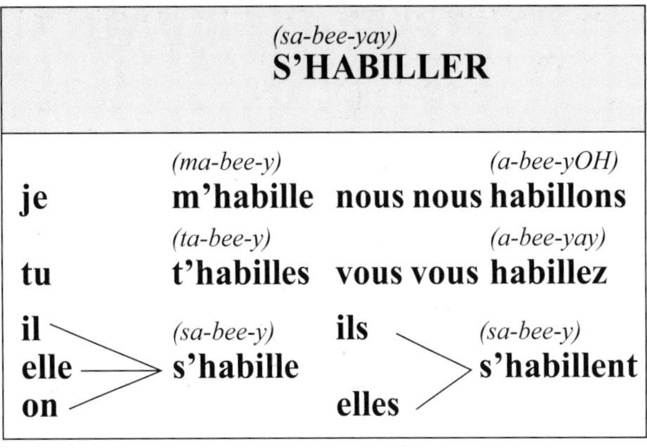

(sa-bee-yay)
S'HABILLER

je	*(ma-bee-y)* **m'habille**	**nous nous**	*(a-bee-yOH)* **habillons**
tu	*(ta-bee-y)* **t'habilles**	**vous vous**	*(a-bee-yay)* **habillez**
il / elle / on	*(sa-bee-y)* **s'habille**	**ils / elles**	*(sa-bee-y)* **s'habillent**

S'HABILLER is a reflexive verb (remember SE LAVER and S'AMUSER in Chapter 6):

Give the correct form of the verb for the persons listed.

	JE, J'	NOUS	ILS
1. **enlever**			
2. **acheter**			
3. **mettre**			
4. **s'habiller**			

Il me faut is another idiomatic way of saying I need (you have encountered **J'ai besoin de**). It means, literally, it is necessary to me (to you, to him, etc.). You use the personal pronoun-indirect object and place it between **il** and **faut**:

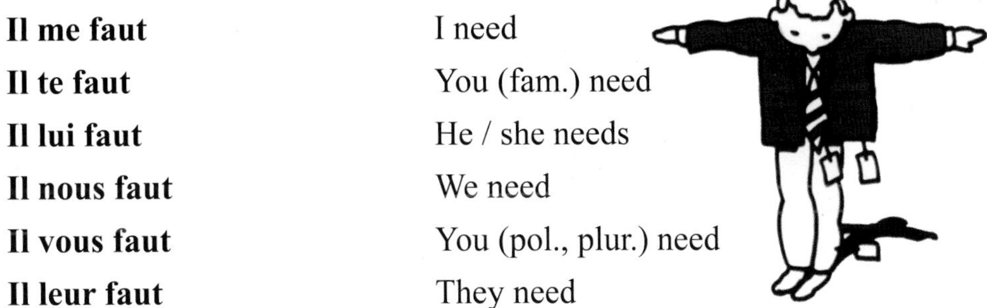

Il me faut	I need
Il te faut	You (fam.) need
Il lui faut	He / she needs
Il nous faut	We need
Il vous faut	You (pol., plur.) need
Il leur faut	They need

When **aller** is preceded by these indirect object pronouns, its meaning changes to **fit**:

Cette chemise vous va bien! This shirt fits you well (or looks nice on you).

ANSWERS

Verbs **1.** enlève, enlevons, enlèvent **2.** achète, achetons, achètent **3.** mets, mettons, mettent **4.** m'habille, nous habillons, s'habillent

VÊTEMENTS D'HOMME

Men's Clothes

	(pahn-ta-lOH) **Ce pantalon est trop petit.**	
CLIENT	**Ce pantalon est trop petit. Pouvez-vous me montrer la taille** *(oh) (duh-sew)* **au-dessus?**	These pants are too small. Can you show me the next larger size?
VENDEUR	**(apportant un pantalon** *(zhOH) (see-trOH)* **jaune citron): Voilà. Nous n'avons** lemon *(blūh)* **pas votre taille en bleu.**	(Bringing bright yellow pants): Here you are. We don't have your size in blue.
CLIENT	*(oh-ruhr)* **Quelle horreur!**	How horrible!
VENDEUR	**C'est la grande mode en France.** *(sew-pehr)* **Essayez-le! Il vous va bien! Super chic!**	It's the fashion in France. Try them on! They look nice on you! Very chic!
CLIENT	*(oh-ruhr)* **Non, vraiment, je ne peux pas** *(por-tay)* **porter ça.**	No, really, I can't wear that.
VENDEUR	*(ruh-vyEH)* **(revient avec un pantalon bleu beaucoup trop grand):**	(comes back with blue pants that are much too big) :
	Excusez-moi! Essayez ce pantalon *(ehg-zak-tuh-mAH)* **bleu exactement de votre taille.**	Excuse me! Try these blue pants that are exactly your size.
CLIENT	*(ehr)* **(l'air épuisé):** the air	(looking exhausted):
	Ça y est. Qu'est-ce que vous pensez?	There . . . what do you think?
VENDEUR	*(par-feht-mAH)* **Il vous va parfaitement!** *(gAH)* **Comme un gant . . .**	They fit you perfectly! Like a glove . . .

Match the French phrases with their English equivalents.

1. Ce pantalon est trop petit.
2. Pouvez-vous me montrer la taille au-dessus?
3. Nous n'avons pas votre taille.
4. C'est la grande mode en France.
5. Il vous va bien.

a. Can you show me the next size?
b. It's the fashion in France.
c. These pants are too small.
d. They look nice on you.
e. We don't have your size.

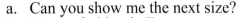

(shoh-seht)
des chaussettes
socks

(shuh-meez)
une chemise
shirt

(kra-vat)
une cravate
tie

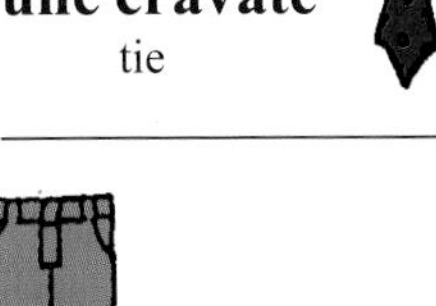

(pAH-ta-lOH)
un pantalon
pants

(pew-lo-vehr)
un pullover
sweater

(sha-poh)
un chapeau
hat

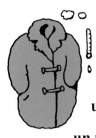

Un client va dans un magasin de confection pour hommes dans la grande ville.

LE VENDEUR **Vous désirez?**

LE CLIENT **Je me marie** *(ma-ree)* (I'm getting married) **ce week-end et il me faut des vêtements neufs** *(nuhf)* (new). **Il me faut des sous-vêtements** *(soo) (veht-mAH)* (underwear) **et aussi une chemise blanche** *(shuh-meez) (blAHsh)* **et une cravate noire** *(kra-vat) (nwar)*.

LE VENDEUR **Est-ce qu'il vous faut un complet** *(kOH-pleh)* (suit)**?**

LE CLIENT **Oui. Pourriez-vous me montrer un complet noir? Je porte du quarante-quatre.**

LE VENDEUR **Nous n'avons rien** (nothing) **dans cette taille. Puis-je vous montrer un veston** *(vehs-tOH)* (sport jacket) **et un pantalon de sport?**

LE CLIENT **D'accord. Puis-je** (Can I) **les essayer?**

(Il les essaie.)

(par-duh-sew)
un pardessus
(mAH-toh)
un manteau
coat

(po-sheht)
une pochette
(moo-shwar)
un mouchoir
handkerchief

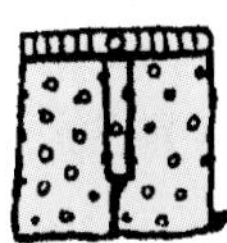

(kal-sOH)
un caleçon
undershorts

(tee-shehrt)
un tee-shirt
T-shirt

(kas-ket)
une casquette
cap

ANSWERS

Matching 1. c 2. a 3. e 4. b 5. d

(pa-ra-plwee)
un parapluie
umbrella

(EH-per-may-ahbl)
un imperméable
raincoat

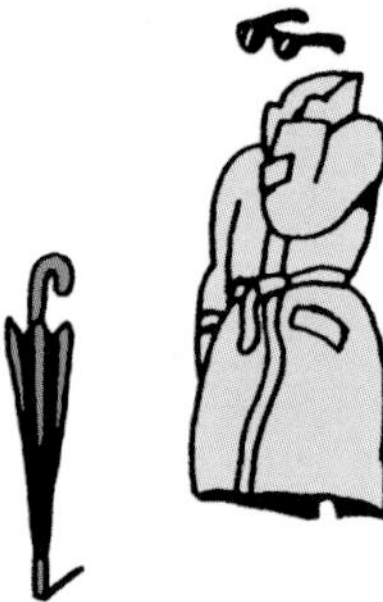

(kOH-ple)
un complet
suit

(gAH)
des gants
gloves

(ves-tOH) *(spor)*
un veston de sport
sport jacket

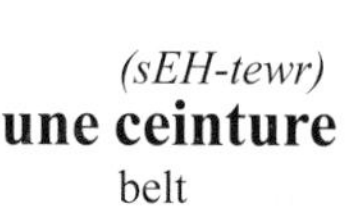

(sEH-tewr)
une ceinture
belt

LE VENDEUR **Ils vous vont à merveille.** *(mer-ve-y)* marvelously

Maintenant je crois qu'il vous faut une nouvelle ceinture! *(sEH-tewr)*

Voilà la facture. *(fak-tewr)* bill **Veuillez payer à la caisse, s'il vous plaît.** *(kes)* cash register

(bot)
des bottes
boots

FACTURE	
3, rue de l'Aiguille du Midi *(eh-gwee-y)* needle	
Chamonix, Haute Savoie	
VESTON	**€ 84**
PANTALON	**€ 44,50**
CHEMISE	**€ 23**
CRAVATE	**€ 13**
CEINTURE	**€ 19,50**
SOUS-VÊTEMENTS	**€ 11**
TOTAL	**€ 198**

LE CLIENT **Monsieur, il y a une erreur dans votre facture.** *(e-ruhr)*

LE VENDEUR **Ah! Vous avez raison.** *(reh-zOH)* You are right. **Cent quatre-vingt-quinze.**

Au revoir Monsieur.
Good-bye.

Le client a raison. The customer is right.

Le vendeur a tort. The clerk is wrong.

Can you tell me if the following statements are correct? Write **vous avez raison** (you are right) or **vous avez tort** (you are wrong):

1. Le client a besoin de vêtements neufs. ______________________________
2. Il ne lui faut pas de sous-vêtements. ______________________________
3. Le client porte du 54. ______________________________
4. Il essaie le pantalon. ______________________________
5. Le pantalon est trop petit pour lui. ______________________________

Tailles

Sizes

VÊTEMENTS D'HOMME Men's Clothes								
CHEMISES (SHIRTS)								
Taille américaine	14	14½	15	15½	16	16½	17	17½
Taille européenne	36	37	38	39	40	41	42	43
AUTRES VÊTEMENTS (OTHER CLOTHING)								
Taille américaine	34	36	38	40	42	44	46	48
Taille européenne	44	46	48	50	52	54	56	58

If you are a man, what size shirt do you wear? (Je porte du ______ .) What size pants, suit and jacket do you wear? (Je porte du _____ .)

If you are a female, look for the sizes of a male friend or relative: (Il porte du ______ pour les chemises et du ______ pour les pantalons, les vestons et les complets).

ANSWERS

True or False **1.** vous avez raison **2.** vous avez tort **3.** vous avez tort **4.** vous avez raison **5.** vous avez tort

Fill in the blanks with the words depicted:

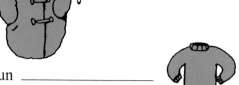

1. Quand il fait froid, je porte un _______________

2. Quand il fait frais, j'enlève mon pardessus et je mets un _______________

3. Quand il neige, je mets mes _______________

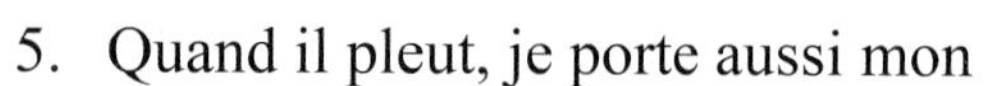

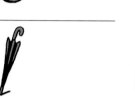

4. Quand il pleut, j'enlève mon pardessus et je mets mon _______________

5. Quand il pleut, je porte aussi mon _______________

(fam)

VÊTEMENTS DE FEMME

Women's Clothes

(koo-luhr) *(prEH-see-pal)*

Les couleurs principales

Basic colors

(shuh-mee-zyay) (vehr)
le chemisier vert
green blouse

(zhew-pOH) (blAH)
le jupon blanc
white slip

(zhewp) (roozh)
la jupe rouge
red skirt

(sak) (mEH)
le sac à main noir
black purse

(sleep) (zhohn)
le slip jaune
yellow panties

(soo-tyEH) (gorzh) (zhohn)
le soutien-gorge jaune
yellow bra

(rob) (blūh)
la robe bleue
blue dress

(foo-lar) (zhohn)
le foulard jaune et noir
yellow and black scarf

ANSWERS

Fill in blanks **1.** un pardessus ou un manteau **2.** pullover **3.** bottes **4.** imperméable **5.** parapluie

Remembering the rules about adjective agreement—final letter E for feminine, ES for feminine plural; no change with an adjective like **rose** and **rouge** in the feminine because the masculine form ends with E; irregular feminine of **blanc**: **blanche**—can you answer these questions about the pictures? Example: De quelle couleur est la jupe? La jupe est rouge.

1. De quelle couleur est le foulard? ______________________

2. De quelle couleur est le chemisier? ______________________

Can you continue asking yourself questions and answering them about the remaining pictures on the previous page?

Tailles

Sizes

VÊTEMENTS DE FEMME

Women's Clothing

LES BLOUSES OU CHEMISIERS (BLOUSES)

Taille américaine	32	34	36	38	40	42	44
Taille européenne	40	42	44	46	48	50	52

AUTRES VÊTEMENTS (OTHER CLOTHING)

Taille américaine	8	10	12	14	16	18
Taille européenne	36	38	40	42	44	46

Et moi, je porte du 48.

And I wear Size 48.

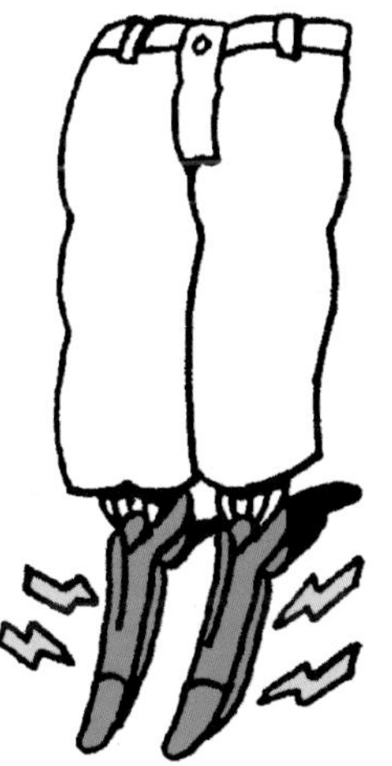

(shoh-sewr)

CHAUSSURES POUR HOMMES ET FEMMES

Shoes for Men and Women

Elles sont trop *(ay-trwat)* **étroites pour moi.** *(sehr)* **Elles me serrent.**

They are too narrow for me. They pinch me.

Elles sont trop. *(larzh)* **larges pour moi.**

They are too wide for me.

ANSWERS

De quelle couleur . . . (sample answers)

1. Le foulard est jaune et noir. **2.** Le chemisier est vert.

Tailles

Sizes

What size shoes do you wear? (Consult the two charts below.)

(shohs)
Je chausse du ________________ **.**

(pwEH-tewr)
Note: Shoe size is usually called **la pointure**.

CHAUSSURES POUR HOMMES (CHAUSSURES DE VILLE *(veel)*, BOTTES, SANDALES *(sahn-dahl)*) Men's Shoes (city shoes, boots, sandals)										
TAILLE AMÉRICAINE	7	7½	8	8½	9	9½	10	10½	11	11½
TAILLE EUROPÉENNE	39	40	41	42	43	43	44	44	45	45
CHAUSSURES POUR FEMMES Women's Shoes										
TAILLE AMÉRICAINE	5	5½	6	6½	7	7½	8	8½	9	
TAILLE EUROPÉENNE	35	35	36	37	38	38	38	39	40	

We don't suppose you are the least bit fussy. But if you were very particular, here are some words and expressions just made to impress the clerk:

(kel-kuh) (shohz)
Je voudrais quelque chose en:
something

	(nee-lOH)		*(kweer)*
nylon	**nylon**	leather	**cuir**
	(dEH)		*(ko-tOH)*
suede	**daim**	cotton	**coton**
	(twahl) (dzheen)		*(swah)*
denim	**toile à jean**	silk	**soie**

Pourriez-vous prendre mes mesures? — Could you take my measurements?

(meh-yuhr)
Je voudrais quelque chose de meilleure *(ka-lee-tay)* **qualité.** — I would like something of better quality.

(a) (la) (mEH)
Est-ce fait à la main? — Is it handmade?

(sAHbl) (lOH) (koor)
Ça me semble un peu long (grand, court, petit). — It looks a little long (big, short, small) on me.

(ruh-toosh)
Pouvez-vous faire une retouche? — Can you do alterations?

Je n'aime pas cette couleur; je préfère le bleu. — I don't like this color; I prefer blue.

Note that, when used as nouns, colors are masculine.

17 Les magasins d'alimentation

(a-lee-mAH-ta-syOH)

Food Stores

Poids et mesures

(pwah)

Weights and Measures

(leh-tree) (krehm-ree) **la laiterie-crémerie** diary	*(boosh-ree)* **la boucherie** butcher shop	*(ay-pees-ree)* **l'épicerie** (fem.) grocery	*(boo-lAHzh-ree)* **la boulangerie** bakery

(leh) **le lait** milk	*(vyAHd)* **la viande** meat	*(frwee) (lay-gewm)* **les fruits, les légumes** fruit, vegetables	*(pEH)* **le pain** bread

(pwa-son-ree) **la poissonnerie** fish store	*(kOH-feez-ree)* **la confiserie** candy store	*(lah-tees-ree)* **la pâtisserie** pastry shop	*(shar-kew-tree)* **la charcuterie** delicatessen	*(vEH) (spee-ree-tew-ūh)* **les vins-spiritueux** liquor store

(pwa-sOH) **le poisson** fish	*(bOH-bOH)* **les bonbons** (m.) candy	*(gah-toh)* **les gâteaux** (m.) cakes	*(soh-see-sOH)* **le saucisson** sausage	*(vEH)* **le vin** wine

(troh) (duh) (kehs-tyOH)

Trop de questions?

Too many questions?

(kew-ryūh)

LE CURIEUX (THE INQUISITIVE ONE) **Excusez-moi, je voudrais vous poser une question. Où puis-je acheter du lait?**

L'AGENT **On vend du lait à la laiterie du coin.**
on the corner

LE CURIEUX **Et si j'ai besoin de légumes et de viande, où est-ce que je vais?**

L'AGENT **À l'épicerie et à la boucherie, bien sûr.**
of course

LE CURIEUX **Et si je veux des fruits et du pain, où est-ce que je peux les acheter?**

L'AGENT **À l'épicerie et à la boulangerie.**

LE CURIEUX **Et s'il me faut du poisson et des bonbons, où puis-je les trouver?**

L'AGENT **Vous pouvez aller à la poissonnerie et à la confiserie.**

LE CURIEUX **Et si je veux des gâteaux?**

L'AGENT **Vous allez à la pâtisserie.**

(glas)

LE CURIEUX **Et pour la glace et le vin?**
ice cream

(shay) (ehg-zas-pay-ray)

L'AGENT **Allez à la pâtisserie et chez le négociant en vin. (exaspéré) Et si vous me posez**
wine merchant exasperated

(kree-yay)

encore une question, je vais crier.
shout

Draw a line through the items that you could *not* find in each store:

1. crémerie—beurre, fromage, vin rosé
2. boucherie—rosbif *(rohs-beef)*, oranges, veau
3. épicerie—petits pains sucrés *(sew-kray)* (sweet rolls), raisins, laitue *(leh-tew)* (lettuce)
4. charcuterie—raisins, pain, salami
5. boulangerie—jambon, crevettes, croissants

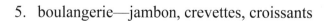

ANSWERS

Items that you could not find

1. vin rosé **2.** oranges **3.** petits pains sucrés **4.** raisins, pain **5.** jambon, crevettes

6. poissonnerie—bonbons, sole, eau minérale

7. confiserie—confiture, asperges, truite *(trweet)* trout

8. pâtisserie—riz *(ree)* rice, lait, petits fours *(foor)* small cakes

9. marchand de vin—poulet, bouteilles, épinards

Notice that many of the store names are formed by adding -ERIE to the end of the product they sell. To name the person who sells the product, we often start the name of his/her store and substitute the ending -ER/-ÈRE Example:

lait	**laiterie**	**laitier**	**laitière**
milk	dairy	milkman	milkwoman

And if we want to say "I am going to the butcher's" instead of "I am going to the butcher shop," we use the preposition CHEZ *(shay)*:

Je vais à la boucherie.	I am going to the butcher shop.
Je vais chez le boucher.	I am going to the butcher's.
Je vais chez la bouchère.	I am going to the butcher's (fem.).

(pwah) *(muh-zewr)*

POIDS ET MESURES

Weights and Measures

(puh-zay)
PESER
To Weigh

____

LE POIDS
The Weight

____

ANSWERS

Items that you could not find

6. bonbons, eau minérale **7.** asperges, truite **8.** riz, lait **9.** poulet, épinards

Although it has not yet caught on in the U.S., the metric system is the standard means for measuring in many other countries. Here are some common weights and measures:

(gram) **100 grammes**	=	3.5 ounces (a little less than ¼ pound)
500 grammes *(leevr)* **une livre**	=	17.5 ounces (1 pound + 1.5 ounces)
1.000 grammes *(kee-loh)* **un kilo**	=	2. 205 pounds

Note: Remember that **une livre** is a measure of weight equal to about one pound; **un livre** is a book.

Note that "one thousand" is 1.000, not 1,000, and that "three point five" is 3,5, not 3.5. *Just the opposite of the American system.*

(mee-lee -leetr) **1 millilitre**	=	0.034 liquid ounces
(sEH-tee-leetr) **1 centilitre**	=	0.33 liquid ounces
(day-see-leetr) **1 décilitre**	=	3.3 liquid ounces
(duh-mee) **1 demi-litre** ½	=	0.53 quarts
1 litre	=	1.06 qu

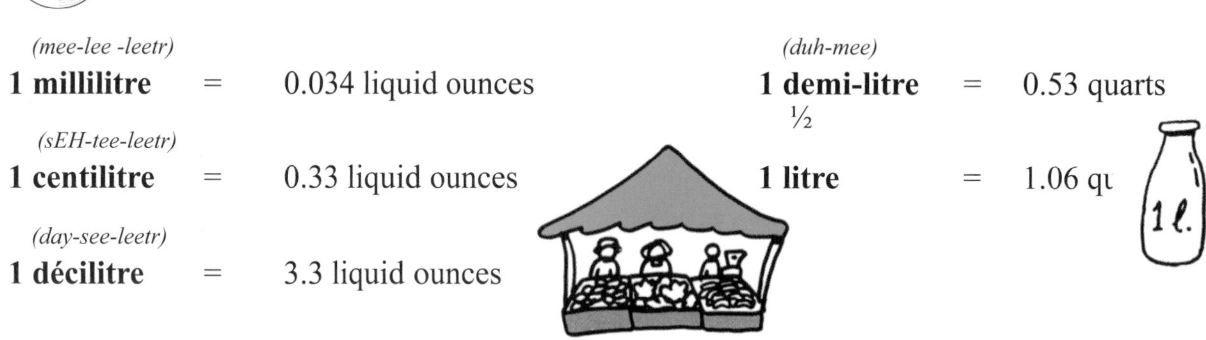

Here are some useful expressions to use when buying food. Try writing them out:

(doo-zen) **une douzaine de (d')**	a dozen of ______________
une demi-douzaine de (d')	a half dozen of ______________
un kilo de (d')	a kilo of ______________
une livre de (d')	a half kilo of ______________
deux cent cinquante grammes de (d')	a quarter kilo of ______________
un litre de (d')	a liter of ______________
Ça pèse combien?	How much does it weigh? ______________
C'est trop.	It's too much. ______________
C'est combien la douzaine?	How much are they per dozen? ______________
C'est combien?	How much does it cost? ______________
Ils/elles sont à combien?	How much do they cost? ______________
C'est trop cher.	It's too expensive. ______________

À L'ÉPICERIE

(roo-loh) *(pa-pyay)*
un rouleau de papier
(ee-zhyay-neek)
hygiénique
a roll of toilet paper

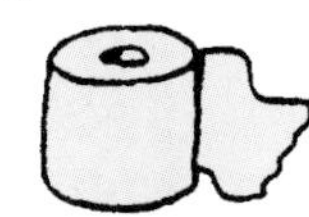

(boh-kal)
un bocal de café
(ans-tAH-ta-nay)
instantané
a jar of instant coffee

Ask the clerk for the items in the pictures. Use the names of the containers they come in or the measurement. Try asking some questions like HOW MUCH DOES IT (DO THEY) COST? HOW MUCH ARE THEY PER DOZEN, PER BOX, and so forth?

(suh-reez)
des cerises pesées
cherries being weighed
(ba-lAHs))
sur une balance
on a scale

(leevr)
une livre de cerises
a pound of cherries

(bwaht) *(bees-kwee)*
une boîte de biscuits
box of cookies

(doo-zehn) *(dūh)*
une douzaine d'oeufs
a dozen eggs

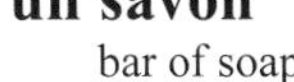

(sa-vOH)
un savon
bar of soap

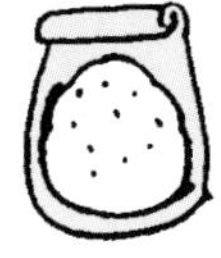

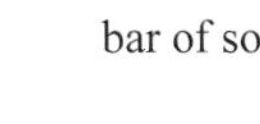

(kee-loh) *(sewkr)*
un kilo de sucre
1 kilo of sugar

1. Je voudrais ______________________ .

   Combien coûte ______________________ ?

(leetr) *(leh)*
un litre de lait
a liter of milk

2. J'ai besoin d'______________________ .

   Combien coûte ______________________ ?

(duh-mee) *(doo-zehn)* *(see-trOH)*
une demi-douzaine de citrons
½ dozen lemons

3. Je voudrais ______________________ .

   Combien coûte ______________________ ?

(lay-gewm) *(kOH-sehrv)*
une boîte de légumes en conserve
can of vegetables

ANSWERS

Fill in blanks (À l'épicerie)

1. un litre de lait **2.** une demi-douzaine de citrons **3.** une boîte de légumes en conserve

Nowadays, it is not always necessary to go to different stores to buy groceries. Many countries have North American style supermarkets where we can buy them in one place: bakery items, meat, eggs, a box of cookies, a roll of toilet paper, a liter of milk, a half-dozen oranges, a kilo of sugar, a package of candy. Of course, it is still interesting to go to the

(mar-shay) (AH) (pleh) (nehr) *(vo-la-y)*
open-air markets (**les marchés en plein air**) to see the great variety of **volaille**, **fruits**,
poultry

(fehr-myay)
légumes, and other products which the **fermiers**
farmers
sell each day. It is a good way to see the foods that are typical of the country or the region .

Indicate the correctness of the statements by writing **vous avez raison** or **vous avez tort**.

(dee-fay-rAH)
1. De nos jours, ill est nécessaire d'aller dans beaucoup de magasins différents pour acheter
Nowadays
(a-lee-mAH-tehr)
des produits alimentaires. ______________________________
food

(sew-per-mar-shay)
2. Il n'y a pas de supermarchés dans les autres pays.

____

3. On ne peut pas acheter de papier hygiénique dans les supermarchés français.

____

4. Dans les marchés en plein air, on peut acheter beaucoup de produits différents.

____

5. Pour trouver les produits typiques de la région, il faut aller dans les supermarchés.

____

ANSWERS

True or false

1. Vous avez tort.
2. Vous avez tort.
3. Vous avez tort.
4. Vous avez raison.
5. Vous avez tort.

18 Le grand magasin — La pharmacie

(ma-ga-sEH) **Le grand magasin** — Department store

(far-ma-see) **La pharmacie** — Pharmacy

In France, you can usually find cosmetics, personal hygiene items, in **un grand magasin** or in **une pharmacie**. Some pharmacies have mainly medical-related products. However, more and more are offering a wider range of products including toothpaste and shampoo along with the prescriptions that one would expect. To find a pharmacy, look for a large, green cross.

AU GRAND MAGASIN

At the Department Store

(ay-pEHgl) **les épingles à** *(shuh-vūh)* **cheveux**
bobby pins

(vehr-nee) **le vernis à** *(ohngl)* **ongles**
nail polish

la crème *(day-ma-kee-yAHt)* **démaquillante**
cleansing cream

(fahr) **le fard**
rouge

(dee-sol-vAH) **le dissolvant**
nail polish remover

(mee-rwar) **un miroir**
mirror

(paht) **la pâte** *(dAH-tee-frees)* **dentifrice**
toothpaste

(bros) **la brosse** *(dAH)* **à dents**
toothbrush

(peh-ny) **un peigne**
comb

(roo-zh) **le rouge** *(lehvr)* **à lèvres**
lipstick

(mas-ka-ra) **le mascara**
mascara

(moo-shwar) **les mouchoirs** *(pa-pyay)* **en papier**
tissues

(lak) **la laque**
hairspray

Monique and Pascale enter the department store and go to the cosmetics section. Monique looks at herself in the mirror.

(poh)
MONIQUE **Je dois acheter des épingles à cheveux, un pot de crème démaquillante**
jar

et des mouchoirs en papier.

(ew-tee-leez)
PASCALE **Je n'utilise jamais de crème démaquillante; c'est trop cher. Tu achètes**

(ma-kee-yahzh) *(reesh)*
toujours ton maquillage ici? C'est un magasin pour les riches, pas pour les

(pohvr)
pauvres comme nous.
poor like

MONIQUE **Tu as raison, mais je ne peux jamais trouver de bons**

(kar-tyay)
produits dans mon quartier.
neighborhood

PASCALE **Je vais te dire quelque chose. Je ne vais rien acheter ici. C'est trop cher.**
something

(may-dam)
LA VENDEUSE **Bonjour Mesdames. Vous désirez?**

(fla-kOH)
MONIQUE **J'ai besoin d'un peigne, d'une brosse à cheveux et d'un flacon de laque.**
bottle

Il me faut aussi une brosse à dents et de la pâte dentifrice. Ça coûte combien?

LA VENDEUSE **La brosse à dents coûte 1 euro 60 et la pâte dentifrice 1 euro 20.**

(day-pAH-say)
PASCALE **Tu vois? Tu vas dépenser beaucoup d'argent!**
to spend

MONIQUE **Maintenant je voudrais voir vos produits de maquillage—le fard,**
make-up

le rouge à lèvres, le mascara, s'il vous plaît. Ah! et

aussi le vernis à ongles et le dissolvant.

PASCALE **Mais tu dépenses trop.**

MONIQUE **Ça ne fait rien. Ce n'est pas**
it doesn't matter

pour moi, c'est pour mon mari.

(ay-to-nay)
PASCALE **(l'air étonné): Qu'est-ce que tu dis?**
astonished

Vrai ou faux?

1. Je peux acheter des mouchoirs en papier au grand magasin. V F
2. On trouve des produits de maquillage **au rayon** *(ray-ohn)* (department) des cosmétiques. V F
3. Les prix *(pree)* (prices) sont chers au grand magasin. V F
4. Pascale ne veut rien dépenser au grand magasin. V F

Ce qu'il faut dire quand vous *devez* faire quelque chose

What you must say when you *have* to do something

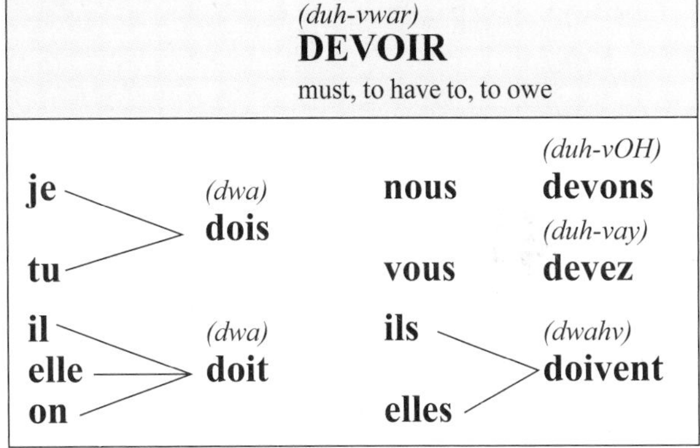

(duh-vwar)
DEVOIR
must, to have to, to owe

je / **tu**	*(dwa)* **dois**	**nous**	*(duh-vOH)* **devons**
		vous	*(duh-vay)* **devez**
il / **elle** / **on**	*(dwa)* **doit**	**ils** / **elles**	*(dwahv)* **doivent**

DEVOIR + INFINITIVE
must, to have to do something

Je dois acheter quelque chose.
I have to buy something.

IL FAUT + INFINITIVE
it is necessary to do something

Il faut aller à la laiterie pour acheter du lait.
It is necessary to go to the dairy to buy milk.

Il faut is a generalization (It is necessary, one must . . .). To make it more specific, you can use the construction **il me faut** (+ infinitive), **il te faut**, and so on, which you learned in Chapter 16.

Let's practice **devoir** + infinitive first. Try starting each sentence with the subjects suggested in parentheses. Say the sentences aloud:

1. **Je dois acheter quelque chose.** (Nous, Tu, Ils, Elle, Vous, Il)
2. **Il ne doit rien manger.** (Je, Nous, Tu, Vous, Ils, Elle)
3. **Elle ne doit pas trop dépenser.** (Vous, Nous, Ils, Je, Elles, Tu)

Can you answer these questions with il faut + INFINITIVE?

1. Est-ce qu'il faut manger pour vivre? ______________________
2. Où faut-il aller pour acheter de la viande? ______________________
3. Qu'est-ce qu'il faut utiliser pour enlever le vernis à ongles? ______________________
4. Où faut-il aller pour acheter du maquillage? ______________________

ANSWERS

True or false **1.** V **2.** V **3.** V **4.** V

Answer questions **1.** Oui, il faut manger pour vivre. **2.** Il faut aller à la boucherie pour acheter la viande. **3.** Il faut utiliser du dissolvant. **4.** Il faut aller au grand magasin ou à la pharmacie.

Let's hope you will never have the problems that this unfortunate traveler has.

HENRI **Est-ce que vous avez des bonbons?**

VENDEUR **Non, nous n'avons pas de bonbons. Pour acheter des bonbons, il faut aller à la confiserie.**

HENRI **Et où trouve-t-on des cigarettes et des briquets?**

VENDEUR **Pour acheter des cigarettes, vous devez aller au bureau de tabac.**
(bew-roh) *(ta-ba)*

HENRI **Merci. Je voudrais un déodorant, un rasoir et des lames de rasoir. Mon rasoir électrique ne marche pas dans ce pays.**
(day-o-do-rAH) *(lahm)* *(marsh)* marche = function

VENDEUR **Il vous faut aller dans un autre magasin pour acheter un transformateur.**
(trAHs-for-ma-tuhr) transformateur = voltage converter

HENRI **Mon Dieu! Que de problèmes!**
Que = what

VENDEUR **J'ai la solution. Laissez-vous pousser la barbe et la moustache comme moi. Les femmes m'adorent.**
(so-lew-syOH) Laissez = Let; pousser = grow; barbe = beard

(bree-keh)
un briquet
lighter

(see-ga-reht)
des cigarettes
cigarettes

(day-o-do-rAH)
le déodorant
(va-po-ree-za-tũhr)
vaporisateur
spray deodorant

(rah-zwar) (ay-lehk-treek)
un rasoir électrique
electric razor

(lahm)
les lames de rasoir
razor blades

(rah-zwar)
un rasoir
razor

1. Name two things you find at the tobacco shop:

_________________ , _________________

2. What things does a man use to shave?

_________________ , _________________

ANSWERS

Tobacco shop (sample answers) **1.** un briquet, des cigarettes **2.** un rasoir, des lames de rasoir

À LA PHARMACIE

At the Pharmacy

You can identify the pharmacy by the green cross displayed outside its door. Pharmacies will not only fill a prescription (**une ordonnance** *(or-do-nAHs)*), some will also treat *minor* emergencies.

Anne va à la pharmacie pour faire des achats *(a-shah)* purchases**. Elle demande des sparadraps, de l'alcool, et un thermomètre. Elle dit au pharmacien** *(far-ma-syEH)* **qu'elle a mal** *(mal)* ache **à la tête** *(teht)* head**, et il lui donne de l'aspirine.**

Elle dit également qu'elle grossit, grows fat **se sent mal le matin et a des nausées** *(noh-zay)* nausea**.**

Le pharmacien dit: "Je crois qu'il vous faut du talc, des épingles de sûreté et des couches!"

Practice writing the new words.

(as-pee-reen)
un flacon d'aspirine
bottle of aspirin

____

(pee-lewl)
les pilules (f.)
pills

____

(spa-ra-dra)
le sparadrap
band-aid

____

(tehr-mo-mehtr)
un thermomètre
thermometer

____

(ay-pEHgl) *(sewr-tray)*
les épingles de sûreté
safety pins

____

(talk)
le talc
talcum powder

____

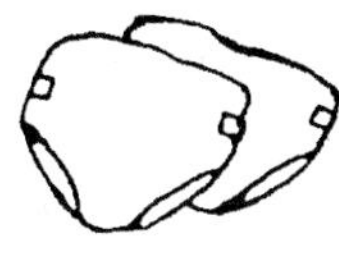

(koosh)
les couches
diapers

____

Here are some useful phrases for your *minor* complaints and hygienic needs:

Il me faut quelque chose pour l'indigestion *(an-dee-zhehs-tyOH)***, le rhume** *(rewm)* cold**, la constipation** *(kohns-tee-pa-syOH)***, le mal de gorge** *(gorzh)* sore throat**.**

(dya-ray)
J'ai . . . la diarrhée

(mee-grehn)
une migraine
migraine

(fyehvr)
de la fièvre

(krahnp)
des crampes
cramps

(greep)
la grippe
flu

(dAH)
mal aux dents
a toothache

(koo) (so-leh-y)
un coup de soleil
sunburn

(toos)
Je tousse
I cough

(koo-pay)
Je me suis coupé (e)
I cut myself

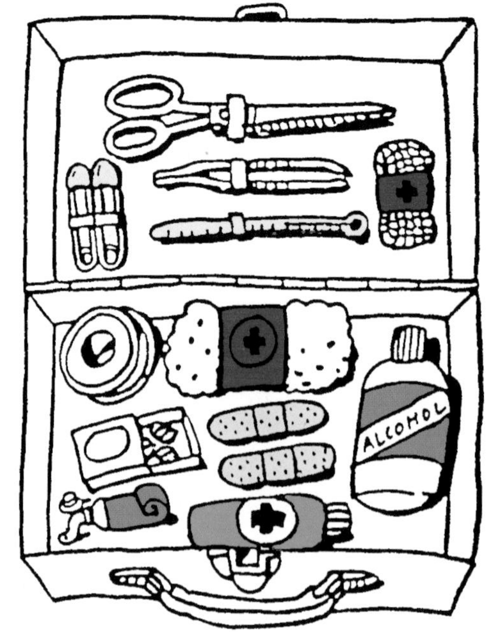

(a-see-dee-tay)
Je voudrais . . . un produit contre l'acidité
acidity

(day-zEH-fehk-tAH)
un désinfectant
antiseptic

(pAHs-mAH)
des pansements
bandages

(ko-tOH) (wat)
du coton (de l'ouate)
aborbent cotton

(see-zoh)
des ciseaux
scissors

(lak-sa-teef)
Je dois acheter . . . un laxatif
laxative

(sehr-vyeht) (ee-zhyay-neek)
des serviettes hygiéniques
sanitary napkins

(see-roh) (too)
du sirop pour la toux
cough syrup

Match the ailment in column 1 with the thing you would most likely ask for at the pharmacy in column 2. Sometimes more than one answer may be possible.

	Column 1	**Column 2**
_____	1. constipation	A. des sparadraps
_____	2. une coupure	B. de l'insuline
_____	3. de la fièvre	C. un laxatif
_____	4. une migraine	D. un produit contre l'acidité
_____	5. des crampes	E. de l'aspirine
_____	6. diabète *(dya-beht)*	F. un désinfectant
_____	7. la toux	G. des couches
_____	8. mal à l'estomac *(es-to-ma)*	H. un thermomètre
		I. du sirop pour la toux
		J. des pansements

ANSWERS

Match **1.** (C) **2.** (A)(F)(J) **3.** (H) **4.** (E) **5.** (E) **6.** (B) **7.** (I) **8.** (D)

19 La blanchisserie / La teinturerie

(blAH-shees-ree) **La blanchisserie** Laundry

(tEH-tew-ruh-ree) **La teinturerie** Dry Cleaning

Laundromats are not as common in France as in the United States. Laundries are very good but fairly slow (3–4 days). For your dry cleaning needs, you can find 24-hour service in most cities. August is vacation month, and many shops are closed at that time. In general, the easiest method is to ask your hotel to take care of your dry cleaning and laundry. Even easier—and cheaper—is to take as many permanent press clothes with you as possible.

Avoir l'air

To seem, to look

This is another very common idiomatic construction with **avoir** (remember **avoir chaud**, **avoir froid**, **avoir envie**, **avoir besoin**, and so forth). It means, literally: to have the air. . . . **Vous avez l'air fatigué aujourd'hui.** You look tired today. **L'agent de police a l'air exaspéré.** The policeman looks exasperated. **Pascale a l'air étonné.** Pascale looks (seems) astonished.

Ça n'a pas l'air suffisant. It doesn't look sufficient. **Il a l'air de mauvaise humeur** *(ew-mūhr)*. He seems to be in a bad mood. **Il a l'air de bonne humeur.** He seems to be in a good mood.

LA LAVERIE AUTOMATIQUE

(la-vree) (oh-to-ma-teek)

The Laundromat

Susan, a foreign exchange student, goes to wash her clothes for the first time at the laundromat. Fortunately for her, a woman who has several children with her is also doing her wash.

le paquet *(pa-keh)* **de lessive** *(le-seev)*
box of soap powder

SUSAN **S'il vous plaît, pouvez-vous m'aider? Combien de lessive** (soap powder) **est-ce que je dois mettre dans la machine** *(ma-sheen)* **à laver** *(la-vay)* **pour laver mon linge** *(lEHzh)* (laundry)**?**

la planche *(plAHsh)* **à repasser** *(ruh-pah-say)*
ironing board

(say-shwar)
le séchoir

(say-shūhz)
la sécheuse
dryer

(kord)
la corde à ligne
clothesline

LA DAME **Jamais plus d'une demi-tasse** *(duh-mee) (tass)* ½ cup **pour si peu de vêtements.**

SUSAN **(à elle-même) Ça n'a pas l'air suffisant.** *(sew-fee-zAH)* sufficient **(Elle met deux tasses de lessive dans la machine à laver. Après quelques minutes, la machine commence à déborder.)** *(day-bor-day)* overflow

LA DAME **Jamais plus d'une tasse.**

Probablement moins . . .

(fehr)
le fer à repasser
iron

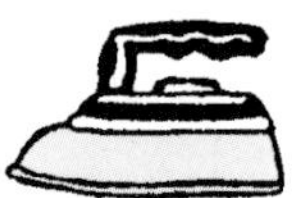

(pEHs)
les pinces à linge (fem.)
clothespins

(kor-beh-y)
la corbeille
(lEHzh)
à linge
laundry basket

Susan is ready to dry her clothes. Another young woman, a student, is nearby.

SUSAN **Pouvez-vous me dire combien de pièces de monnaie il faut mettre dans la fente du séchoir? Et, à propos, où est la fente? (Le séchoir ne marche pas.)**
(pyehs) pieces *(mo-neh)* change *(fahnt)* slot *(a) (proh-poh)* on the subject

L'ÉTUDIANTE **Il faut appuyer sur ce bouton. Comme ça, la machine marche et sèche vos habits.**
(a-pwee-yay) press *(boo-tOH)* button *(kom) (sa)* This way *(a-bee)* clothes

SUSAN **C'est la première fois que je lave mes habits depuis que je suis étudiante ici.**
(duh-pwee) since

L'ÉTUDIANTE **Tu es une nouvelle étudiante? C'est ma troisième année.**

SUSAN **Tu es étudiante aussi? J'aimerais bien te revoir. J'ai tant de questions à te poser!**
(ehm-reh) would like *(ruh-vwar)* see again *(tAH)* so many

1. If you are going to the laundromat, what should you take along?

____________________, ____________________

ANSWERS

Going to the laundromat **1.** un paquet de lessive, une corbeille à linge

2. In the laundromat, which machines do you need to use?

______________________, ______________________

TRACK 41

(*blAH-shee-sahzh*)

LES SERVICES DE BLANCHISSAGE

(*neh-twa-yahzh*) (*a*) (*sehk*)

ET DE NETTOYAGE À SEC DANS LES HÔTELS

Hotel Laundry Services and Dry Cleaning

If you decide to use the laundry services of the hotel where you are staying, these expressions might get you by:

Est-ce que vous avez un service de blanchissage? — Do you have a laundry service?

J'ai du linge à faire laver. — I have some clothes to be washed.

Pouvez-vous coudre un bouton sur ma chemise? — Can you sew a button on my shirt?

(*ruh-koodr*) (*mAHsh*)
Pouvez-vous recoudre la manche de ce chemisier? — Can you mend the sleeve of this blouse?

(*na-mee-do-nay*)
N'amidonnez pas mes caleçons. — Don't use starch on my undershorts.

Pourriez-vous repasser cette chemise encore une fois? — Could you iron this shirt again?

(*neh-twa-yay*)
Pourriez-vous faire nettoyer à sec ce complet? — Could you have this suit dry cleaned?

(*tash*)
Pouvez-vous enlever cette tache? — Can you take out this spot?

Try filling in the blanks with the key words from the sentences above. Then read the sentences aloud:

1. Pouvez-vous enlever cette ______________?

2. Pouvez-vous ______________ un bouton sur ma chemise?

3. Est-ce que vous avez un service de ______________?

ANSWERS

Going to the laundromat 2. une machine à laver, un séchoir

Fill in blanks 1. tache? 2. coudre 3. blanchissage?

4. Pouvez-vous faire ______________ ce complet?

5. Pouvez-vous ______________ la ______________ de ce chemisier?

(AH-vwah)
Jean envoie toujours son linge à la blanchisserie de l'hôtel. Mais cette fois, il y a des
sends · time

(par-tee) (ra-port) (a-par-tyehn) (kel-kUH)
problèmes. Une grande partie des vêtements qu'on lui rapporte appartiennent à quelqu'un
part · brings back · belong · somebody else

(dohtr) (plEHdr) (zhay-rAH) (soo-tyEH) (gorzh)
d'autre. Il va se plaindre au gérant. D'abord, il ne porte jamais de soutien-gorge ou de
compalin · manager · First of all · never · bra · or

(ko-lAH) (a-mee-do-nay) (ah-bee-may) (brew-lay)
collants. Ensuite, ses chemises sont trop amidonnées et une d'elles est abîmée; elle est brûlée.
pantyhose · Next · starched · ruined · scorched

(ahn) (plews) (mAHk) (ruh-swah)
En plus, il lui manque deux chaussettes, une rouge et une verte. Le complet qu'il reçoit
in addition · he's missing · receives

(tash)
de la teinturerie a une tache sur la manche. Il a raison de se plaindre, vous ne trouvez pas?
spot · complain

How would you complain about such things? You might want to use some of the following phrases:

I have to complain.	**Je dois me plaindre.**
There is a mistake.	**Il y a une erreur.**
These clothes are somebody else's.	**Ce linge est à quelqu'un d'autre.**
This shirt has too much starch.	**Cette chemise est trop amidonnée.**
My clothes are ruined.	**Mes habits sont abîmés.**
This shirt is scorched.	**Cette chemise est brûlée.**
There's a button missing.	**Il manque un bouton.**
There's a spot on these trousers.	**Il y a une tache sur ce pantalon.**
I'm missing a pair of socks.	**Il me manque une paire de chaussettes.**

ANSWERS

Fill in blanks **4.** nettoyer à sec **5.** recoudre manche

20 Le salon de beauté (sa-lOH) (boh-tay)
The Beauty Shop

Le coiffeur pour dames (kwah-fuhr) (dam)
The Hairdresser

Le coiffeur pour hommes (om)
The Barber Shop

AU SALON DE BEAUTÉ
At the Beauty Shop

Henriette goes to the beauty shop for her weekly visit.

LA COIFFEUSE **Qu'est-ce que vous désirez cette semaine, Madame?**

HENRIETTE **Un shampooing—mise en plis,** (mee) (zAH) (plee) set **s'il vous plaît. Et une retouche.** (ruh-toosh) touch up

Pouvez-vous aussi me faire un massage facial et une manucure?

LA COIFFEUSE **Vous êtes brunette maintenant.** (brew-neht) **Vous voulez un rinçage de quelle teinte?** (rEH-sahzh) rinse (tEHt) **De la même couleur ou plus foncé?** (fOH-say) darker

HENRIETTE **Un peu plus clair, s'il vous plaît.** (kler) lighter **Je voudrais aussi des boucles sur le côté et** (bookl) curls

(shuh-vūj)
on lave les cheveux de la jeune femme
young woman's hair being washed

(shAH-pwan)
le shampooing
shampoo

(per-ma-nAH)
la permanente
permanent

(bee-goo-dee)
les bigoudis
curlers

(ma-new-kewr)
la manucure
manicure

(ma-sahzh) (fa-syal)
le massage facial
facial massage

(bro-say)
brosser
to brush

(say-shwar)
le séchoir
hair dryer

(OH-dew-la-syOH)
des ondulations sur la tête. Pourriez-vous
waves
(ra-koor-seer)
raccourcir un peu mes cheveux sur
shorten
(newk)
la nuque? Je n'aime pas avoir les cheveux
back of neck
(lOH) (koor)
longs, je préfère les avoir courts.
long short

(Une heure plus tard, la coiffeuse brosse les cheveux d'Henriette, et Henriette se regarde dans le miroir.)

(blOHd)
HENRIETTE **Je suis blonde!**
blond

une brosse à cheveux
hairbrush

se regarder
(meer-wahr)
dans le miroir
to look at oneself in the mirror

FOR WOMEN ONLY: You are going to the "salon de beauté." What would you say to the "coiffeuse"?

Je désire 1. ______________________________

2. ______________________________

3. ______________________________

Here are some useful expressions a woman might want to know before she goes to the beauty shop. Try writing them out:

I'd like to make an appointment for tomorrow.	(rah-day) (voo) **Je voudrais prendre rendez-vous pour demain.**

____

Could you give me a rinse?	(rEH-sahzh) **Pourriez-vous me faire un rinçage?**

____

Could you cut my hair?	(koo-pay) **Pourriez-vous me couper les cheveux?**

____

ANSWERS

FOR WOMEN ONLY **1.** un shampooing—mise en plis. **2.** une retouche. **3.** une manucure.

Don't use any hairspray. — **Ne mettez pas de laque.**

I would like my hair cut in bangs. — *(frahnzh)* **Je voudrais une frange.**

CHEZ LE COIFFEUR

At the Hairdresser

Unisex hairdressers are just beginning to appear but are not widespread. Here are a few more useful expressions you may need at **LE COIFFEUR POUR DAMES**, **LE COIFFEUR POUR HOMMES** (or **MESSIEURS**) or **LE COIFFEUR UNISEXE** *(ew-nee-sehks)*.

Could you blow dry my hair? — **Pourriez-vous me faire un brushing?** *(bra-sheeng)*

I would like a light trim. — **Je voudrais me faire égaliser les cheveux.** *(ay-ga-lee-zay)*

Can you give me a light tint? — **Pouvez-vous me teinter légèrement les cheveux?** *(tEH-tay) (lay-zhehr-mAH)*

I would like an Afro. — **Je voudrais une coiffure afro.** *(kwah-fewr) (a-froh)* (coiffure = hairdo)

I would like my hair frosted. — **Je voudrais une légère décoloration** *(day-ko-lo-ra-syOH)* / **des mèches.** *(mehsh)* (mèches = locks)

Can you tease my hair just a little? — **Pouvez-vous me crêper les cheveux un tout petit peu?** *(kreh-pay)*

After practicing these expressions aloud, try to fill in the blanks in the sentences below, using the words on the right-hand side of the page.

1. Pourriez-vous me faire _______________ ?
2. Je voudrais me faire _______________ les cheveux.
3. Je voudrais _______________ afro.

égaliser

un brushing

une coiffure

ANSWERS

Fill in blanks **1.** un brushing **2.** égaliser **3.** coiffure

4. Pouvez-vous me ____________ les cheveux un tout petit peu? **décoloration des mèches**

5. Je voudrais une légère ____________ . **crêper**

CHEZ LE COIFFEUR POUR HOMMES

At the Barber Shop

Mince! Je suis chauve!

(rah-zay)
raser
to shave

(moos-tash)
une moustache

(barb)
une barbe
beard

(peh-nyay)
peigner
to comb

se raser
to shave oneself

(pat)
des pattes
sideburns

se peigner
to comb one's hair

le rasoir

(tOH-dūhz)
une tondeuse à cheveux
clippers

la crème à raser
shaving cream

(see-zoh)
les ciseaux

(see-zoh)
une coupe de cheveux
haircut

un homme
(shohv)
chauve
bald

ANSWERS

Fill in blanks **4.** crêper **5.** décoloration des mèches

Philippe va chez le coiffeur parce qu'il a besoin d'une coupe de cheveux. D'abord, le

(ra-freh-shee)

coiffeur le rase et lui rafraîchit la barbe. Puis il lui fait un shampooing et lui coupe les

trims then

cheveux. Comme Philippe aime avoir les cheveux très courts, le coiffeur coupe beaucoup

(sAH-dor) *(foh-tuh-y)*

sur la tête et sur la nuque. Philippe est très fatigué, et il s'endort dans son fauteuil. Le

falls asleep armchair

(plew) (zAH) (plew)

coiffeur coupe de plus en plus. Finalement il déclare: "Voilà, Monsieur." Philippe se

more and more

regarde dans le miroir et voit qu'il est chauve. "Combien est-ce que je vous dois?"

demande-t-il. Le coiffeur répond: "Vous pouvez me payer pour six mois. Je ne crois pas

(byEH-toh) (ruhv-neer)

que vous allez bientôt revenir."

soon come back

Try writing out these expressions, which could come in handy. Then read the sentences aloud:

Where is there a good barber shop? **Où y a-t-il un bon coiffeur pour hommes?**

___

Do I have to wait long? *(lOH-tAH)* **Faut-il attendre longtemps?**

___

Whose turn is it? **C'est à qui le tour?**

___

I would like a shave. **Je voudrais me faire raser.**

___

I would like a haircut. **Je voudrais une coupe de cheveux.**

___

Long in back, short in front. **Longs derrière, courts devant.**

___

Cut a little bit more here. *(plews)* **Coupez un peu plus ici.**

___

21 Le kiosque à journaux La papeterie

(kyosk) (zhoor-noh) (pa-pe-tree)

Newsstand — Stationery Store

AU KIOSQUE

TRACK 44

(ma-ga-zeen)
le magazine
magazine

(zhoor-nal)
le journal
newspaper

(kart) (pos-tahl)
les cartes postales
postcards

(tEHbr)
les timbres (avion)
postage stamps (air mail)

(see-ga-reht)
les cigarettes

LE JEUNE HOMME **Pardon. Avez-vous des** (zhoor-noh) **journaux en anglais?**

Excuse me. Do you have newspapers in English?

(pro-pry-ay-tehr)
LE PROPRIÉTAIRE DU KIOSQUE (owner) **Oui, nos avons un bon choix** (shwah; selection) **de journaux anglais et américains.**

Yes, we have a good selection of English and American newspapers.

LE JEUNE HOMME **Je voudrais aussi des cartes postales de Paris.**

I would also like some postcards of Paris.

LE PROPRIÉTAIRE	**Voilà des vues** *(vew)* **intéressantes de la capitale.** *(ka-pee-tahl)*	Here are some interesting views of the capital.
LE JEUNE HOMME	**Avez-vous des timbres-poste?**	Do you have postage stamps?
LE PROPRIÉTAIRE	**Non, mais vous pouvez en trouver au bureau de tabac.**	No, but you can find some at the tobacco shop.
LE JEUNE HOMME	**Et du tabac?** *(ta-ba)* **Je voudrais un paquet de cigarettes américaines.**	And tobacco? I would like a package of American cigarettes.
LE PROPRIÉTAIRE	**Vous voyez l'enseigne** *(AH-sehn-y)* **là-bas?**	You see the sign with a plug of tobacco on it down there?
	Ça veut dire qu'on vend des cigarettes.	That means they sell cigarettes.
LE JEUNE HOMME	**Merci. Est-ce que vous avez des magazines avec des photos?** *(foh-toh)* ***Paris Match*** **par exemple? Ce n'est pas pour moi, mais pour mon grand-père.**	Thank you. Do you have picture magazines? *Paris Match*, for example? It's not for me, but for my grandfather.
LE PROPRIÉTAIRE	**(il fronce** *(frOHs)* frowns **les sourcils** *(soor-see)* eyebrows**):** **Oui, naturellement.**	Yes, of course.
LE JEUNE HOMME	**Bon. Je prends le journal, les cartes postales et le magazine. Je vous dois combien?**	Good. I'll take the newspaper, the postcards, and the magazine. How much do I owe you?

NOTE: Au bureau de tabac, on peut aussi acheter des bonbons, du chocolat, des allumettes, *(a-lew-met)* **du papier à lettres,** *(letr)* stationery **quelquefois** *(kehl-kuh-fwa)* sometimes **de la glace. Les bureaux de tabac sont souvent** *(soo-vAH)* often **ouverts** *(oo-vehr)* open **le dimanche matin.**

Try reading the conversation several times. When you feel confident of its meaning, see if you can match the phrases on the next page.

Match these French words or phrases from the dialogue with their English equivalents:

1. les journaux
2. les cartes postales
3. les timbres-poste
4. le bureau de tabac
5. le paquet de cigarettes

a. postcards
b. tobacco store
c. newspapers
d. package of cigarettes
e. postage stamps

À LA PAPETERIE

At the Stationery Store

(stee-loh) (bee-y)
un stylo à bille
ballpoint pen

(ka-yay)
un cahier
notebook

(AHv-lop)
une enveloppe
envelope

(blok)
un bloc-notes
writing pad

(kreh-yOH)
un crayon
pencil

(skotsh)
du scotch
transparent tape

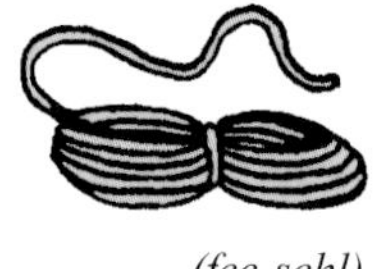

(fee-sehl)
de la ficelle
string

(lehtr)
du papier à lettres
stationery

Si j'ai besoin d'un stylo à bille ou d'un crayon, je vais à la papeterie. Si je veux écrire une lettre, j'utilise du papier à lettre, et je mets la lettre dans une enveloppe. On vend aussi des cahiers à la papeterie. Je peux écrire des notes dans un cahier ou dans un bloc-notes. Si je veux envelopper *(AHv-lo-pay)* (wrap) **un paquet, il me faut du scotch, de la ficelle, et du papier d'emballage** *(AH-ba-lahzh)* (wrapping paper)**.**

Pour demander quelque chose, je dis: *Je voudrais . . .* (I would like . . .)

ANSWERS

Matching 1. c 2. a 3. e 4. b 5. d

Now, let's take a trial run.

1. What two objects can you write with? ______________ , ______________ .
2. If you write a letter, what do you write it on? ______________ .
3. What two things do you use to wrap a package? ______________ , ______________ .
4. What two things can you write notes on? ______________ , ______________ .
5. Where can you buy des timbres-avion *(a-vyOH)* (airmail stamps)? ______________ .
6. Can you find the following words below? Circle them as in the example. (You should be able to find six more): envelope, pencil, newspaper, cigarettes, stamp, paper

E	M	I	G	U	J	O	N	B	L	O	C
N	E	X	C	E	O	T	R	O	S	U	A
V	I	C	E	S	U	S	D	U	R	E	T
E	C	I	G	A	R	E	T	T	E	S	I
L	S	R	E	C	N	L	E	E	E	H	M
O	A	M	A	L	A	P	A	I	E	R	B
P	U	T	I	Y	L	P	A	P	I	E	R
P	T	E	D	E	O	R	E	L	A	T	E
E	B	L	I	M	S	N	E	E	A	Q	U

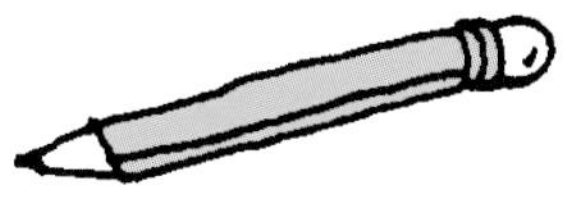

ANSWERS

Fill in the blanks **1.** un stylo, un crayon **2.** du papier à lettres **3.** de la ficelle, du scotch **4.** un bloc-notes, un cahier **5.** au kiosque **6.** enveloppe, crayon, journal, cigarettes, timbre, papier

22 La bijouterie L'horlogerie (fém.)

(bee-zhoo-tree) **La bijouterie**
Jewelry store

(or-lozh-ree) **L'horlogerie** (fém.)
Watchmaker's shop

À LA BIJOUTERIE

At the Jeweler's

Practice writing the new words on the lines provided under the pictures

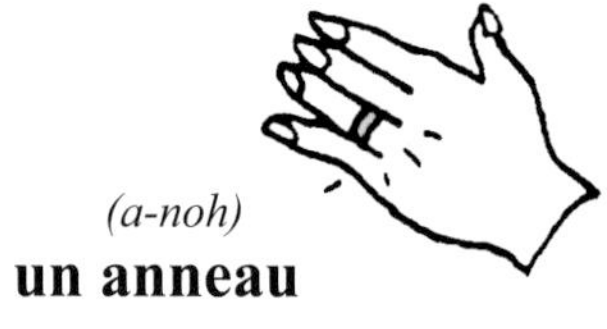

(a-noh)
un anneau
ring without stone

____

(ko-lyay)
une bague
ring (with setting)

____

(ko-lyay)
un collier
necklace

____

LE BIJOUTIER **Vous désirez Monsieur?**

LE CLIENT **Je voudrais acheter un cadeau** *(ka-doh)* (present) **pour ma femme.**

LE BIJOUTIER **Voulez-vous regarder ces bracelets et ces bagues en argent?** *(ar-zhAH)* (silver)

LE CLIENT **Je n'aime pas l'argent. Je préfère l'or.** *(gold)* (gold)

LE BIJOUTIER **Voudriez-vous voir une broche ou un collier?** *(voo-dray)* (would you like)

(bras-leh)
un bracelet
bracelet

____

(brosh)
une broche
broach

____

(bookl)
les boucles (fem.)
(o-reh-y)
d'oreille
earrings

(sheh-neht)
une chaînette
chain

LE CLIENT **Je ne sais pas. Montrez-moi un**
(pūh-tehtr)
bracelet, un anneau en or, ou peut-être
maybe
une paire de boucles d'oreille, s'il
vous plaît.

LE BIJOUTIER **À pendentif?**

(mOH-tewr)
LE CLIENT **Oui. Et une bague avec une monture**
setting
(pyer) 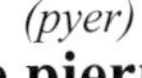 *(pray-syūhz)*
de pierres précieuses, et une chaînette en or.
stones precious

(em-rohd)
LE BIJOUTIER **Que pensez-vous de cette émeraude?**
(nes-pah)
Elle est superbe, n'est-ce pas?
isn't it true?

(fOH)
LE CLIENT **Combien font les boucles d'oreille, la**
make
(AH) (too)
bague et la chaînette en or en tout?
altogether

les boucles d'oreille
(pAH-dAH-teef)
à pendentif
pendant earrings

LE BIJOUTIER **8.400 euros.**

(oh-see)
LE CLIENT **La Place Vendôme est aussi chère que**
as . . . as . . .
la Cinquième Avenue à New York!
(me-tAH) *(mEH)*
(Mettant sa main dans sa poche) haut les
putting hand pocket hands up
mains, s'il vous plaît!

1. Name two items of jewelry you might wear on your fingers.

________________, ________________

2. What two sorts of jewelry do women wear on their ears?

________________, ________________

ANSWERS

Jewelry **1.** une bague, un anneau **2.** des boucles d'oreille, des boucles d'oreille à pendentif

3. What two types of jewelry are worn around the neck?

______________________ , ______________________

4. What is worn on the wrist? ______________________

5. What might a woman pin on her dress? ______________________

If you're a big spender and well-heeled, you might want to know the names of some valuable **pierres précieuses**. Try writing them out even if your wallet is not too thick.
precious stones

(pehrl)
des perles
pearls

____

(aym-rohd)
une émeraude
emerald

____

(to-pahz)
une topaze
topaz

____

(dya-mAH)
un diamant
diamond

____

(sa-feer)
un sapphir
sapphire

____

(rew-bee)
un rubis
ruby

____

(pla-teen)
le platine
platinum

____

(ar-zhAH)
l'argent
silver

____

(or)
l'or
gold

____

ANSWERS

Jewelry **3.** un collier, une chaînette **4.** un bracelet **5.** une broche

L'HORLOGERIE

The Watchmaker's Shop

TRACK 47

(mOHtr)
une montre-bracelet
wristwatch

(ray-veh-y)
un réveil
alarm clock

(or-lozh-ree)
l'horlogerie
watchmaker's shop

(or-lo-zhay)
l'horloger
watchmaker

Practice writing the new words by filling in the blanks under the pictures. Once you have done this, read the sentences below out loud. This may help you when you visit the watchmaker's. After you have practiced pronouncing the words, try writing them out in the spaces that are provided.

(ray-pa-ray)
Pouvez-vous réparer cette montre? Can you fix this watch?

Pouvez-vous nettoyer ma montre? Can you clean my watch?

(a-vAHs)
Ma montre avance. My watch is fast.

Mon réveil retarde. My alarm clock is slow.

(a-reh-tay)
Ma montre s'est arrêtée. My watch has stopped.

Elle ne marche pas bien. It doesn't run well.

Notice: In France, watches, clocks (as well as cars, washing machines and other machines) don't run; they're more liesurely; they walk (the verb *marcher* literally means to walk).

Il me faut une pile.	I need a battery.
Quand est-ce qu'elle va être prête?	When will it be ready?
Pouvez-vous me donner un reçu? *(ruh-sew)*	Can you give me a receipt?

Try reading this paragraph to see if you can understand it. You may need to refer to the previous sentences.

Ma montre ne marche pas bien. Un jour elle avance; un autre jour elle retarde. Aujourd'hui elle s'est arrêtée et je ne peux pas la réparer moi-même *(mwa-mem)* myself**. Je vais l'apporter chez l'horloger et l'horloger va la réparer. Il va aussi la nettoyer. Si je dois laisser** *(leh-say)* leave **ma montre à l'horlogerie, l'horloger va me donner un reçu.**

1. If you are always arriving late, what could be wrong with your watch?

   Ma montre ne ________________ bien. Elle ________________ .

2. When you always seem to be early for appointments, what might be the matter?

   Ma montre ________________ .

ANSWERS

Fill in blanks **1.** marche pas retarde. **2.** avance.

23

(ka-doh)

La boutique de cadeaux

Gift Shop

(tek-no-lo-zhee) *(mew-zeek)*

La technologie, la musique,

Technology, Music,

(fo-to-gra-fee) *(EH-tehr-net)*

La photographie, l'Internet

Photography, The Internet

(ka-doh)
un cadeau
present

(foo-lar)
un foulard
scarf

(ruh-pro-dewk-syOH)
une reproduction
reproduction

(par-fUH)
du parfum
perfume

(por-tuh-fuh-y)
un portefeuille
wallet

(por-tuh) (klay)
un porte-clés
key ring

(port) (bo-nūhr)
un porte-bonheur
lucky charm

(bee-zhoo)
un bijou
jewel

(port) (mo-neh)
un porte-monnaie
change purse

(sa) (ka) (mEH)
un sac à main
handbag

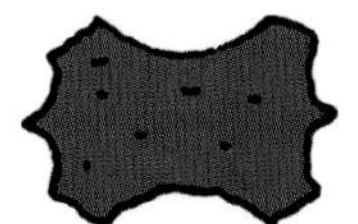

(kweer)
du cuir
leather

(ar-zhAH-tree)
de l'argenterie
silverware

(boo-teek)
UN BOUTIQUE
boutique

Here are a few adjectives that may be useful when shopping for gifts and souvenirs:

(boh) (bel) **beau, belle**	beautiful	*(tee-peek)* **typique**	typical
(zho-lee) **joli, jolie**	pretty	*(fOH-say)* **foncé, foncée**	dark
(ra-vee-sAH) (ra-vee-sAHt) **ravissant, ravissante**	lovely	*(klehr)* **clair, claire**	light
cher, chère	expensive	*(bOH) (mar-shay)* **bon marché**	inexpensive

À LA BOUTIQUE DE CADEAUX

At the Gift Shop

LA VENDEUSE **Vous désirez?**	Can I help you?
LE TOURISTE **Je voudrais un cadeau typiquement français.**	I would like a typically French present.
LA VENDEUSE **Pour un monsieur ou pour une dame?**	For a man or for a woman?
LE TOURISTE **Pour une dame.**	For a woman.
LA VENDEUSE **Un foulard en soie peut-être? Un sac en cuir, du parfum? Nous avons aussi ces belles reproductions des tableaux du Louvre et du Musée d'Orsay.**	A silk scarf perhaps? A leather bag, some perfume? We also have these beautiful reproductions of paintings from the Louvre and from the Musée d'Orsay.
LE TOURISTE **Combien coûte ce foulard?**	How much does the scarf cost?
LA VENDEUSE **Quarante-huit euros. C'est un beau souvenir. Regardez: c'est une carte de la France avec tous les monuments.** *(mo-mew-mAH)*	Forty-eight euros. It is a beautiful souvenir. Look: it is a map of France with all the monuments.
LE TOURISTE **Je le prends. Pouvez-vous faire un joli paquet?**	I'll take it. Can you gift-wrap it?

(While the clerk gift-wraps the package, the tourist takes out his wallet.)

LE TOURISTE	**Zut! Je n'ai pas assez d'argent. (À ce moment, sa femme entre dans le magasin.)**	Darn it! I don't have enough money. (At this moment, his wife enters the store.)
LA TOURISTE	**Mais qu'est-ce que tu fais ici?**	But what are you doing here?
LE TOURISTE	**Euh . . . j'achète un cadeau pour toi. . . . Chérie** *(shay-ree)* darling**, peux-tu me prêter** *(pre-tay)* lend **vingt-cinq euros?**	Uh . . . I'm buying you a present. . . . Darling, can you lend me 25 euros?

Answer these questions based on the dialogue in French.

1. Qu'est-ce que le touriste voudrait acheter?
2. Pour qui?
3. Qu'est-ce que la vendeuse suggère?
4. Combien coûte le foulard?
5. Quel est le problème du touriste?
6. Le touriste a besoin de combien d'euros?

LA TECHNOLOGIE

Technology

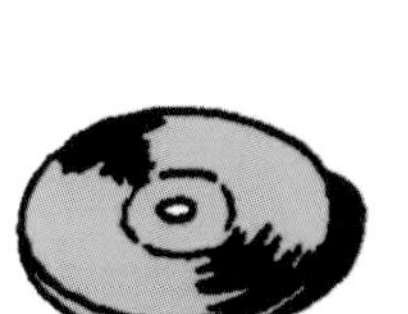

(por-tabl)
le portable
cell phone

(lek-tūhr) (em-pay-twa)
le lecteur MP3
MP3 player

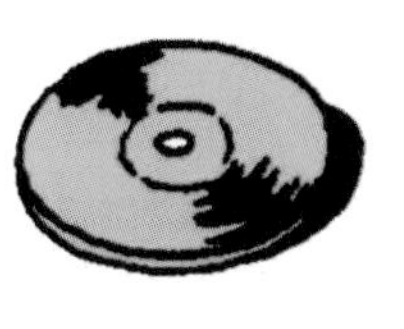

(tay-lay-shar-zhay)
télécharger
to download

(say-day)
le CD
CD

(por-tabl)
le portable
laptop computer

(kOH-pakt)
le disque compact
compact disk

(tay-lay-vee-zyOH)
la télévision
television

(You can use **le portable** to talk about a cell phone or a laptop computer. After all, they're both portable!)

ANSWERS

Dialogue **1.** Le touriste voudrait acheter un cadeau typiquement français. **2.** Pour une dame. **3.** La vendeuse suggère un foulard en soie, un sac en cuir, du parfum, et des belles reproductions. **4.** Le foulard coûte quarante-huit euros. **5.** Il n'a pas assez d'argent. **6.** Il a besoin de vingt-cinq euros.

MARIE **Zut! Mon lecteur MP3 ne marche plus.**

(sAH-tr)
ANNE **Allons au centre commercial.**
shopping mall

MARIE **Tu veux prendre l'autobus ou le métro?**

ANNE **Prenons le métro. C'est plus facile.**

(ko-neh) *(pree)*
MARIE **Super! Je connais un magasin où les prix sont très bas.**
know prices

(ah-nee-mahl-ree)
Et c'est à côté d'une animalerie.
pet store

(ah-lOH-zee)
ANNE **Allons-y!**
Let's go!

Answer the following questions in French.

1. Pourquoi est-ce que Marie a besoin d'aller au magasin?

___

2. Où vont-elles?

___

3. Est-ce qu'Anne et Marie prennent l'autobus ou le métro?

___

4. Qu'est-ce qu'il y a juste à côté du magasin?

___

ANSWERS

Dialogue **1.** Son lecteur MP3 ne marche pas. **2.** au centre commercial **3.** Elles prennent le métro. **4.** Il y a une animalerie.

LA MUSIQUE

Music

La musique française
French music

(rok)
Le rock
Rock

(rahp)
Le rap
Rap

(kla-seek)
La musique classique
Classical music

(blooz)
Le blues
Blues

(eep-ohp)
Le hip-hop
Hip hop

La musique pop
Pop music

(shAH-sOH)
Les chansons folkloriques
Folk songs

(vyEH)
Marie vient d'acheter un nouveau lecteur MP3. Elle veut télécharger
just bought

(ay-koo-tay) (pAH-dAH)
quelques chansons pour les écouter pendant qu'elle fait du jogging.
listen to while

(dzh-ug-een) (re-kom-AHd)
MARIE **Je vais faire du jogging. Qu'est-ce que tu recommandes comme musique?**

ANNE **Peut-être du rock?**

(bun-ee-day) (koo-reer)
MARIE **Bonne idée! Mais je vais courir trop vite.**
Good idea! to run

(tay-lay-char-zhay)
ANNE **Tu peux télécharger un peu de musique classique aussi.**
to download

(mAH-dor-meer)
MARIE **Non. Je vais m'endormir.**
to fall asleep

ANNE **Le hip-hop?**

(reet-me)
MARIE **Excellente idée. J'aime bien le rythme.**

(AH-vee)
ANNE **Et après, as-tu envie d'aller au zoo?**
want

(troh)
MARIE **Je vais être trop fatiguée. Allons en ville pour écouter du blues.**
too

Vrai ou faux?

1. Marie a acheté un nouveau lecteur MP3.
2. Anne recommande le jazz.
3. Marie aime le hip-hop.
4. Anne et Marie vont aller au zoo.

ANSWERS

Dialogue 1. V 2. F 3. V 4. F

LA PHOTOGRAPHIE

Photography

(a-pa-reh-y) (foh-toh) (new-may-reek)
un appareil photo numérique
digital camera

(ka-may-rah)
une caméra numérique
digital movie camera

(EH-pree-mAHt)
une imprimante
printer

FRANÇOIS **Ce n'est pas possible!**

(kess-keel-ya)
MADELEINE **Qu'est-ce qu'il y a?**
What's wrong?

FRANÇOIS **J'ai perdu mon appareil photo.**

(say) (do-mazh)
MADELEINE **C'est dommage! Et nous allons visiter la ville cet après-midi.**
Too bad!

FRANÇOIS **J'ai besoin d'acheter un nouvel appareil photo.**

François et Madeleine vont au magasin pour acheter un appareil photo.

VENDEUR **Bonjour, monsieur. Je peux vous aider?**

FRANÇOIS **Bonjour, monsieur. Je cherche un appareil photo numérique.**

(shwa)
VENDEUR **Nous avons un très grand choix. À quel prix?**
choice

une photo
photo

FRANÇOIS **Qu'est-ce que vous avez pour cent euros?**

(may-gah-peek-sehl)
VENDEUR **À ce prix, nous avons un appareil de seize mégapixels. Avec une carte**

(may-mwahr) (zhee-gah-ok-te)
mémoire de huit gigaoctets.
memory card

(stok-ay)
FRANÇOIS **Je prends beaucoup de photos. Combien de photos est-ce que la carte peut stocker?**
store

VENDEUR **Vous pouvez prendre plus de mille photos!**

(EH-pree-may)
FRANÇOIS **C'est beaucoup! Et pour imprimer les photos?**
print

VENDEUR **Vous pouvez les faire imprimer ici ou sur Internet. J'ai aussi une imprimante**

pour 120 euros, et elle imprime en couleur ou en noir et blanc.
black and white

FRANÇOIS **C'est un peu cher. Je vais seulement prendre l'appareil-photo.**

Il parle à Madeleine.

FRANÇOIS **Madeleine, tu préfères le rouge ou le bleu?**

MADELEINE **Le rouge!**

Answer the following questions in French.

1. Qu'est-ce que François va acheter?
2. Combien coûte l'appareil photo?
3. Combien de photos peut-il prendre?
4. Est-ce que Madeleine préfère le rouge ou le bleu?

(EH-tehr-net)
L'INTERNET
The Internet

(or-dee-na-tūhr)
un ordinateur
computer

(ta-blet) (tahk-teel)
une tablette tactile
touchscreen tablet computer

(koo-ree-yay) (ay-lehk-tro-neek)
le courrier électronique

(koo-ree-yel)
le courriel
e-mail

(vee-rews)
le virus
virus

(wehb)
le Web
World Wide Web

(soo-ree)
la souris
mouse

(seet)
le site Web
website

AU CAFÉ

Daniel, un jeune étudiant américain, est à Montpellier, où il étudie le marketing. Il décide d'aller dans un café pour se brancher *(brAH-shay)* [to plug in/connect] au réseau *(ray-zoh)* [network] Wi-Fi et envoyer un courriel à sa famille. Sa famille lui manque *(mAHk)* [he misses his family] beaucoup et il a le cafard *(ka-far)* [he is feeling low]. Daniel décide d'acheter un billet d'avion pour aller voir sa famille pendant les vacances de Toussaint *(too-sEH)* [All Saints' Day].

LA SERVEUSE **Que désirez-vous boire?**

DANIEL **Un café au lait, s'il vous plaît.**

LA SERVEUSE **Vous voulez autre *(oh-tr)* chose *(shohz)*?**

DANIEL **Non, merci. Quel est le mot de passe *(mohd-pahs)* [password] pour le réseau Wi-Fi?**

LA SERVEUSE **Le nom d'utilisateur *(ew-tee-lee-za-tuhr)* [user name] et le mot de passe sont écrits sur cette fiche *(feesh)* [card].**

Elle lui *(lwee)* [to him] donne une petite fiche pour l'aider à brancher son portable au réseau Wi-Fi.

ANSWERS

Dialogue **1.** un appareil photo numérique **2.** cent euros **3.** plus de mille photos **4.** le rouge

(troov)
Daniel commence à surfer l'Internet. Il trouve un site où il peut acheter des billets très
finds

(bOH mar-shay)
bon marché. Sa famille habite à Trenton, dans le New Jersey, aux États-Unis. Après
cheap
quelques minutes, Daniel trouve un billet aller-retour, de Paris à Jersey, pour 250 €.

DANIEL **Quel bon prix! Et quelle bonne surprise pour mes parents.**

(kahrt duh kray-dee) (AH leenye)
Il sort sa carte de crédit et il achète le billet en ligne. Avec la souris, il clique sur le
credit card on line

(rAH-tr) (kOH-tAH)
bouton marqué «acheter.» Il finit son café au lait et il rentre chez lui, très content.
returns home happy

(lAH-duhmEH) (kah-mah-rahd)
Le lendemain, il montre son billet électronique à son camarade de chambre, Jules.
next day e-ticket roommate

(ruh-gard)
DANIEL **Regarde. Je vais passer les vacances de la Toussaint avec ma famille.**
Look

JULES **Mais, tes parents, n'habitent-ils pas aux États-Unis?**

DANIEL **Si. Ils habitent dans le New Jersey.**

(eel-duh-zher-zay)
JULES **Mais tu as acheté des billets pour l'île de Jersey. C'est une des**
bought Isle of Jersey

(AH-glow nohr-mAHd) (mAHsh)
îles anglo-normandes, dans la Manche.
Channel Islands English Channel

(mEHs) (trOH-pay) (rAH-boor-sahbl)
DANIEL **Mince! Je me suis trompé! Et le billet n'est pas remboursable.**
Darn! I made a mistake refundable

JULES **Qu'est-ce que tu vas faire?**

DANIEL **Je vais visiter l'île de Jersey!**

Vrai ou faux?

1. Daniel va au café pour envoyer un courriel à sa famille.
2. Daniel prend un coca.
3. Daniel achète un billet aller-retour pour le New Jersey.
4. Daniel va visiter sa famille pendant la Toussaint.

ANSWERS

Dialogue 1. V 2. F 3. F 4. F

24

(ray-pa-ra-syOH)
Les réparations:
Repair Services

(kor-do-nyay)
Le cordonnier
The Shoemaker (cobbler)

(op-tee-syEH)
L'opticien
The Optometrist

TRACK 50

Pour vraiment bien voir une ville ou un village, il faut marcher. Vous faites partie de la (are part) **foule** (fool) (crowd) **et la foule ne fait pas attention** (a-tAH-syOH) (pays no attention) **à vous. Vous pouvez observer** (op-sehr-vay) **les visages** (vee-zahzh) (faces)**, entrer dans les magasins, examiner** (ehg-za-mee-nay) **les étalages** (ay-ta-lahzh) (displays) **des marchés en plein air** (AH) (plEH) (ehr)**, marchander** (mar-sHAn-day) (bargain) **dans les marchés aux puces** (pews) (flea markets)**, flâner** (fah-nay) (stroll) **dans les jardins publics** (zhar-dEH) (pew-bleek) (public gardens)**, lire les inscriptions** (ans-kreep-syOH) **sur les statues** (sta-tew)**.**

Pour tout cela (suh-la) (that)**, il vous faut posséder** (po-seh-day) (own) **de bonnes chaussures de marche, ou** (or) **connaître les expressions suivantes** (swee-vAHt) (following)**:**

Pardon, pourriez-vous me dire s'il y a un cordonnier près d'ici?

Excuse me. Could you tell me if there is a shoemaker near here?

CHEZ LE CORDONNIER

At the Shoemaker/Shoe Repair Shop

(shoh-sewr)
des chaussures
shoes

(la-seh)
des lacets
shoelaces

(sAH-dahl)
des sandales
sandals

le cordonnier
shoemaker

(ta-OH) (kah-say)
Mon talon est cassé.
heel broken

My heel is broken.

(ray-pa-ray)
Est-il possible de réparer ma chaussure
(pAH-dAH) (kuh) (zha-tAH)
pendant que j'attends?

Is it possible to fix my shoe while I wait?

Pour quand pouvez-vous la réparer?
for when

When can you fix it?

Retenez . . .

Remember . . .

ouvert	open
jusqu'à	until
(suh-mel) **la semelle**	sole
(ew-zay) **usé**	worn
(ruh-suh-muh-lay) **ressemeler**	to resole
le plastique	plastic
temporaire	temporary
le talon	heel

CHEZ L'OPTICIEN

At the Optometrist's

l'opticien
optometrist

(lew-neht) (kah-say)
des lunettes cassées
broken glasses

LA TOURISTE **La monture et un verre de mes lunettes sont cassées. Je ne vois rien sans lunettes.**

(pehr) (ruh-shAHzh)
L'OPTICIEN **Avez-vous une paire de rechange?**
extra pair

(ma-lūh-rūhz-mAH)
LA TOURISTE **Malheureusement pas.**

(myop) (ee-pehr-may-trop)
L'OPTICIEN **Vons êtes myope ou hypermétrope?**
near-sighted far-sighted

(mOH-tewr)
la monture
frame

(vehr)
un verre
lens
(de contact)
(contact)

LA TOURISTE **Hypermétrope.**

(eh-say-ay)
L'OPTICIEN **Essayez cette paire . . . Qu'est-ce que vous voyez?**
try on

LA TOURISTE **Elles me vont bien! Écoutez:**
fit me well listen

(say)
C

(oh) (ew) (vay)
o u v

(dooble vay) (day) (es) (er) (tay) (kah) (ee grek)
w d s r t k y

L'OPTICIEN **Hum . . . Asseyez-vous là. Je vais essayer**
Sit there

de réparer vos lunettes tout de suite. . . .

(tar)
(Quelques minutes plus tard).
later

(fra-zheel) (tAH-po-rehr)
L'OPTICIEN **Voilà. Attention! Vos lunettes sont très fragiles. C'est une réparation temporaire.**
fragile temporary

(ruh-ko-ne-sAHt)
LA TOURISTE **Merci mille fois, Monsieur. Je vous suis très reconnaissante.**
grateful

Retenez . . .

Remember . . .

réparer	to fix
(se-ray) **serrer**	to tighten
(so-leh-y) **les lunettes de soleil**	sunglasses
remplacer	to replace
(tood-sweet) **tout de suite**	right away
cassé	broken
(ruh-shAHzh) **une paire de rechange**	a spare pair

After studying the optometrist and shoemaker vocabulary, try to draw lines between the French words and their English equivalents:

1. réparer	A. the cobbler
2. des lunettes	B. the shoelaces
3. des chaussures	C. to tighten
4. cassé	D. the heel
5. la monture	E. shoes
6. le talon	F. glasses
7. serrer	G. lens
8. les lacets	H. frame
9. les verres	I. to repair
10. le cordonnier	J. broken

ANSWERS

Matching **1.** I **2.** F **3.** E **4.** J **5.** H **6.** D **7.** C **8.** B **9.** G **10.** A

ESSENTIAL SERVICES

(ser-vees) *(eh-sAH-syel)*
Services essentiels

25 La banque

(bAHk)
Bank

LES BILLETS ET LA MONNAIE

(bee-yeh) *(mo-neh)*
Bills and Coins

In 2002 the French franc passed into history and was replaced by the euro (*er-ro*). The new currency is identical throughout the European Union countries. The seven euro notes come in different colors and sizes, and the eight new French coins go from 1 cent to 2 euros.

French bank notes (un billet = a bill)

5 euros	**100 euros**
10 euros	**200 euros**
20 euros	**500 euros**
50 euros	

French coins (la monnaie = coins)

1 cent	**1 euro**
2 cents	**2 euros**
5 cents	
10 cents	
20 cents	
50 cents	

To obtain the best exchange rate for your foreign currency, you will want to go to the nearest bank. Most French banks remain open from 9:30 A.M.–4:30 P.M. Some close for lunch, especially during the slower summer months. All banks close at noon on the day before a holiday.

Most large hotels will exchange your dollars if you are staying there. You can find *(bew-roh)* **BUREAUX DE CHANGE** in large banks, in airports and railroad stations, and at the border. **Attention!** If you are traveling during the weekend, don't forget to change your money promptly, as you may have difficulty finding a **bureau de change** open in small towns.

Une pièce de dix cents A 10-cent coin

Un billet de cinquante euros A 50-euro bill

The abbreviation for euro is €. Bear in mind that when using numbers, the French use commas where we use periods. 5.000,50 € is five thousand euros and fifty cents.

(shAHzh)

LES BANQUES, LE CHANGE,

(shehk) (vwa-yahzh)

LES CHÈQUES DE VOYAGE

Banks, Money Exchange, Traveler's Checks

Les gens et les choses

People and things

(AH-plwah-yay)
l'employé de banque
l'employée de banque
bank employee
(male and female)

la banque
bank

(u-toh-mah-teek)
le guichet automatique
automatic teller, ATM

(AH-prUH)
l'emprunt (masc.)
loan (money you borrow)

(keh-syeh) *(keh-syehr)*
le caissier, la caissière
cashier (male and female)

l'argent
money

(lee-keed)
l'argent liquide
cash

le billet de banque
banknote

(gee-sheh)
le guichet
teller's window

(bewl-tan) *(vehr-suh-mAH)*
le bulletin de versement
deposit slip

(kOHt)
le compte
account

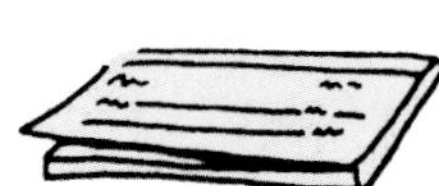

(keh-syeh)
le carnet de chèques
checkbook

(vwa-yahzh)
le chèque de voyage
traveler's check

(mo-neh)
la monnaie
small change

Read the following dialogue out loud several times. It contains expressions you will need to conduct business in a bank.

Mr. Smith and his wife enter a bank in Paris in order to exchange some American dollars and traveler's checks.

M. SMITH	**Bonjour Monsieur. Je voudrais changer ce chèque de voyage de 100 dollars en euros.** (chèque de voyage: traveler's checks)	Good day sir. I would like to exchange this $100 American traveler's check for euros.
LE CAISSIER	**J'ai besoin de votre passeport.**	I need your passport.
M. SMITH	**Pourquoi?**	Why?
LE CAISSIER	**C'est comme ça. Il faut montrer une carte d'identité.** *(ee-dAH-tee-tay)*	That's the way it is. You have to show some identification.
M. SMITH	**Je l'ai oubliée à 'hôtel.**	I left it at the hotel.
MME SMITH	**J'ai mon passeport.**	I have my passport.
L'EMPLOYÉ	**Très bien, Madame.**	Very well, Madam.
MME SMITH	**Je voudrais aussi changer 500 dollars américains.**	I would also like to change 500 American dollars.
L'EMPLOYÉ	**Bon. Alors ça fait 600 dollars américains en tout?**	Okay. Then, it is 600 American dollars in all?
MME SMITH	**Oui.**	Yes.

L'EMPLOYÉ	(Speaking in English:)	That will be 730 euros. Take this slip to the cashier.
M. SMITH	**Mais vous parlez anglais?**	But you speak English?
L'EMPLOYÉ	**Bien sûr. J'ai fait un stage de deux ans à une banque à New York.**	Of course. I did a two-year internship at a bank in New York City.
M. SMITH	*(for-mee-dabl)* **C'est formidable! Mais vous auriez pu nous le dire plus tôt . . .**	That's wonderful! But you could have told us earlier . . .
L'EMPLOYÉ	(souriant) **Au revoir . . . et bon séjour en France!**	(smiling) Good-bye . . . and enjoy your stay in France!

(ko-mAH)

COMMENT. . .

How to . . .

(shAH-zhay)
changer
to exchange

(toh) (shAHzh)
le taux de change
exchange rate

(pay-yay)
payer
to pay

(day-poh-zay)
déposer
to deposit

(prayl-yay)
prélever
to withdraw

(oo-vreer) (kOHt)
ouvrir un compte
to open an account

(too-shay) (shek)
toucher un chèque
to cash a check

(see-nyay)
signer
to sign

Now see if you can remember these useful things. Match each expression or word to each picture by checking off the appropriate box:

1. ☐ la monnaie
   ☐ le coin

2. ☐ le carnet de chèques
   ☐ l'argent liquide

3. ☐ le directeur
   ☐ le billet

4. ☐ le guichet
   ☐ le directeur

5. ☐ le dépôt *(day-poh)*
   ☐ le chèque de voyage

6. ☐ le bulletin de versement
   ☐ le bulletin de prélèvement

Now, try to complete the following:

1. Je voudrais ________________ (exchange) dix dollars américains.

2. Je voudrais ________________ (withdraw) soixante-quinze euros.

3. Je voudrais ________________ (cash) un chèque.

4. Je voudrais ________________ (deposit) 75 euros.

ANSWERS

Match each expression **1.** la monnaie (**le coin** = the corner) **2.** le carnet de chèques **3.** le billet **4.** le guichet **5.** le chèque de voyage **6.** le bulletin de versement

Complete the following **1.** changer **2.** prélever **3.** toucher **4.** déposer

Match up the French expressions at the left with the English terms on the right:

1. L'emprunt
2. Les chèques de voyage
3. La monnaie
4. Le taux de change
5. Le caissier
6. Le guichet
7. Le compte
8. Le carnet de cheques

A. Exchange rate
B. Cashier
C. Loan
D. Small change
E. Teller's window
F. Traveler's checks
G. Checkbook
H. Account

Comment aller à la banque?

(bAHk) — banque

Which way to the bank?

Suppose someone stops you on the street and asks for directions to get to the bank. You are now at the shoemaker's shop. Can you give him or her proper instructions? Use the map below.

ANSWERS

Banking 1. C 2. F 3. D 4. A 5. B 6. E 7. H 8. G

Which way to the bank Tournez à gauche. Allez tout droit. Tournez à gauche. Tournez à droite.

26	*(sehr-vees)* *(post)* # Le service de poste Postal Service

(vyEH)

Je viens de . . .

I just . . .

Remember the immediate future, simply formed with **aller** in the present tense followed by an infinitive? To express the immediate past, you simply use **venir** (to come) + **de** or **d'** before a vowel + infinitive. The English equivalent of this construction is: "I just went to the post office." (*Je viens d'aller à la poste.*)

(AH-vwa-yay) **Je viens d'envoyer une lettre à ma mère.**	I just sent a letter to my mother.
Tu viens d'arriver?	Did you (familiar) just arrive?
Il vient d'acheter une voiture.	He just bought a car.
Nous venons d'aller à Paris.	We just went to Paris.
Vous venez d'apprendre quelque chose de nouveau.	You just learned something new.
Marc et Marie viennent de partir.	Marc and Marie just left.

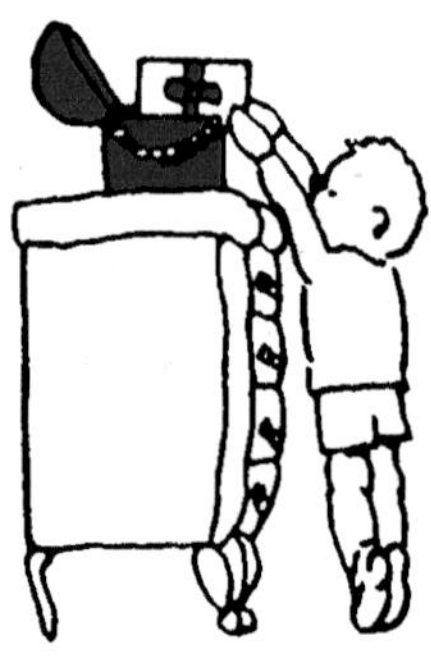

It's lunch time. Jeannot, 5 years old, comes home, out of breath and looking happy.

JEANNOT **Je viens de jouer au facteur,** *(fak-tuhr)* **maman!** *(ma-mAH)*	I just played mailman, mommy.
MAMAN **Au facteur? Comment peut-on jouer au facteur sans lettres?**	Mailman? How can one play mailman without letters?

JEANNOT **Mais j'ai des lettres.**	But I do have letters.
MAMAN **Quelles lettres?**	What letters?
JEANNOT **Dans la commode** *(ko-mod)* **de ta chambre, tu sais bien . . . le paquet de lettres avec un beau ruban** *(rew-bAH)* **rose autour** *(oh-toor)* **. . .**	In the bureau of your room, you know . . . the package of letters with a beautiful pink ribbon around . . .
MAMAN **Oui . . . eh bien?**	Yes . . . so?
JEANNOT **Eh bien! Je viens de mettre une lettre sous chacune** *(shah-kewn)* **des portes de notre rue.**	So! I just put one letter under each door of our street.

The French post office, **La Poste**, is much more than a post office. You can, of course, go to **La Poste** to send letters and packages. However, you can also do banking, buy a cell phone, or set up a web site. You can even set up an e-mail account through the post office's web site. The services have been expanding and changing drastically in recent years. Your best bet is to go to a post office near where you are staying to see what new services are available.

le facteur
(fak-trees)
la factrice
letter carrier

la boîte aux lettres
mailbox

(ko-lee)
le paquet/le colis
package

(rehs-tAHt)
la poste restante
general delivery

(gee-shay)
le guichet
window

la poste
post office

(a-frAH-sheer)
affranchir
to put stamps on a letter or package

(koo-ryay)
le courrier
mail

faire suivre
to forward

TRACK 54

Jean et Françoise vont à la poste.

(John has quite a few chores to do. His Parisian friend Françoise helps him out.)

JEAN	**Combien de timbres faut-il mettre sur cette lettre pour Seattle?**	How many stamps should be put on this letter to Seattle?
FRANÇOISE	**Je ne sais pas. Allons la faire peser à la poste.**	I don't know. Let's go and have it weighed at the post office.
JEAN	**Dans ce cas** *(kah)*, **je vais aussi envoyer ce colis à New York. Et je voudrais ouvrir un compte d'épargne** *(ay-parn-y)*.	In that case, I'll also mail this package to New York. And I would also like to open a savings account.
FRANÇOISE	**À la poste.**	At the post office.
JEAN	**C'est commode. Je dois aussi acheter un téléphone portable.**	That's handy. I must also buy a cell phone.
FRANÇOISE	**À la poste.**	At the post office.
JEAN	**Et il me faut faire une photocopie.**	And I have to make a photocopy.
FRANÇOISE	**À la poste.**	At the post office.

(ehks-tror-dee-nehr)
JEAN **Extraordinaire!** — Extraordinary!

Est-ce que je peux aussi faire nettoyer mon complet, louer une voiture, faire ma réservation d'avion et manger de la glace au chocolat à la poste? *(ray-zehr-va-syOH)* — Can I also have my suit cleaned, rent a car, make my plane reservation and eat a chocolate ice cream at the post office?

À LA POSTE

At the Post Office

JEAN **Où est le guichet pour envoyer un colis?** — Where's the window to send a package?

FRANÇOISE **Là-bas.** — Over there.

LE POSTIER (postal employee) **Je suis désolé, mais ce guichet est fermé.** — I'm sorry, but this window is closed.

(Jean va à un autre guichet.)

JEAN **Bonjour, madame. J'ai besion d'envoyer ce colis.** — Hello, ma'am. I need to send this package.

LA POSTIÈRE (another postal employee)

Pourriez-vous remplir cette formule s'il vous plaît? *(for-mewl)* — Could you please fill out this form?

JEAN **D'accord. Avez-vous des timbres?** — Okay. Do you have stamps?

LA POSTIÈRE **Malheureusement, il ne me reste plus de timbres. Mais il y a un distributeur de timbres dans le coin.**

(mal-ūhr-ūhz-mAH) *(dee-stree-bew-tūhr)* *(kwEH)*

Unfortunately, I don't have any more stamps. But there is a stamp machine in the corner.

JEAN **Merci, madame. Et pourriez-vous peser cette lettre?**

Thank you, ma'am. And could you weigh this letter?

LA POSTIÈRE **Il y a une balance self-service à côté du distributeur de timbres.**

(ba-lAHs)

There is a self-service scale next to the stamp machine.

JEAN **Et est-ce que vous avez de la glace au chocolat?**

And do you have any chocolate ice cream?

How about changing the immediate future into an immediate past as in the example below:

Je vais aller à la poste. — **Je viens d'aller à la poste.**

1. Jean va envoyer un colis. — Jean ____________ envoyer un colis.
2. Jean va aussi acheter des timbres. — Jean ____________ acheter des timbres.
3. Nous allons oublier nos passeports. — Nous ____________ oublier nos passeports.

4. Anne et Jean vont voyager en Europe. — Anne et Jean ____________ voyager en Europe.
5. Qu'est-ce que vous allez faire? — Qu'est-ce que vous ____________ faire?

Fill in blanks with French words:

Pour envoyer son ________________, Jean va au guichet.

Jean achète aussi des ________________.

Les employés de la poste s'appellent les ________________.

Les employées de la poste s'appellent les ________________.

ANSWERS

Immediate past **1.** vient d' **2.** vient d' **3.** venons d' **4.** viennent de **5.** venez de

Fill in blanks colis (paquet) timbres facteurs factrices or les postiers les postières

27 Le service téléphonique

(sehr-vees) (tay-lay-foh-neek)

Telephone Service

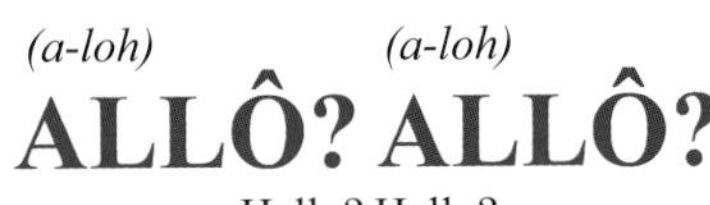

(a-loh) (a-loh)

ALLÔ? ALLÔ?

Hello? Hello?

(a-loh) **Allô? Allô?**	Hello . . . Hello?
(kee) (eh) (ta) (la-pa-reh-y) **Qui est à l'appareil?**	Who is it?
Je voudrais parler à . . .	I would like to speak to . . .
(me-sahzh) **Puis-je laisser un message?**	May I leave a message?
Dites . . . que Marc Smith *(ra-play) (tar)* **va rappeler plus tard.**	Say . . . that Mark Smith will call back later.
Madame/Monsieur!	Operator! (Address an operator as "madame" or "monsieur.")
(ko-mew-nee-ka-syOH) (moh-vehz) **La communication est mauvaise.**	This is a bad connection .
(ay-tay) (koo-pay) **Nous avons été coupés.**	We have been cut off.
Vous vous êtes trompé de numéro.	This is the wrong number.
(kee-tay) **Ne quittez pas!**	Don't hang up. (Wait a minute.)
(kOH-poh-say) **Composer un numéro**	To dial a number
(day-kro-shay) (ray-sehp-tuhr) **Décrocher (le récepteur)**	To pick up the receiver
(ra-kro-shay) **Raccrocher (le récepteur)**	To hang up
(a-new-ehr) **L'annuaire**	Telephone book

AU RESTAURANT

Paul et Sophie sortent au restaurant. Ils sont pressés parce qu'ils veulent aller au cinéma à vingt heures. Il est maintenant dix-huit heures.

Paul and Sophie go out to a restaurant. They're in a hurry because they want to go to the movies at 8 P.M. It is now 6 P.M.

LE SERVEUR **Bonjour, madame, monsieur. Vous désirez?** *(day-zee-ray)*	Hello, sir, ma'am. Can I help you?
PAUL **Un coca, s'il vous plaît.**	A coke, please.
SOPHIE **Moi aussi. Et une carafe d'eau, s'il vous plaît.**	Me too. And a pitcher of water, please.
PAUL **Et la soupe du jour aussi.**	And the soup of the day too.
LE SERVEUR **Et pour madame?**	And for the lady?
SOPHIE **Rien pour le moment, merci.**	Nothing for now, thank you.
LE SERVEUR **Bien.**	Very well.
Le serveur part chercher leurs boissons et la soupe. Il revient.	The server leaves to get their drinks and the soup. He returns.
LE SERVEUR **Vous avez choisi?**	Have you decided?
PAUL **Pour moi, un steak-frites, bien cuit.** *(kwee)*	For me, a steak with fries, well done.
SOPHIE **La salade césar au poulet.** *(say-zar)*	The Cesar salad with chicken.

LE SERVEUR **Excellent.**	Excellent.
Vingt minutes plus tard . . .	Twenty minutes later . . .
SOPHIE **Où est le serveur?**	Where is the waiter?
PAUL **Je ne sais pas. Je ne vois personne!**	I don't know. I don't see anyone!
Je vais téléphoner au restaurant.	I'm going to call the restaurant.
Paul sort son portable et il appelle le restaurant. Le téléphone sonne.	Paul takes out his cell phone and calls the restaurant. The phone rings.
SOPHIE **Pas de réponse!** *(ray-pOHs)*	No answer!
PAUL **Personne!**	Nobody!
SOPHIE **Qu'est-ce que nous allons faire? Le film commence à vingt heures. Nous allons être en retard!** *(AH re-tar)*	What are we going to do? The movie starts at eight. We're going to be late!
PAUL **La pizzeria Chez Antoine est très rapide.**	Chez Antoine pizza is very quick.
SOPHIE **Oui, mais ils n'ont pas de tables.**	Yes, but they don't have any tables.
PAUL **Je le sais.**	I know.
Paul sort son portable.	Paul takes out his cell phone.
CHEZ ANTOINE **Allô. Chez Antoine. C'est pour livraison ou pour emporter?** *(lee-vreh-zOH) (AH-por-tay)*	Hello. Chez Antoine. Is it for delivery or takeout?
PAUL **C'est pour livraison.**	It's for delivery.
CHEZ ANTOINE **Votre adresse, s'il vous plaît.**	Your address, please.
PAUL **Je suis au restaurant Chez Henri, rue Dufour.**	I'm at Chez Henri, on Dufour Street.
SOPHIE **Bonne idée! Je préfère la cuisine chinoise.**	Good idea! I prefer Chinese food.

Sophie sort son portable aussi.

Sophie takes out her cell phone too.

SOPHIE **Quel est le numéro de téléphone du restaurant chinois rue Dufour? Je vais commander un pâté impérial—pour livraison!**

What's the phone number of the Chinese restaurant on Dufour Street? I'm going to order an egg roll—for delivery!

After studying the expressions at the beginning of this section and the dialogue, can you come up with the appropriate expressions?

1. Hello. ____________________
2. I would like to speak to . . . ____________________
3. This is the wrong number. ____________________
4. Don't hang up. ____________________
5. What's the phone number of . . . ? ____________________

ANSWERS

Expressions **1.** Allô. **2.** J'aimerais parler à . . . **3.** Vous vous êtes trompé de numéro. **4.** Ne quittez pas. **5.** Quel est le numéro de téléphone de . . .

28 Les docteurs/Les médecins

(dok-tūhr) *(mayd-sEH)*

Doctors

Les dentistes / Les hôpitaux

(dAH-teest) *(o-pee-toh)*

Dentists / Hospitals

(ray-pay-tee-syOH) *(zhay-nay-rahl)*

UNE RÉPÉTITION GÉNÉRALE

A Once Over . . .

(Paul and Anne are at it again. This time they test each other on the parts of the human body.)

PAUL	**Alors, qui commence, toi ou moi?**	Well, who starts, you or me?
ANNE	**Tu me demandes en premier.**	You ask me first.
PAUL	**Bon. Qu'est-ce que tu as là?**	Good. What do you have there?
ANNE	*(shuh-vūh)* **Les cheveux.**	Hair.
PAUL	*(yūh)* **Entre les cheveux et les yeux?**	Between the hair and the eyes?
ANNE	*(frOH)* **Le front.**	The forehead.
PAUL	*(oh) (duh-sew)* **Au-dessus des yeux?**	Over the eyes?
ANNE	*(soor-see)* **Les sourcils.**	The eyebrows.

PAUL **Et qu'est-ce qu'on ferme quand on dort?**

And what does one close when one sleeps?

(poh-pyehr)
ANNE **Les paupières.**

The eyelids.

PAUL **Et sur les paupières il y a . . .**

And on the eyelids there are . . .

(seel)
ANNE **les cils.**

lashes.

PAUL **Et entre les yeux il y a . . .**

And between the eyes there is

(nay)
ANNE **le nez.**

the nose.

PAUL **Et entre le nez et la** *(boosh)* **bouche, beaucoup d'hommes ont**

And between the nose and the mouth, many men have

(moos-tash)
ANNE **une moustache.**

a moustache.

PAUL **Tu as deux . . .**

You have two . . .

(o-reh-y)
ANNE **oreilles**

ears

PAUL **et deux . . .**

and two . . .

(zhoo)
ANNE **joues**

cheeks

PAUL **mais seulement un . . .**

but only one . . .

(vee-zahzh)
ANNE **visage**

face

PAUL **et seulement une . . .**

and only one . . .

(let)
ANNE **tête.**

head.

(ree)
PAUL **Quand tu ris, on voit . . .**

When you laugh, one sees . . .

(dAH)
ANNE **les dents**

the teeth

PAUL **et quand tu vas chez le docteur, tu lui montres la**

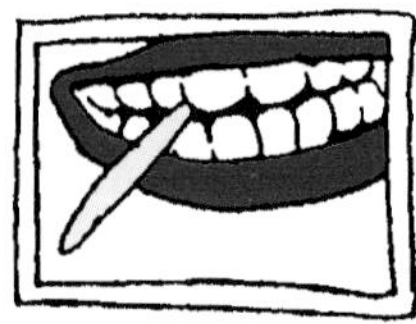

and when you go to the doctor's, you show him the

ANNE *(lAHg)* **langue, aaaaaaah . . .** — tongue, aaa . . .

PAUL **Ça, c'est le . . .** — This is the . . .

ANNE *(mAH-tOH)* **menton** — chin

PAUL **et ça, le . . .** — and this, the . . .

ANNE *(koo)* **cou.** — neck.

PAUL **Voilà deux . . .** — Here are two

ANNE *(ay-pohl)* **épaules** — shoulders,

PAUL **deux . . .** — two . . .

ANNE *(brah)* **bras** — arms

PAUL **et deux . . .** — and two . . .

ANNE *(kood)* **coudes** — elbows

PAUL **deux . . .** — two . . .

ANNE *(mEH)* **mains** — hands

PAUL **et dix . . .** — and ten . . .

ANNE *(dwa)* **doigts.** — fingers.

PAUL **Mon tour maintenant.** — My turn now.

ANNE **Ça, c'est le** — This is the . . .

PAUL *(doh)* **dos** — back

ANNE **et là-devant, la . . .** — and here in front, the . . .

PAUL *(pwa-treen)* **poitrine.** — chest.

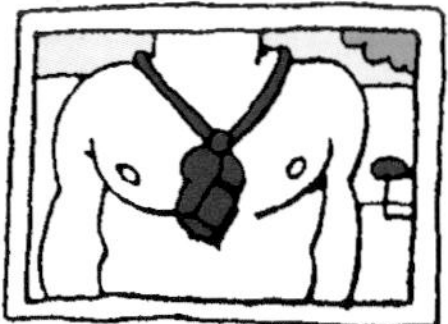

ANNE **Quelque chose te fait mal quand tu manges trop de gâteau:** — Something hurts you when you eat too much cake:

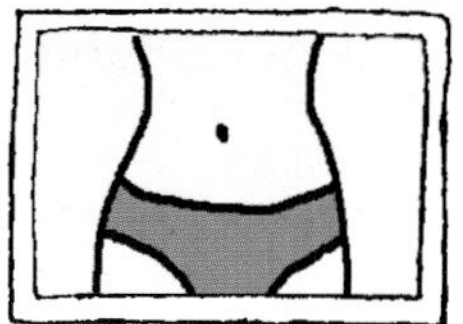

PAUL	*(es-to-ma)* **l'estomac.**	the stomach.
ANNE	**Et un peu plus bas il y a le . . .**	And a little lower is the
PAUL	*(vAHtr)* **ventre.**	belly.
ANNE	**Et derrière il y a le ...**	And behind there is the . . .
PAUL	*(de-ryer)* **derrière**	behind
ANNE	**et d'ici jusque là tu as deux . . .**	and from here to there you have two . . .
PAUL	*(kwees)* **cuisses**	thighs
ANNE	**et ensuite deux**	and then two . . .
PAUL	*(zhuh-noo)* **genoux**	knees
ANNE	**et plus bas les deux . . .**	and farther down the two . . .
PAUL	*(mo-le)* **mollets**	calves
ANNE	**jusqu'aux deux . . .**	down to the two . . .
PAUL	*(shuh-vee-y)* **chevilles.**	ankles.
ANNE	**Et ce que tu te laves une fois par an, ce sont les . . .**	And what you wash once a year are the . . .
PAUL	*(pyay)* **pieds**	feet
ANNE	**avec les dix . . .**	with the ten . . .
PAUL	*(or-te-y)* **orteils.**	toes.

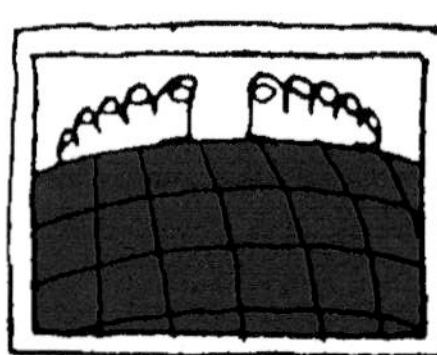

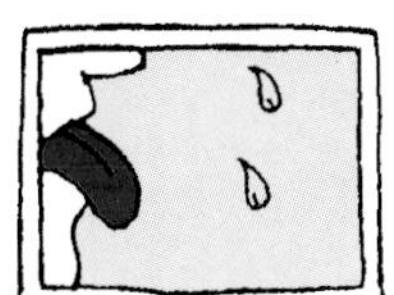

Draw lines between the matching words:

1. le front	A. tongue
2. les orteils	B. face
3. la bouche	C. eyelids
4. les chevilles	D. forehead
5. la langue	E. ankles
6. les paupières	F. toes
7. l'estomac	G. stomach
8. le visage	H. mouth
9. la moustache	I. teeth
10. les dents	J. moustache

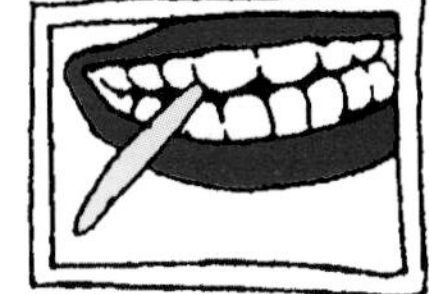

(sAH-teer)

Se sentir (bien, mal)

To feel

Do you remember the second group of **IR** verbs you studied in Chapter 5? When the verb **SENTIR** (to smell, to feel) is made reflexive, it is used to describe the state of one's health.

Toilettes (W.C.)

Dames Messieurs

Je me sens bien.	I feel well.
Je me sens mal.	I feel sick.
Je ne me sens pas très bien.	I don't feel very well.

Parts of the body are usually preceded with the definite article **LE**, **LA**, **L'**, **LES**.

Je me lave les mains.	I wash my hands.
J'ai mal à la tête.	My head hurts, I have a headache.

Remembering that À + LE becomes **AU** and À + LES **AUX**, can you practice this construction with parts of the body?

Example: **J'ai mal à la tête.**

J'ai mal au dos.

J'ai mal aux oreilles.

ANSWERS

Matching **1.** D **2.** F **3.** H **4.** E **5.** A **6.** C **7.** G **8.** B **9.** J **10.** I

Draw lines between the expressions that match:

1. **J'ai mal aux dents.**
2. **J'ai mal au dos.**
3. **J'ai mal à la tête.**
4. **J'ai mal au pied.**
5. **J'ai mal aux oreilles.**
6. **J'ai mal aux yeux.**
7. **J'ai mal à l'estomac.**
8. **J'ai mal au genou gauche.**
9. **Je me suis fait mal.**
10. **Je me suis fait mal au doigt.**

A. I have a headache.
B. I have an earache.
C. My foot hurts.
D. I have a toothache.
E. I have a backache.
F. My left knee hurts.
G. My eyes hurt.
H. I hurt my finger.
I. I have a stomach-ache.
J. I hurt myself.

In case of a minor medical complaint that cannot be solved with **des aspirines**, you can always walk into a **pharmacie** and say:

Excusez-moi Monsieur/Madame.	Excuse me.
Pouvez-cous me donner un conseil? *(kOH-se-y)*	Can you give me some advice?
J'ai très mal ____________________ .	My ____________________ hurts badly.

If the **pharmacien** *(far-ma-syEH)* or **pharmacienne** *(far-ma-syehn)* cannot help you, he/she will give you the address of a doctor. So will the hotel's receptionist. Doctors usually have consultation hours for patients who do not have an appointment. You may have to wait a long time, so it's better, if possible, to make an appointment ahead of time. In case of an emergency, you can call an emergency number (see page 243) and you can even ask for an English-speaking doctor. The emergency numbers are on page one of the telephone book. A few pharmacies remain open all night and during the weekend. The local paper carries a list. In case of a toothache, the procedure is the same.

ANSWERS

Matching 1. D 2. E 3. A 4. C 5. B 6. G 7. I 8. F 9. J 10. H

TRACK 58

DITES AAAAAAAAAH . . .

Say Aaaaaaaaah . . .

(gorzh)
Marie a mal à la gorge. (Mary has a sore throat.) She makes an appointment with Dr. Rebouteux, a general practitioner (**généraliste**). *(zhay-nay-rah-leest)*

LE DOCTEUR	**Bonjour, Madame.**	Hello, madam.
	(khes) (keen) (va) (pah) **Qu'est-ce qui ne va pas?**	What's wrong?
MARIE	*(gor-zh)* **J'ai mal à la gorge.**	I have a sore throat.
LE DOCTEUR	**Ouvrez la bouche et dites "trente-trois."**	Open your mouth and say "trente-trois."
MARIE	**Pourquoi trente-trois?**	Why 33?
LE DOCTEUR	**C'est comme ça. Oui, la gorge est un peu rouge. Comment vous sentez-vous autrement?** *(oh-truh-mAH)*	That's the way it is. Yes, your throat is a little red. How do you feel otherwise?
MARIE	*(boo-shay)* **Mal. J'ai le nez bouché et j'ai mal à la tête.**	Poorly. I have a stuffy nose and a headache.
LE DOCTEUR	**Prenons votre température.**	Let's take your temperature.
	(Mary opens her mouth).	
LE DOCTEUR	**La température est normale.** *(may-shAH) (rewm)* **C'est un méchant rhume avec un peu** *(AH-zheen)* **d'angine. . . .**	Your temperature is normal. It's a bad cold with a little angina . . .
MARIE	**Angine?**	Angina?
LE DOCTEUR	*(EH-fek-syOH)* **Oui, une petite infection à la gorge.**	Yes, a mild throat infection.
	Je vais vous donner une ordonnance.	I'll give you a prescription.
	(kohn-pree-may) **Prenez un comprimé toutes les quatre heures.**	Take one pill every four hours.

(oo-vray) *(boosh)*

OUVREZ LA BOUCHE!

Open Wide!

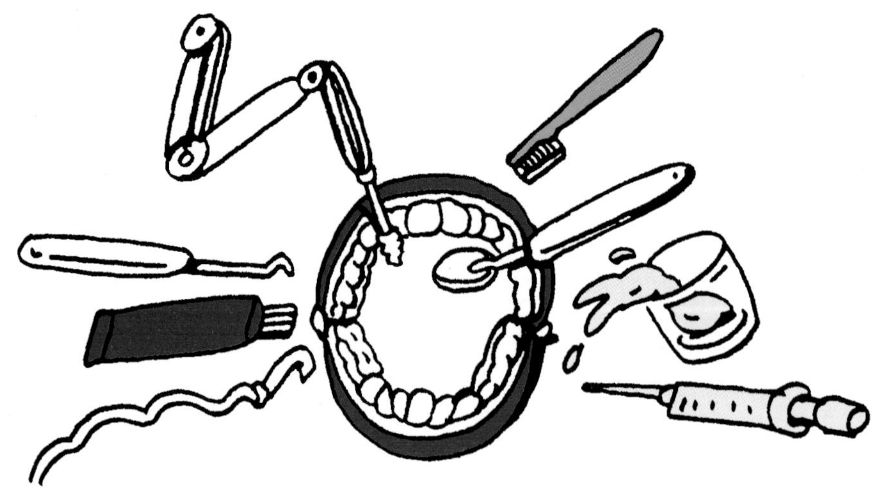

Mark has a toothache. A friend recommends a dentist that she likes very much. Mark's appointment is today at 2:00 P.M.

MARC (à la réceptionniste) **J'ai un rendez-vous.**	(To the receptionist) I have an appointment.
LA RÉCEPTIONNISTE **Avec le Docteur** *(bwee-sOH)* **Buisson?**	With Dr. Buisson?
MARC **Oui, pour deux heures.**	Yes, for 2 o'clock.
LA RÉCEPTIONNISTE **Votre nom, s'il vous plaît?**	Your name, please?
MARC **Marc Smith.**	Mark Smith.
LA RÉCEPTIONNISTE (Elle examine le livre de rendez-vous.) *(ehfeh)* **En effet.**	(She examines the appointment book.) That's correct.
LA RÉCEPTIONNISTE *(plas)* **Prenez place, s'il vous plaît. Il y a du monde aujourd'hui. C'est votre première visite?**	Please take a seat. There are a lot of people today. Is this your first visit?
MARC **Oui.**	Yes.

LA RÉCEPTIONNISTE **Pourriez-vous remplir cette carte s'il vous plaît?**	Could you fill out this card please?
(Une heure plus tard)	(One hour later)
L'ASSISTANTE DENTAIRE **Monsieur Smith?** *(a-sees-tAHt) (dAH-ter)*	Mr. Smith?
MARC **Oui?**	Yes?
L'ASSISTANTE **Asseyez-vous dans ce fauteuil. Le docteur arrive.** *(a-say-ay) (foh-tuh-y)*	Sit in this armchair. The doctor will be here soon.
(Quinze minutes plus tard.)	(15 minutes later)
LE DENTISTE **Monsieur Smith? Où avez-vous mal? Ici? Voyons . . . Ça fait mal? Et ça? Oui—et ça branle un peu par ici. Le plombage est tombé. Je vais vous faire une anesthésie locale. Puis je vais boucher la dent avec un plombage temporaire. Ce bridge ici est mal placé et cette couronne est à moitié fichue. Dans deux ou trois ans vous allez avoir besoin d'un dentier.** *(braH) (plOH-bahzh) (a-nehs-tay-zee) (lo-kahl) (boo-shay) (plOH-bazh) (tAH-po-rehr) (koo-ron) (mwa-tyay) (fee-shew) (dAH-tyay)*	Mr. Smith? Where does it hurt? Here? Let's see . . . It hurts? And that? Yes—and it wobbles a bit around here. The filling has fallen out. I'm going to give you a local anesthetic. Then I'll fill the tooth with a temporary filling. This bridge here doesn't sit well and this crown is half-finished. In two to three years you're going to need a denture.
MARC **Cela me réjouit le coeur.** *(ray-zwee) (kuhr)*	That makes my heart rejoice.
LE DENTISTE **Au revoir Monsieur, et bonnes vacances!** *(bon) (va-kAHs)*	Good-bye, and enjoy your vacation!

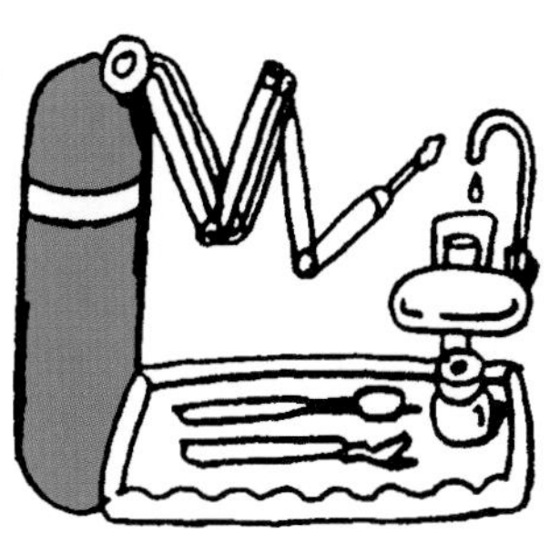

Can you match up the words in the left column with the definitions in the right column?

1. **généraliste**
2. **mal à la gorge**
3. **le nez bouché**
4. **rendez-vous**
5. **anesthésie locale**
6. **plombage**
7. **dentier**

A. stuffy nose
B. appointment
C. general practitioner
D. filling
E. sore throat
F. denture
G. local anesthesia

A L'HÔPITAL

At the Hospital

(André, Aunt Agnes's husband, has symptoms that look like a heart attack. The ambulance takes him to the hospital; Agnes and Suzanne stay in the waiting area.)

AGNÈS	**Tu es vraiment gentille d'être** *(zhAH-te-y)* **venue avec moi. Je suis un peu inquiète.** *(EH-kyet)*	You are really kind to have come with me. I am a little worried.
SUZANNE	**Où est-il maintenant?**	Where is he now?
AGNÈS	**Dans la salle des urgences.** *(ewr-zhAHs)*	In the emergency room.
SUZANNE	**Est-ce qu'il est souvent malade?**	Is he often sick?
AGNÈS	**Pas du tout. Il est costaud comme** *(kos-toh)* **un boeuf.** *(buhf)*	Not at all. He's as strong as an ox.
SUZANNE	**Voilà l'infirmière.** *(EH-feer-myehr)* nurse	Here is the nurse.

ANSWERS

Matching 1. C 2. E 3. A 4. B 5. G 6. D 7. F

AGNÈS **Comment va mon mari?**	How is my husband?
L'INFIRMIÈRE **Tout va bien! Le docteur** *(muh-zewr)* **mesure** **sa** *(tAH-syOH)* **tension** *(ar-tay-ryehl)* **artérielle.**	Everything is fine! The doctor is taking his blood pressure. Follow me.
Suivez-moi.	(In the room)
AGNÈS **Alors, mon trésor, comment te sens-tu?**	So, my treasure, how are you feeling?
ANDRÉ **Un peu fatigué, mais bien autrement.**	A little tired, but fine otherwise.
AGNÈS (au docteur): **Docteur, qu'est-ce qu'il a?**	Doctor, what's the matter with him?
LE DOCTEUR **Un peu de** *(fa-teeg)* **fatigue, c'est tout.**	A little fatigue, that's all.
AGNÈS (à André) **Tu vois, mon chou? Je te répète tout le temps que tu travailles trop, tu ne fais pas assez d'exercice et tu fumes trop.**	You see, my darling? I'm always telling you that you work too much, don't do enough exercise and smoke too much.

Retenez

Remember

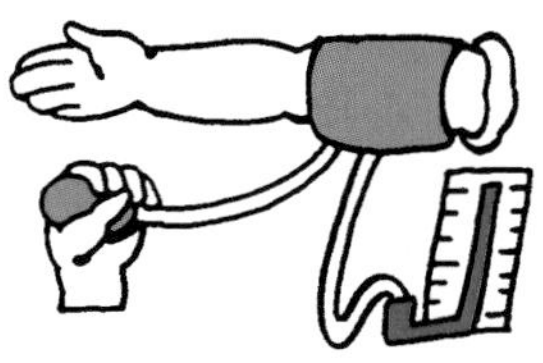

(fyehvr) **la fièvre** fever	*(or-do-nAHs)* **l'ordonnance** prescription	*(tAH-syOH) (ar-tay-ryel)* **la tension artérielle** blood pressure	*(zhay-nay-ra-leest)* **le généraliste** general practitioner
(vee-zeet) **la visite** visit	*(spay-see-men) (ew-reen)* **le spécimen d'urine** urine specimen	*(tAH-pay-ra-tewr)* **la température** temperature	*(spay-sya-leest)* **le spécialiste** specialist
la gorge throat	*(ma-lad)* **le malade/la malade** patient	*(AH-feer-myehr)* **l'infirmière, l'infirmier** nurse (female and male)	*(pwah)* **le poids** weight

See if you can answer the following questions pertaining to the dialogues on the doctor, dentist, and hospital:

1. Pourquoi Marie va-t-elle chez le docteur? Parce qu'elle a

   A. mal à l'estomac
   (ma-la-dee)
   B. une maladie cardiaque
   illness
   C. mal à la gorge

2. Le docteur donne à Marie

   A. un conseil
   B. des comprimés
   C. une ordonnance

3. Marc va chez le dentiste

   A. parce qu'il a mal aux dents
   B. parce qu'il a besoin d'un dentier
   C. pour trouver une couronne

4. Qui est dans la salle d'attente du docteur Buisson?

   A. Jean
   B. beaucoup de monde
   C. un dentiste très patient

5. Qui a une petite crise?

   A. André
   B. Jean
   C. Agnès

ANSWERS

Dialogue 1. C 2. C 3. A 4. B 5. A

Have fun with the following puzzle:

ACROSS
3. prescription
5. hand
6. throat
7. nose
8. illness

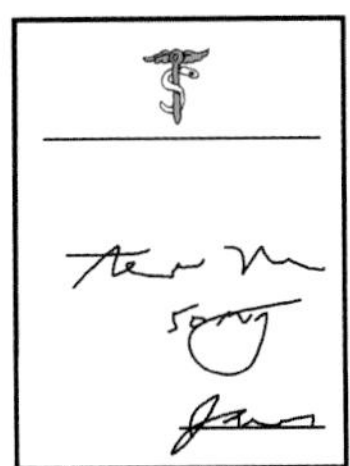

DOWN
1. arm
2. hospital
3. ear
4. pill
9. tooth

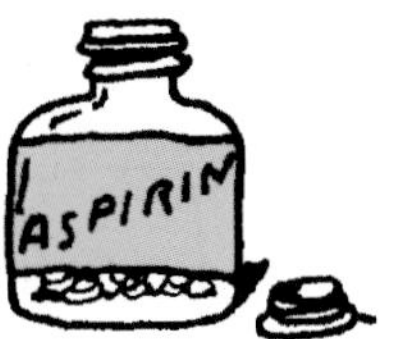

ANSWERS

Puzzle ACROSS **3.** ordonnance **5.** main **6.** gorge **7.** nez **8.** maladie
DOWN **1.** bras **2.** hôpital **3.** oreille **4.** comprimé **9.** dent

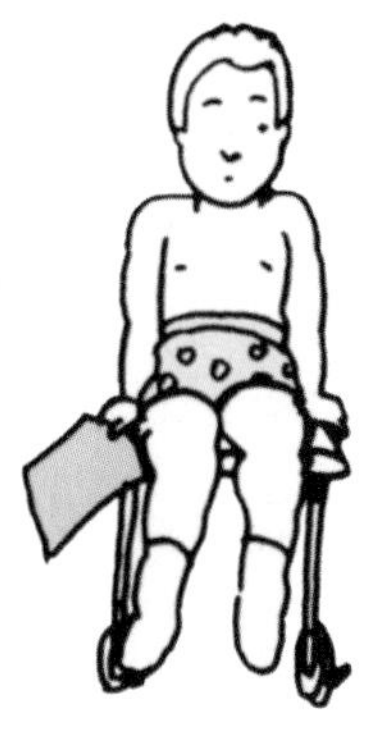

Un jeune homme entre dans la salle *(say-lehbr)* **d'attente d'un célèbre spécialiste des** *(o-suhz)* **maladies osseuses. Il dit à l'infirmière qu'il voudrait parler au docteur en** *(pree-vay)* **privé. "Entrez ici," dit l'infirmière,** *(day-za-bee-yay)* **"déshabillez-vous et attendez."**

A young man walks into the waiting room of a famous specialist of bone diseases. He tells the nurse that he would like to talk with the doctor in private. "Come in here," the nurse says, "get undressed and wait."

"Mais . . . ."

"But . . . ."

LE DOCTEUR **Qu'est-ce qui ne va pas?**

What's wrong?

"Je suis ici," répond le jeune homme, "pour vous demander si vous voulez *(ruh-noov-lay)* **renouveler votre** *(a-bon-mAH)* **abonnement à *Paris Match*."**

"I am here," replies the young man, "to ask you if you want to renew your subscription to *Paris Match*."

Can you remember? Just answer **vrai ou faux**.

1. _______ Le jeune homme voudrait parler au docteur et à l'infirmière.
2. _______ Le jeune homme est malade.
3. _______ Le docteur est un spécialiste du coeur.
4. _______ Le jeune homme demande au docteur s'il veut continuer son abonnement à *Paris Match*.

ANSWERS

Vrai ou faux **1.** F **2.** F **3.** F **4.** V

29 Comment obtenir de l'aide

(ob-tuh-neer) *(ehd)*

How to Get Help

Here is a little courtroom drama. As in English, the speakers use the present tense to give a sense of immediacy to their remarks.

(zhewzh) LE JUGE (judge)	**Donc vous cassez votre parapluie sur le crâne** *(krahn)* **de votre mari.**	So you break your umbrella over your husband's skull.
(ay-pooz) L'ÉPOUSE (the wife)	**Un accident, Monsieur le Juge.**	An accident, your honor.
LE JUGE	**Comment est-ce possible?**	How is that possible?
L'ÉPOUSE	**Je n'ai pas l'intention** *(EH-tAH-syOH)* **de casser le parapluie.**	I do not intend to break the umbrella.

COMMENT APPELER UNE AMBULANCE

(AH-bew-lAHs)

How to Call an Ambulance

If you need an ambulance, the fire department, or the police in France, you can dial the general European number 112 from any phone. For specific services, dial 15 for an ambulance (**le SAMU—le Service d'Aide Médical d'Urgence**), 18 for the fire department (**les pompiers**), or 17 for the police (**la police**). You should also check a local phone book for more exact information. Don't count on using 911 from your cell phone. It may not be transferred to the emergency services you need. Check with your phone service provider before your travel. Obviously, if you have a serious crisis, contact any local citizen for help (hotel receptionist, store clerk, someone with a cell phone).

(At a party, Jack meets Dr. Henri Lasanté, a health officer of the French government.)

JACQUES	**Qu'est-ce que je dois faire si ma femme a une crise cardiaque?**	What should I do if my wife has a heart attack?

LE DR. LASANTÉ **Pas de problème. Vous appelez ou demandez à quelqu'un d'appeler le secours et une ambulance va venir immédiatement. Ne dites pas: "Ma femme a mal au coeur" parce que "avoir mal au coeur" veut dire "avoir la nausée."** *(noh-zay)* **Dites: "*Ma femme vient d'avoir une crise cardiaque.*"**

No problem. You call or ask somebody to call **for help** and an ambulance will come immediately. Do not say: "My wife has mal au coeur" because this means to be nauseated. Say: "My wife just had a heart attack."

JACQUES **Les ambulances ont de l'oxygène** *(ok-see-zhehn)* **et tout l'équipement** *(ay-keep-mAH)* **nécessaire?** *(nay-se-sehr)*

The ambulances have oxygen and all the necessary equipment?

LE DR. LASANTÉ **Bien sûr. Ne vous inquiétez pas.**

Of course. Don't worry.

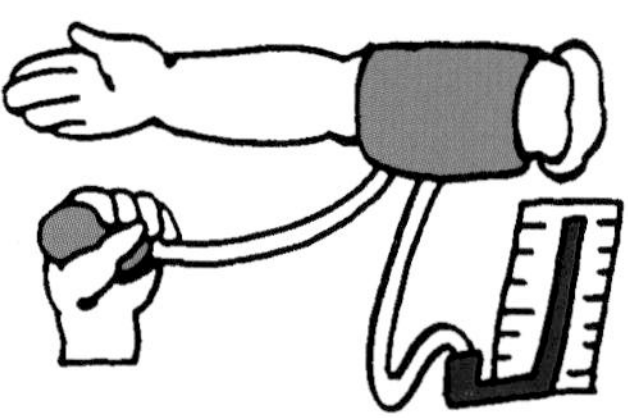

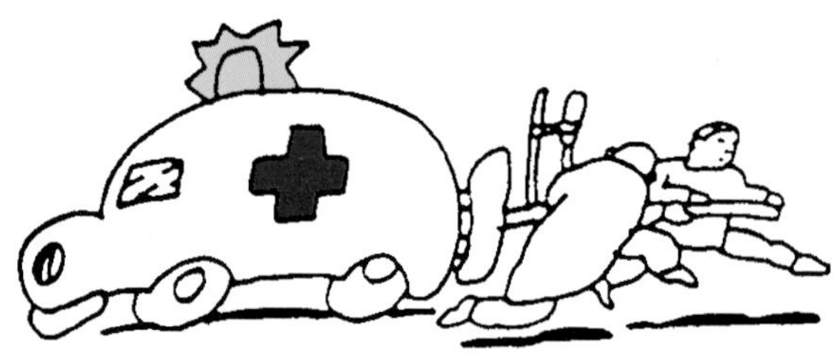

(po-lees)

COMMENT APPELER LA POLICE

How to Call the Police

In case of emergency, ask the hotel's receptionist to call the police. If you are walking, ask a pedestrian or an **agent de police**:

Pouvez-vous me dire où est le commissariat?

Can you tell me where the police station is?

(At the same party, Jack meets a retired police official, Pierre Leflic.)

JACQUES **Quelle est la différence entre un agent** *(a-zhAH)* **de police, un gendarme** *(zhAH-darm)* **et un C.R.S.?** *(say-ehr-es)*

What's the diference between an "agent de police," a "gendarme" and a C.R.S.?

LEFLIC ***L'agent de police*** **dirige la circulation dans les villes.** ***Le gendarme*** **est sur les routes, en voiture ou à moto.** *(moh-toh)* **Le** ***C.R.S.*****, un militaire,** *(mee-lee-tehr)* **est mobilisé** *(mo-bee-lee-zay)* **pour assurer l'ordre en cas de manifestation** *(ma-nee-fehs-ta-syOH)* **publique.**

The *agent de police* regulates traffic in the cities. The *gendarme* is on the roads, in a car or on a motorcycle. The *C.R.S.,* a soldier, is mobilized to keep order in case of public demonstrations.

JACQUES **Est-ce que les piétons** *(pyay-tOH)* **traversent la rue quand c'est interdit,** *(an-tehr-dee)* **comme en Amérique?**

Do pedestrians cross the street illegally as in America?

LEFLIC **Hélas!** *(ay-lahs)* **Tout** *(tool)* **le temps.** *(tAH)* **Mais vous connaissez le dicton:** *(deek-tOH)* **"À Rome,** ***ne*** **faites** ***pas*** **comme les Romains . . . "**

Alas! All the time. But you know the saying: "When in Rome, do *not* do as the Romans do . . ."

BEFORE YOU LEAVE

Avant de partir

Now we have come to the final step in the learning process, and the most important one. What will you do in the following situations? It may be worthwhile to look over each unit before answering.

Situation 1: Faisons connaissance

1. It is day and you meet someone. What do you say in order to start a conversation?
   A. À bientôt
   B. Bonjour
   C. Au revoir
2. You have just run into a friend. What do you say?
   A. Merci
   B. Salut
   C. Au revoir
3. You introduce the friend to your wife. You say:
   A. Je te présente . . .
   B. Je vous en prie . . .
   C. Je vais bien merci . . .

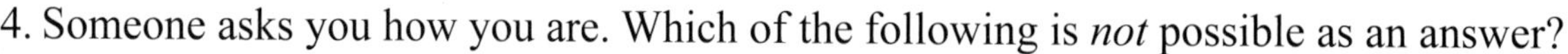

4. Someone asks you how you are. Which of the following is *not* possible as an answer?
   A. Pas mal, merci
   B. Très bien, merci
   C. Bonjour, merci

Situation 2: L'arrivée

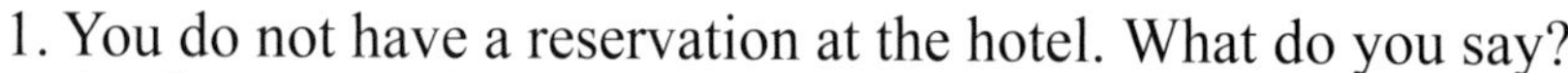

1. You do not have a reservation at the hotel. What do you say?
   A. Comment allez-vous, Monsieur?
   B. Excusez-moi, Monsieur, je n'ai pas de réservation.
   C. Bonjour, Monsieur, comment vous appelez-vous?
2. You want to say that you would like a room. You say:
   A. S'il vous plaît, je voudrais une chambre.
   B. S'il vous plaît, je ne veux pas de salle de bains.
   C. S'il vous plaît, je veux une fenêtre dans ma chambre.
3. You want to inquire about price and what is included. So you say . . .
   A. Pouvez-vous me dire où sont les toilettes?
   B. Pouvez-vous me dire combien coûte la chambre et si le service est compris?
   C. Pouvez-vous me dire comment vous vous appelez?

ANSWERS

Situation 1 1. B 2. B 3. A 4. C **Situation 2** 1. B 2. A 3. B

Situation 3: Allons visiter la ville

1. You are on foot and you want to find a certain street. You ask a passerby the following:
   A. Pardon, où allez-vous?
   B. Pardon, où est la rue du Cherche-Midi?
   C. Pardon, où habitez-vous?

2. The passerby might give you various directions such as . . .
   A. À gauche, à droite, tout droit . . .
   B. Demain, hier, aujourd'hui . . .
   C. Le bureau de poste, la banque, le bureau de tabac . . .

3. Now you have just gotten onto a bus. You want to ask where to get off. You say . . .
   A. Excusez-moi, combien coûte le billet?
   B. Excusez-moi, où dois-je descendre pour la rue . . .
   C. Excusez-moi, comment vous appelez-vous?

4. You have flagged down a taxi, but before getting in you want to know how much it would cost to get to **la rue Molière**.
   A. Excusez-moi, est-ce que la rue Molière est loin?
   B. Excusez-moi, savez-vous où est la rue Molière?
   C. Excusez-moi, c'est combien pour aller à la rue Molière?

5. You have forgotten your watch. You stop a passerby to ask what time it is. You say . . .
   A. Pardon, quelle heure est-il?
   B. Pardon, j'ai une montre.
   C. Pardon, quel temps fait-il?

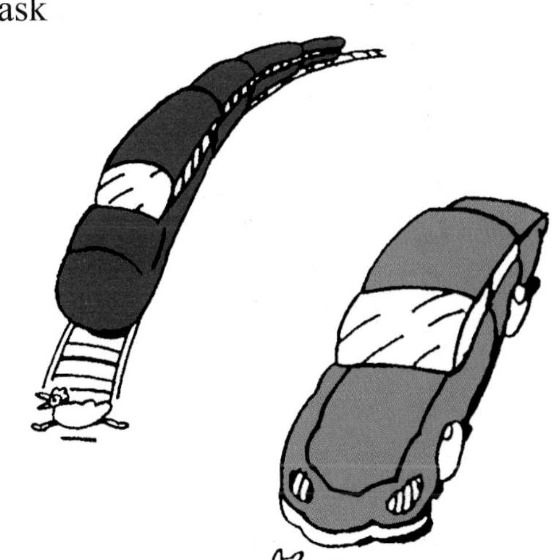

6. The passerby would *not* answer . . .
   A. Il est deux heures vingt-cinq.
   B. C'est demain.
   C. Il est une heure et demie.

7. You are at the train station and want to buy a ticket.
   A. Excusez-moi, combien coûte un billet pour Lyon?
   B. Excusez-moi, où est Lyon?
   C. Excusez-moi, quelle heure est-il?

8. The clerk answers that there is no room left on the train. He might say something like . . .
   A. Je suis désolé, mais vous êtes porteur.
   B. Je suis désolé, mais vous ne parlez pas français.
   C. Je suis désolé, mais il n'y a pas de place.

9. You want to say to someone that you are American and speak only a little French. You might say . . .
   A. Je suis américain, je parle un tout petit peu le français.
   B. Je parle américain, je ne suis pas français.
   C. Je ne suis pas français, je suis américain.

ANSWERS

Situation 3 **1.** B **2.** A **3.** B **4.** C **5.** A **6.** B **7.** A **8.** C **9.** A

10. You want to rent a car cheaply. You might ask the clerk . . .
   A. Je voudrais une voiture pas trop chère.
   B. Je voudrais une voiture pas trop sale.
   C. Je voudrais une voiture pas trop bon marché.

11. You want to fill up your car. You might say . . .
   A. S'il vous plaît, une voiture jaune.
   B. S'il vous plaît, faites le plein.
   C. S'il vous plaît, c'est trop cher.

12. A service station attendant might tell you that your car needs repairs. He would *not* say . . .
   A. Votre voiture est belle.
   B. Votre voiture a besoin de nouveaux freins.
   C. Votre voiture a besoin d'un nouveau moteur.

13. You ask a "camping employee" if there are essential services. You would *not* say . . .
   A. Est-ce qu'il y a de l'eau?
   B. Est-ce qu'il y a des toilettes?
   C. Est-ce qu'il y a un cinéma?

14. As an answer to "Quelle est la date d'aujourd'hui?" (What's today's date?), you would *not* hear . . .
   A. C'est le trente mars.
   B. C'est le deuxième jour.
   C. C'est le trois mai.

15. To ask an airline employee at what time your flight leaves, you would say . . .
   A. Pardon, à quelle heure part mon vol?
   B. Pardon, quand arrive mon vol?
   C. Pardon, vous volez souvent?

16. With which statement does the picture go?
   A. Je voudrais louer une voiture pour une semaine.
   B. Je voudrais deux billets aller-retour pour Paris en deuxième classe.
   C. À quelle heure part le vol pour Zurich?

Situation 4: Les divertissements

1. You are at a ticket agency. The clerk would *not* ask you . . .
   A. Vous voulez un billet d'opéra?
   B. Vous voulez un billet de cinéma?
   C. Vous voulez un billet d'avion?

2. If someone were to ask you what your favorite sport was (**Quel est votre sport préféré?**), you would *not* say . . .
   A. J'aime le tennis.
   B. J'aime la natation.
   C. J'aime le français.

ANSWERS

Situation 3 **10.** A **11.** B **12.** A **13.** C **14.** B **15.** A **16.** B **Situation 4** **1.** C **2.** C

Situation 5: Comment commander un repas

1. You want to ask what the restaurants in France are like. You would ask . . .
   A. On mange bien en France?
   B. Comment sont les restaurants?
   C. Où sont les restaurants?

2. As a possible answer, you would *not* hear . . .
   A. Ils sont à Paris.
   B. Il y a beaucoup de restaurants.
   C. Ils sont bons.

3. When a waiter asks you to order, he might say . . .
   A. Vous désirez?
   B. Vous payez?
   C. Vous finissez?

4. To see the menu, you would say . . .
   A. Puis-je voir la cuisine?
   B. Puis-je voir la carte?
   C. Puis-je voir le directeur?

5. One of the following is not connected with eating . . .
   A. pharmacie
   B. restaurant
   C. assiette

6. If you wanted to order some vegetables you would say . . .
   A. Une assiette de soupe chaude, s'il vous plaît.
   B. Un plat de légumes, s'il vous plaît.
   C. Des pamplemousses, s'il vous plaît.

7. After which course would you expect to be served your salad?
   A. l'entrée
   B. le fromage
   C. le dessert

8. An example of a dessert you might order is . . .
   A. du poisson
   B. de la glace
   C. de la confiture

9. At the end of a meal you say to the waiter/waitress . . .
   A. Le couteau, s'il vous plaît.
   B. Le pourboire, s'il vous plaît.
   C. L'addition, s'il vous plaît.

10. How would you ask if the tip is included on your bill?
   A. Le petit déjeuner est servi?
   B. La taxe est correcte?
   C. Le service est compris?

ANSWERS

Situation 5 1. B 2. A 3. A 4. B 5. A 6. B 7. A 8. B 9. C 10. C

Situation 6: Au magasin

1. Which of the following would you *not* say in a clothing store?
   A. Pardon, combien coûte cette chemise?
   B. Pardon, combien coûte ce pain?
   C. Je voudrais des chaussures, des chaussettes et des cravates.

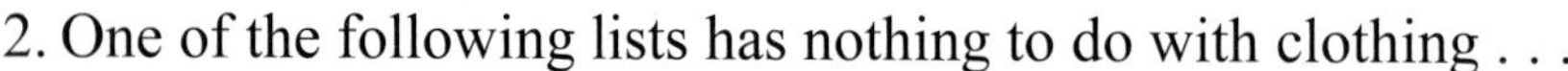

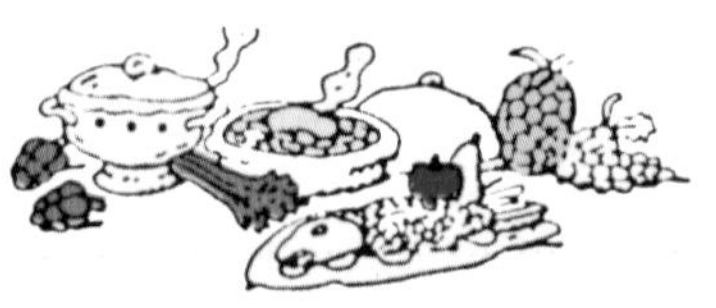

2. One of the following lists has nothing to do with clothing . . .
   A. complet bleu, robe de laine, chemise blanche
   B. gants de cuir, chaussures du soir, chemise de soie
   C. légumes, viandes, fruits

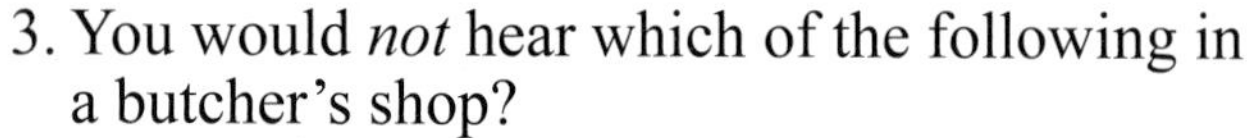

3. You would *not* hear which of the following in a butcher's shop?
   A. Combien coûtent les fruits?
   B. La viande coûte 11 euros le kilo.
   C. Le veau est frais.

4. You want to order a drug at the pharmacy. You might say . . .
   A. Je voudrais ces légumes, s'il vous plaît.
   B. Je voudrais ce médicament, s'il vous plaît.
   C. Je voudrais ces fruits, s'il vous plaît.

5. A pharmacist would *not* ask you one of the following . . .
   A. Voulez-vous une bouteille de vin?
   B. Voulez-vous des aspirines?
   C. Avez-vous une ordonnance?

6. You are at the laundry. You would *not* ask one of the following . . .
   A. Pouvez-vous laver et repasser ces chemises pour demain?
   B. Faites-vous aussi le nettoyage à sec?
   C. Combien coûtent les chaussures?

7. You are at the barber's and want a haircut. You might say . . .
   A. S' il vous plaît, donnez-moi un paquet de cigarettes.
   B. S'il vous plaît, coupez-moi les cheveux très courts.
   C. S'il vous plaît, donnez-moi un billet.

8. The hairdresser might ask you . . .
   A. Voulez-vous une mise en plis?
   B. Voulez-vous un biscuit?
   C. Voulez-vous un journal?

ANSWERS

Situation 6 1. B 2. C 3. A 4. B 5. A 6. C 7. B 8. A

9. Choose the store for each sentence (match them up):
   A. Combien coûte la réparation de mes chaussures?
   B. Est-ce qu'il me faut une nouvelle montre?
   C. Combien coûtent un journal et une revue?
   D. J'ai besoin de faire le plein.
   E. Avez-vous de l'aspirine?
   F. Est-ce que vous vendez du papier à lettres?
   G. Combien coûte cette robe?
   H. Cette bague est magnifique.

   1. la cordonnerie
   2. la papeterie
   3. la station service
   4. la pharmacie
   5. l'horlogerie
   6. le bureau de tabac
   7. la bijouterie
   8. le magasin de confection-dames

10. Each of these stores is selling an item that should be carried by another store. Can you correct the situation?

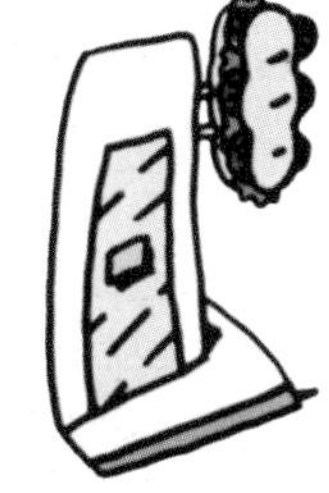

A. PRÊT-À-PORTER
   1. robes
   2. collants
   3. saucisson
   4. jupes

B. SOUVENIRS
   1. viande froide
   2. reproductions
   3. cartes postales
   4. foulards

C. BOULANGERIE
   1. croissants
   2. pain
   3. linge
   4. petits fours

D. CHARCUTERIE
   1. bagues
   2. jambon
   3. pâté
   4. salami

Situation 7: Services essentiels

1. You are at a bank and wish to exchange a traveler's check . . .
   A. Excusez-moi, pourriez-vous me dire l'heure?
   B. Excusez-moi, pourriez-vous me changer ce chèque de voyage?
   C. Excusez-moi, pourriez-vous me donner un cadeau?

2. A bank employee would *not* ask you . . .
   A. S'il vous plaît, remplissez cette formule.
   B. S'il vous plaît, signez ici.
   C. S'il vous plaît, mangez du pain.

3. You want to buy stamps at a post office. You would say . . .
   A. S'il vous plaît, je voudrais acheter du fromage .
   B. S'il vous plaît, je voudrais acheter des journaux.
   C. S'il vous plaît, je voudrais acheter des timbres.

4. Which of the following would you *not* say in a post office?
   A. Je voudrais envoyer cette lettre par avion.
   B. Je voudrais envoyer ce colis.
   C. Je voudrais écrire une lettre maintenant.

ANSWERS

Situation 6 **9. A.** 1 **B.** 5 **C.** 6 **D.** 3 **E.** 4 **F.** 2 **G.** 8 **H.** 7 **10. A.** 3 **B.** 1 **C.** 3 **D.** 1

Situation 7 **1.** B **2.** C **3.** C **4.** C

5. You answer a phone call with . . .
   A. Allô
   B. Au revoir
   C. À bientôt

6. When you call for Mr. Smith, you find out that he is not there. You decide to leave a phone message for him. You would say . . .
   A. Je voudrais votre numéro de téléphone.
   B. Je voudrais laisser un message.
   C. Qui est à l'appareil?

7. You want to ask someone how to dial a number. You would say . . .
   A. S'il vous plaît, comment faut-il composer le numéro?
   B. S'il vous plaît, où est le téléphone?
   C. S'il vous plaît, combien coûte la communication?

8. Which of the following would *not* be used to seek help in an emergency?
   A. S'il vous plaît, appelez une ambulance.
   B. S'il vous plaît, appelez la police.
   C. S'il vous plaît, dites-moi où vous habitez.

9. You would not say one of the following to a doctor.
   A. Docteur, j'ai mal à la tête.
   B. Docteur, j'ai besoin d'un parapluie.
   C. Docteur, j'ai de la fièvre.

10. Can you match the questions in the left column with statements in the right column?

A. Comment vous appelez-vous?
B. Où descendons-nous pour aller au cinéma Broadway?
C. Quelle heure est-il?
D. Où puis-je acheter du lait?
E. Pourriez-vous me couper les cheveux?
F. Avez-vous des jounaux en anglais?
G. Il y a un trou dans ma chaussure. Pouvez-vous la réparer?
H. Avez-vous des timbres?
I. Combien coûte un billet aller-retour à Cannes pour quatre personnes?
J. Est-ce qu'il y a un garage près d'ici?
K. Quel temps fait-il?
L. Qu-est-ce que tu veux faire ce soir?

1. On pourrait aller au théâtre.
2. Un temps magnifique!
3. À la laiterie.
4. Allez au guichet-timbres.
5. Aimez-vous les cheveux courts?
6. Je ne peux pas la réparer.
7. Oui, nous avons un bon choix de journaux anglais et américains.
8. À l'arrêt après la Concorde.
9. Il est midi.
10. Oui, au coin de la prochaine route.
11. 125 euros par personne.
12. Je m'appelle Marc Smith.

ANSWERS

Situation 7 **5.** A **6.** B **7.** A **8.** C **9.** B **10.** A.12 B.8 C.9 D.3 E.5 F.7 G.6 H.4 I.11 J.10 K.2 L.1